There's a Cockroach in My Regulator!

Bizarre and Brilliant True Diving Tales
from Thirty-Five Years of
*Undercurrent, the Private, Exclusive
Guide for Serious Divers*

Written and Edited by:
Ben Davison
Larry Clinton

Printed in the United States of America
ISBN 978-0-615-33301-4

Cover Photograph: David Haas
Cover and Interior Design: Rich Gelber

Undercurrent Books
2030 Bridgeway
Sausalito, CA 95965
415-289-0501
www.undercurrent.org
bendavison@undercurrent.org

Printed on recycled paper

Table of Contents

Introduction

Acknowledgments

Chapter 4: Unconventional Wisdom

Chapter 5: Diving Poets? Well . . .

Chapter 6: Two Divers, Diving Together

Chapter 7: Deeds of Derring-Do

Acknowledgments

As a reader-driven forum, *Undercurrent* has had thousands of contributors over the years, all of whom merit our gratitude. Contributions from many of them are included in this book.

A number of *Undercurrent* readers volunteered to proof these pages and make suggestions, a job far greater than I had imagined. We are very appreciative for their help. So I thank Annie Griffiths, Mike Thompson, Dorothy Levine, Gabriel Peñagarícano, Corinne Halberg, Lisa Kuriscak, Mark Scoble, Alice Ribbens, Linda Cober, John McMinn, D. Jonathan Blake, Amy Gallatin, Cindy Darling, Alvin Rosenfeld, Diana Abarshkin, Laurie Richardson and . . . Rich Gelber, Lori Lundberg, Michelle Jordan, Lynda Peterson, Bill Tubbs, Michael H. Smith, Arthur Hardman, Dave Van Rooy, Pong Yoopin, John Shobe, Doc Vikingo, Dr. Ern Campbell, and Vanessa Richardson also made significant contributions. Many subscribers submitted their photographs for our cover, and we picked one by David Haas. Our thanks.

In particular, I must mention Bret Gilliam, who has had made prolific contributions to *Undercurrent*. Bret has had a forty-year diving career logging more than 18,000 dives in military, commercial, scientific, filming, and technical diving operations. I first reviewed his operation in the Virgin Islands in 1976. He founded the training agency, SDI/TDI and *Fathoms Magazine* and was the CEO of UWATEC. Author of nearly 1000 articles, his photos have graced more than one hundred magazine covers. Our special thanks.

Thanks to Larry Clinton, who put in more hours than he ever bargained for searching through, rewriting and correcting thirty-five years of articles that went to print long before we had a computer with a spell checker.

Finally, thanks to thousands upon thousands of *Undercurrent* subscribers who make this long journey worth every minute. I've been diving with a lot of you, listened to your stories about *Undercurrent*, and often your kind words, and never once identified myself. Sorry about that, but I then again you have been paying for anonymity and I've kept my promise. But it's been fun keeping the secret. Thanks for your loyal support.

– Ben Davison

vii

Introduction

Thirty-five years of *Undercurrent, the private exclusive guide for serious divers* has produced some marvellous stories, insightful articles and, upon reflection, a unique look at the history of diving. Because we have always been a simple newsletter, relying on reporting, not photographs, and taking no advertising and no favors, we have been free to write as we wished. Many of our stories would have never seen the light of day in the diving industry had we not published them. We provided regular commentary on rigid and overbearing dive operators, shark attacks on divers, the dive industry's resistance to shark conservation and its lack of attention to reef conservation, dive operators who leave divers at sea, silly and faulty equipment (especially the early decompression meters), resorts and liveaboards that failed to deliver, and much more. Insiders criticized *Undercurrent* for being negative about diving, when all we did was tell the truth so our fellow sport divers were assured of diving safely while getting their money's worth. Our stories carried weight. The industry and especially our fellow divers are better for it.

For years, I've been hoping to collect many of these stories in one volume, not only to entertain our fellow divers, but also to enlighten them about the real history of diving, sort of the "people's" history.

This volume is unlike any other dive book you have read. *Undercurrent* has been fortunate to attract many knowledgeable contributors, some of them legends in the sport (you will see their by-lines on

Introduction

many pieces). Our goal was to recreate the atmosphere of a salon on a comfortable liveaboard, with divers sharing stories among their peers. In this compilation, we have tried to preserve the flavor of the original articles as much as possible — including the personality of the individual contributors. Therefore, you will encounter many different voices and points of view, just as you would while enjoying a post-dive beer on a liveaboard.

While searching for a title, I ran across a short piece about an instructor who was teaching his students that they should always purge their regulators before inserting them into their mouths. However, he didn't follow his own advice and when he put his mouthpiece between his lips and pressed the purge button a cockroach flew into the back of his throat.

Gross, you say? Yes indeed. And funny as well. Something we figure would have happened only once, until we got this letter from one of our readers, Judy Foester, when she learned about *There's a Cockroach in My Regulator*.

"My husband was killed in a car crash in December 1975. We had been traveling to Grand Cayman since the mid-60s and he always wanted to take up scuba diving, but I was afraid. So, after he died, I didn't care if I lived or died. I went to New York City and bought a complete Nikonos III outfit. Then, I was off to Grand Cayman. I took a three-hour resort course on Seven Mile Beach, with Bob Soto (Don Foster was my instructor) and learned underwater photography from Dave Woodward at the East End Inn and Diving Center.

"We dove at the Arches, at Sand Slide . . . just great places. We had great laughs. One day I got seasick on the way to the dive site and the guides said how happy the fish would be as I fed them. I asked Dave, "what happens if I get sick under the water?" He said, "there's nothing you can do on land that you can't do underwater. Just throw up into your regulator." The next day, I got down to about ninety feet and noticed all this movement in my mouth. I took out the regulator and this big cockroach started doing the breast stroke for the surface. . . ."

We have plenty of other odd tales in *There's a Cockroach in My Regulator*, and plenty of information, criticism and speculation. Take Ralph Osterhaus' 25-year-old predictions of what diving equipment would be like today. Or Bret Gilliam's take on how narcosis may be a figment of a diver's imagination. Or what divers did when they found bundles of cocaine floating at sea.

We hope you enjoy our effort to pull together some of the best yarns, research and opinions of our thirty-five years of publishing. It was no easy task. Truth is Larry Clinton, my co-conspirator, and I realized there is enough material for another book. If you and your fellow readers find enough here to entertain yourselves, let us know. *There's a Bee in My Snorkel,* is just around the corner. We'd love to tell you that story and a hundred more.

– Ben Davison

Chapter 1
Dangerous Denizens of the Deep

Shark infested waters? Poisonous sea snakes on the attack? Giant octopuses guarding sunken treasure chests? We divers scoff at such descriptions; however, over the years we've encountered some hair-raising stories about strange encounters with sea creatures big and small. Just about every diver has a chilling shark story (or two), and while we won't vilify our favorite marine animal, these incidents from 2004 remind us that we're not in an underwater petting zoo.

Shark Tales

First, there's the story about an Australian who swam 300 yards with a two-foot wobbegong shark clamped to his leg before driving a mile to get the creature removed. Luke Tresoglavic, 22, was snorkeling off a beach 100 miles north of Sydney when the shark bit into his left leg and wouldn't let go, even after Tresoglavic "staggered onto the beach where two sunbathers tried to pry open the creature's mouth," according to the *Chicago Sun Times*. He got into his car and wedged the two-foot shark against the gear lever as he drove with one hand to a surf club. Lifeguards there couldn't break the wobbegong's grip, so they plunged Tresoglavic's leg into a bucket of fresh water, drowning the shark. You can bet that shark grows at least a foot every time Tresoglavic retells the story.

1

Undercurrent reader Gerry Lauro (Wyckoff, NJ) reported a grisly shark feeding incident in the Galapagos National Park. The dive operator, Scuba Iguana, took its group to a small island where sea lions were swimming. "As we arrived," says Lauro, "a tour boat was chumming for sharks to show the tourists. That this was going on in a national park is horrible, but our boat let several of our divers go snorkeling around the circling sharks. Within fifteen minutes, one diver was bitten in the midsection by a smaller shark (five feet or so). The diver sustained multiple cuts and lacerations but nothing fatal. The crew basically took no action toward helping him, other than driving to the nearest dock and getting him a cab and accompanying him to the hospital. How a dive boat allows guests in the water in a shark feeding situation mystifies me. Needless to say, I left the boat with the injured diver. They were ready to go for the second dive after this!"

Our last shark tale comes from our own fearless correspondent who visited North Caicos many years ago. He had made several dives and saw no sharks, until he happened to look up and see a six-footer speeding directly toward him. He raised his arm and shouted so loud his regulator popped from his mouth, so he pressed his octopus regulator's purge button to blow bubbles. The shark scraped his wet suit, but kept right on going and didn't return. Our correspondent reported: "I've seen hundreds of sharks in my twenty years of sport diving, and this is only my second incident. I was busy poking around the bottom and did nothing to provoke this fellow, but he came anyway. I suspect the bubbles from my regulator or the shout kept him from coming back a second time, but then he may not have seen me since I immediately found myself engulfed in my own brown cloud."

Humans, like squid and octopus, seem to have their own techniques of self-defense.

Protect Yourself

While it is extremely rare for a diver to meet an aggressive shark and even more rare to be attacked, keep in mind your defense. Bob Hueter, the director for Mote's Center for Shark Research, says, "If attacked by a shark, the general rule is: Do whatever it takes to get away!" Some people have successfully chosen to be aggressive by yelling, blowing bubbles, or fending the shark off with their fists, cameras, or other objects. Other survivors have remained passive."

And, there's more — like hang with a group if you're in waters filled with sharks. Avoid murky waters, harbor entrances, and areas near stream mouths, especially after heavy rain. Do not provoke or harass a shark, even a small one, even a nurse shark; they bite hard. If fish or turtles start to behave erratically, leave the water. And if you hear ominous two-beat music off in the distance, start saying your prayers.

Now if you've seen enough sharks to be ho-hum about them, here are some truly frightening creatures to dive with.

Crocs, Cobras and Polar Bears

In October 2004, scuba diver Russell Butel, 55, collecting fish for his own aquarium business, was killed by a crocodile in Australia's Northern Territory. A crocodile expert told reporters that "The croc would have lined him up and gone underwater from 100-200 meters. The animal may then have surfaced right next to him and attacked. It would have all been over in seconds."

Divers said Mr. Butel was working where there was a high risk of attack, but his friends said he knew the risks and accepted them as an occupational hazard. A crocodile had killed a snorkeler in the Northern Territory five days previously.

In 1987, an Australian skindiver was attacked a few hundred yards offshore in the Arafura Sea. His wife saw him suddenly surface, screaming and struggling in the jaws of a 13-foot salt water crocodile. Seconds later both diver and crocodile disappeared underwater. Several hours later a search party found his body on shore, where the crocodile had apparently dragged it prior to dining. There were few marks on the body since crocodiles normally kill their prey by drowning, rather than with their teeth.

But divers have also survived croc attacks.

Also in 1987, Gustav Kietzman went out for a little spearfishing on Lake Kariba, near his home in the African nation of Zambia. While diving in 20 feet of water, reports the Associated Press, he felt something nudge him from behind. Turning, he faced a 16-foot crocodile. "He was so close," Kietzman said, "that I couldn't use the speargun. I grabbed for a tree and he grabbed me. He shook me like a dog shakes a rat. It was very painful. I thought I was going to die."

Chapter 1: Dangerous Denizens of the Deep

The crocodile took a chunk out of Kietzman's leg as he hauled himself up a petrified tree. Then it thrust itself out of the water, snapping at the man's heels as he clung to a branch with his fins dangling three feet above the water.

"The driftwood became a mass of writhing cobras."

One of his friends leaped from a motor boat to rescue him, then drove him 225 miles to the nearest hospital for treatment. Kietzman claimed that when the wound healed, he would try spearfishing again. "I hear that if you're farther out, towards the middle of the lake, there are fewer crocs," he said.

Now if this isn't enough, consider polar bears. We have heard that polar bears can't open their mouths and bite underwater, which may be an old husband's tale, but they can indeed take a healthy swat with a paw and knock a diver senseless, then wait for him to bob to the surface. Italian filmmaker Paolo Curto was filming a documentary in 1979 entitled *Dear Monsters of the Sea*, and reports that the defense used by the camera crew against polar bears was to dive with several extra pounds of weight and an inflated BC. "If a diver became a target for an angry bear, he would pull his dump valve and dip down to below 16 feet, where no polar bear can follow because they cannot compensate." During the filming only one bear showed any aggressive tendencies, and Curto, who for a while couldn't find his dump valve, only received a light scrape from the bear's enormous paw. On the other hand, most bears ignored the cameramen and the biggest problem was to get them off the ice floes and into the water for filming. In one case, a frustrated cameraman dragged a seal carcass away from a feeding bear, to which the bear responded by rolling over and falling asleep.

Even non-aquatic animals can be dangerous to divers. Len Charlton, Assistant Editor of the British *Subaqua Scene*, visited Thailand in 1979 in search of new dive sites and had this to relate about his first dive there:

"My son and I hired a boat and boatman to take us to a good dive site. When we arrived I asked the boatman to put the ladder in the water for our entry, but he refused. I insisted and pushed the ladder into the water. He shook his head again and pulled it up. Then he went to the anchor and started to pull it up. By this time I was getting slightly angry. He spoke no 'Engerish,' he said, but I tried to find out what was the matter. I could see no reason for us not to dive in this beautiful, calm sea. Finally, he pointed to several lots of driftwood floating about 100 meters away. He took a piece of wood from the boat deck and threw it at the driftwood. Suddenly all hell broke loose. The driftwood became a mass of writhing cobras. There had been a few big storms, I was to learn later, and the snakes drifted down the rivers into the sea, where they would float in clusters to the nearest islands. I saw six lots of big and small snakes. Imagine coming up after a dive among them. I apologized to the boatman and rather quickly helped him pull up the anchor."

Whales, demonized in early fiction like Moby Dick, are now known to be intelligent creatures. But it's still not wise to invade their space, as the following piece (based on an article by Charles Petit that appeared in the San Francisco Chronicle *and our own interview with Lee Tepley) tells us.*

Whale Nearly Drowns Free Diver

In 1996, a nationwide *I-Witness Video* television audience watched in horror as a 20-foot pilot whale closed its jaws around Lisa Costello's leg and dragged her 40 feet under the sea off the Hawaii coast. A large species of dolphin, just a bit smaller than killer whales, pilot whales are not known to attack humans.

It all began when Costello and Lee Tepley, a California professional underwater photographer, went out in his 15-foot inflatable boat off the island of Hawaii. They encountered about a half-dozen pilot whales, so Tepley grabbed his video camera and he and Costello leaped in to snorkel with the animals.

> *The whale grabbed the woman's right leg, whirled her around and pulled her as deep as 40 feet for nearly a minute.*

When a young male whale swam slowly over to Costello, she reached out and stroked its back. She spent about 20 seconds with the animal while other whales in the group milled nearby. The whale, after

Fish Head

If you've ever been diving along the Great Barrier Reef, you may have encountered one of those enormous, Volkswagen-sized potato cod. They look big enough to swallow a man. The smaller ones look big enough to swallow a man's head, which is exactly what seafood processors in Cairns found in 1996 when they cleaned a six-foot fish. The head, not yet decomposed, may have come from a man who "fell" off a trawler just days before the fish was caught. Either a fish bit it off or someone on board cut it off. Can the movie be far behind?

drifting off a short distance, returned and grabbed the woman's right leg, whirled her around and pulled her as deep as 40 feet for nearly a minute. In the dim depths at the limit of the camera's range, she looked like a slender, fluttering bird in the jaws of an immense retriever. Finally, the whale slowly brought her up as the terrified woman continued to struggle. With Tepley's help, Costello climbed back into the boat, exhausted, bleeding and nearly unconscious. She had no broken bones or muscle injuries and recovered in a week or two.

Federal attorney Lisa Caplan, representing the National Oceanic and Atmospheric Administration, said that as a professional underwater photographer, "Tepley should have known that the law forbids any close contact between people and whales in U.S. waters without a permit. It is the same law used to keep whale-watching tour boats from getting too close to whales."

Susan H. Shane, a marine mammalogist at the University of California, suspects that the whale may have been protecting his "toy" from the attentions of other whales that came near. Scientists agree that the footage of the pilot whales reveals behavior never seen before and is a valuable guide to further research into their nature.

Even the best-intentioned divers need to be wary of whale interactions.

Whale Rider

When the Mayday call came about a stricken humpback whale caught in lines off New Zealand's Kaikoura coast in 2003, Tom Smith strapped on his tank and raced into action. On two earlier occasions the 38-year-old fisherman had responded to a roped whale and both times he had managed to free them.

He said that saving a humpback whale was "a real once-in-a-lifetime encounter" after he freed one from craypot lines in Kaikoura in June 2001. He said he had donned scuba gear and made eye contact to let the whale know he was there. "As I swam up I could see it drop its head and thought it was going to dive, but what it did was to lift its tail and lay dead still while I cut off the float and the last of the rope." After the whale was freed, it came up right beside the boat, where it stayed for a few moments, before lifting its tail and slowly swimming away.

The big fish flipped him around and then flung him away.

This time, thirty tourists on a whale watching adventure watched a tragedy unfold. Smith was on board his vessel the *Bounty* with his wife, father-in-law, and a friend, when fishermen alerted him to a trapped whale, about 30 feet long. The tourists were watching the whale when Smith arrived and leaped into the water. He was trying to cut the line attached to a crayfish pot when the whale lifted its tail, smashing it down on its rescuer underneath. Smith and the bubbles from his tank disappeared.

The New Zealand Herald reported that the Coast Guard and locals searched the area, giving up after four hours when they knew there was no hope of finding him alive. The whale apparently broke free of the nylon rope and survived.

Some sea critters come with built-in weapons that are best avoided, as the following 2003 reports confirm.

Critters with Weapons

Scientists have found a new deadly jellyfish off Australia's tropical northeast coast. Researchers had previously thought the thumbnail-sized Irukandji jellyfish was responsible for the deaths of an American and a Briton in 2001, when 160 other swimmers were also treated in hospitals because of jellyfish stings. But a James Cook University expert said another, yet unnamed, jellyfish had been linked to Irukandji syndrome, which causes severe pain, anxiety, a potentially fatal rise in blood pressure and cerebral hemorrhaging. The jellyfish species are believed to be related to the deadly box jellyfish that infests northern waters in summer months.

Don't ignore sea urchins. Taiwanese doctors report a case of a woman diver who stepped on one while beach diving in Palau. She felt immediate and intense pain. After having the spine removed and her foot painted with Betadine, she later developed fever, chills, nausea, and persistent discharge and tenderness. Seven days later, she was admitted to the hospital with toxic hepatitis. *(Wu ML, et. al., Taipei Veterans General Hospital, Taiwan).*

> *The swordfish turned on Ferrari, ramming its 5-foot bill into his right shoulder beneath the collarbone.*

In 2003, off west Maui, whale researcher Mark Ferrari was underwater videotaping a frenzied pod of 50 false killer whales, a dolphin species. He assumed the pod was attacking schooling fish, but then realized that a 15-foot broadbill swordfish was the target. Fascinated by the teamwork and strategy of the false killer whales, he continued to film. However, without warning, the swordfish turned on Ferrari, ramming its 5-foot bill into his right shoulder beneath the collarbone. The big fish flipped him around and then flung him away. Debbie Ferrari helped her bleeding husband climb aboard their boat and raced to Lahaina where Ferrari was taken to a local hospital. Miraculously, no major arteries or organs were pierced, though nerves were damaged and bones broken.

At what might be the most dangerous patch of underwater real estate anywhere, critters continue to attack humans at Grand Cayman's Stingray City.

On April 1, 2005 according to the *Wisconsin State Journal*, eleven-year-old Justin Weber was scuba diving with his parents at Stingray City on Grand Cayman when a six-foot green moray chomped down on his forearm, severing several arteries. The eel held on tight until Justin's dad pried its jaws apart. Justin underwent six hours of surgery on Grand Cayman, where doctors used a vein from his leg to help restore blood flow to his hand. The Webers arranged for a chartered medical jet, which cost $21,400, to fly Justin to Madison, Wisconsin, for further surgery. His mother Laura said the family will resume diving, but not where fish are fed. "We believe this changes the way the animals react to human beings," she said.

Two Fathom Hickey

The following item appeared in the *New England Journal of Medicine* in 1993. It was submitted by Robert E. Falcone, M.D., and Anne P. Miller, M.D., of the Grant Medical Center in Columbus, OH.

"We recently treated a 'two-fathom hickey,' an entity not previously described in the medical literature.

"A 37-year-old woman scuba diving in 12 feet of water near the Cayman Islands was hand-feeding stingrays that were from three to five feet long. One of the fish missed the offering and sucked the woman's wrist into its mouth, producing a partial-thickness contusion-avulsion wound. Feeding 'tame' stingrays is a popular tourist activity in the Cayman Islands. 'Hickeys' are not uncommon and are apparently self-limiting injuries. The wounds are superficial and contain neither venom nor retained stingray integument. Local therapy, which includes careful scrubbing with soap and water, appears to be adequate. Neither topical nor systemic antibiotics appear to be indicated.

"Another matter, however, are defensive stingray 'attacks,' which result in puncture or laceration by the ray's tail. An estimated 1500 injuries occur yearly in the United States. Envenomation produces an intense local reaction, with pain and systemic symptoms that range from nausea and vomiting to arrhythmias and death. Treatment includes immediate local suction and irrigation to remove the venom and hot-water soaks (45 to 50 degrees C) to attenuate the venom. Necrotic material and retained stingray integument should be removed and the wound closed loosely with drainage. Secondary infection is common, and broad-spectrum antibiotics are often administered."

If only Steve Irwin had heeded these warnings . . .

Crikey! Irwin's Death Stirs Backlash
Should anyone confront wildlife?

The tragic 2006 encounter between flamboyant Australian naturalist Steve ("Crikey!") Irwin and a stingray has generated a storm of media criticism regarding his confrontational approach to wildlife.

Irwin, 44, was snorkeling at Batt Reef, off northeastern Queensland state, while shooting a series called *Ocean's Deadliest*, when he swam too close to a six-foot-wide stingray that thrust its eight-inch barb into his chest, piercing his heart. The TV star's last act was to yank the dagger-sharp barb from his chest. According to eyewitness reports, Irwin was barely conscious as his production team rushed him to his vessel, *Croc One*. He was pronounced dead shortly afterward by Queensland Rescue Service officers. Companions who had been filming Irwin told the Australian media that the self-proclaimed "Crocodile Hunter" did not provoke the stingray when he was attacked. They suggested that the ray "probably felt threatened because Steve was alongside and there was the cameraman ahead, and it felt there was danger and it balked."

> *"There was not an animal he was not prepared to manhandle."*

Typically, rays are more likely to flee than fight. Before this incident, only seventeen fatal stingray attacks had been recorded throughout the world, according to the *Sydney Daily Telegraph*. A more typical incident occurred in September 2006, when a New Zealand crayfish diver was stung at Okiwi Bay. Joe McKnight was stabbed in the leg by a one-meter-wide stingray that attached to him for five seconds. His leg went numb. Friends on his dive boat bandaged it and took him to shore, where he was taken to a hospital, treated and discharged.

A ray's barb is a fragile defense mechanism, and although rays can regenerate lost barbs, until they do, they're more vulnerable than usual. The ray that defended itself against Steve Irwin must have felt particularly threatened to react with its barb. Irwin's crew turned their footage over to Queensland police, but they and his family are opposed to releasing it to the public.

As word of the bizarre tragedy flashed around the world, Queensland Premier Peter Beattie, describing Irwin as possibly the best-known Australian in the world, offered a state funeral. But others were not so kind. In the *Guardian*, expatriate Australian academic Germaine Greer wrote, "The animal world has finally taken its revenge on Irwin." She quoted marine biologist Dr. Meredith Peach as saying, "It's really quite unusual for divers to be stung unless they are grappling with the animal." Greer pointed out: "What Irwin never seemed to understand was that animals need space . . . There was no habitat, no matter how fragile or finely balanced, that Irwin hesitated to barge into, trumpeting his wonder and amazement to the skies. There was not an animal he was not prepared to manhandle." Greer also said she hoped Irwin's death would signal the end of what she described as the exploitative nature of such documentaries.

San Francisco Chronicle columnist Debra Saunders added, "When human beings mistake wildlife for Walt Disney characters, they fail to appreciate wild animals for what they truly are — wild. Read: Not susceptible to boyish charm . . . "

Even comic Bill Maher weighed in: "It shouldn't be surprising when a stingray stings someone," he suggested. "They're not called HUG rays!"

Many guides and some divers often display their own versions of Irwin's hubris, including the handling of nurse sharks, moray eels, scorpion fish, lionfish and sea snakes. In the June 2002 *Undercurrent*, we reported about Dr. Erich Ritter, a leader against the Florida shark feeding ban, who claimed that he could keep sharks away by modifying his heart rate. According to the *South Florida Sun-Sentinel*, Ritter was in waist-deep water at Walker's Cay in the Bahamas when a big lemon shark bit a large hunk out of his left calf. "That was an accident waiting to happen," said Samuel Gruber, a University of Miami professor. "Erich takes certain chances based on what he thinks he knows about shark behavior, but there is no evidence to support his theories," he said.

The most bizarre twist to the Irwin tragedy came in a *London Times* online report that fans' mourning had taken a new focus: stingray rage. Within days of his death, at least ten stingrays were found dead and mutilated on Australia's eastern coast "in what conservationists believe could be revenge attacks for the death of Steve Irwin," according to the *Times*.

They Bite!

In September 2000 we noted that a bite from the Indo Pacific blue ring octopus is deadly. That prompted reader Samuel Johnson to ask, "Do the octopuses that I encounter in the Caribbean bite, if given the opportunity? I've had friends report allowing octopuses to wander over and sit on and explore their bare hands. Is there any reason not to do this, either for my own health and safety or that of the octopus?"

"This cute little fish has teeth like a parrotfish and the ability to crush shells if necessary. I was in pain."

Yes, indeed there is. All octopuses are equipped with a beak-like mouth and powerful jaw muscles. They seize prey with their arms and use their beaks to bite while injecting a venom to paralyze the victim. So, just about any octopus large enough to be noticed by a diver is also capable of biting. How severe that bite might be depends on the size of the octopus and where it bites you. A large octopus biting with full force on lightly or unprotected flesh could inflict some real damage. Five species of octopus live in the Caribbean at depths frequented by divers; the largest approaches seven feet in arm spread. While there is no indication of anything comparable to the danger posed by a blue ring octopus (whose bite can be fatal within twenty minutes), one cannot rule out the possibility of a bad reaction in some individuals, given injection of sufficient quantities of poison into their blood. As to the possible negative effects on the octopus' health from being handled by divers, such encounters, no matter how benign the activity may appear, have the capacity to cause stress, alter behavior, disorient animals, and possibly cause infections. Wild marine animals deserve the same respect as do their wild terrestrial cousins. Look, but don't touch. And remember: Other innocent creatures bite as well.

In November 2003, Randy Jordan, who runs Jupiter Dive Center in Florida, was leading a group through a local underwater cavern when he spotted a porcupine puffer fish in a hole. He figured he'd coax the little guy out of the hole to show his divers.

First he stroked the fish's head with one Kevlar-gloved finger. The puffer stayed put. So he waggled his fingers in front of its face, doing his best imitation of food (porcupine puffers usually feed on shrimp and smaller fish). "My hope was to entice him to come out and play," Randy said. "That is when he launched forward and got hold of my pinkie. Playtime over! Man that hurt. This cute little fish has teeth like a parrotfish and the ability to crush shells if necessary. I was in pain, but relieved that my glove wasn't cut."

However, when Randy took the glove off underwater, "I realized half my finger was still in the glove. The stump that extended from my hand was clouding the water with green smoke. It was so thick I couldn't see my hand. I grabbed the base of my finger to attempt to stop the blood cloud and was shocked to see the damage inflicted."

At the emergency room, Randy recalls, "the guffaws were endless." Most people aren't aware that normally shy puffers even have teeth, but this one did enough bone damage that they couldn't reattach the severed fingertip. Randy underwent plastic surgery to close off the stump, and was back in the water ten days later, a humbler diver.

Though he has always cautioned his customers not to touch fish, and has spoken out against the practice of shark feeding (which he feels creates a "Pavlovian response" toward humans and their boats), Randy overlooked his own warnings in this case, and paid quite a price. He told *Undercurrent* he now realizes that "Touching fish is not good for them and may not be good for you. All fish will do what they need to do to defend themselves."

In 1982, Britain's *Diver* magazine reported one of the oddest and yuckiest scuba diving accidents we've ever heard about. An Australian woman complained of being deaf in one ear after a lake dive. Upon examination, she was found not only to be deaf, but also was bleeding profusely from that same ear. The injury was not permanent. A leech had crept under her hood, imbedded its incisors into her ear canal, and then, when the leech swelled up with the blood it had ingested, blocked the ear canal, rendering her deaf until it could be removed. She required two days' hospitalization.

Cockroaches?

Over the years, I've reported on a couple of unusual problems with a scourge of dive resorts: the cockroach. In reviewing a manifest of injuries to PADI instructors, I was taken by one that occurred in Jakarta, Indonesia, in March 1993. Seems that an instructor was lecturing his students about the importance of purging their second stages before taking a breath. So he purged his own regulator's second stage. But for some unexplained reason he then breathed from his Air 2 alternate air source . . . and sucked in a cockroach. He couldn't exhale it, no matter

We Have Met the Enemy and He is ....

Perhaps, we should fear ourselves more than anything we are about to encounter below the surface. In January 2009, Aussie diver Greg Robertson, 25, was using a spear gun for the first time. A big wave knocked him off the rocks north of Brisbane and pushed his spear gun out of his hands. The six-foot-long spear rebounded off the rocks, pierced his inside upper thigh just millimeters from his genitals and femoral artery. Paramedics unscrewed the long pole so there was only six inches sticking out and a rescue helicopter performed a winch rescue in front of hundreds of onlookers. Robertson had surgery to remove the spear that night.

His friend Casey Jensen told the *Sunshine Coast Daily* "The spear's barbed on the end, so it's locked in there. We joked about it...we told buddies not to not spear themselves and mistake themselves for a fish, and then it actually happened."

how hard he tried. It took a physician at the local hospital to surgically remove it. Gross, is about all I can say.

Cockroaches can bug divers in other ways, as well. When a cockroach the size of your thumb scampers from your dive bag, you must take two actions. In my $250 a night beachfront room at the Ramada Hotel in Grand Cayman in 1996, I did the first: I nailed that puppy.

But I ignored the second and went diving the next day without checking the lip of my mask. When I got underwater my spanking new Tabata mask leaked. Cockroaches love to munch on that silicon lip, a lesson I apparently forgot. You see, years before Honduran cockroaches had devoured another Tabata of mine.

Protection is simple: keep your mask in a sealed container or wrapped in a towel or bathing suit. In fact, more than masks are susceptible to these omnivores. Once in Fiji, I slipped a new mouthpiece on my regulator, only to have a roach nibble on it the first night in the dive shop.

So, keep your silicon under wraps so it doesn't become a roach restaurant. Nothing is more frustrating than diving with the sea dribbling into your mask.

– Ben Davison

They Sting, Itch, and Raise Angry Welts
Sea lice season in the Caribbean

This you knew: sea lice are not something you get from wearing your buddy's dive hood.

The aggravating rash comes compliments of stinging cells called nematocysts, most of which come from the miniscule larvae of thimble jellyfish. Even a brief encounter can yield dime-sized red welts that itch intensely for days. Serious exposure can cause nausea, vomiting, diarrhea, headache, muscle spasms, a sense of malaise, and trouble sleeping.

Subscriber Randy Harris (Trinidad, TX) describes sea lice irritation as "chiggers x 10." Sea lice, which resemble specks of finely-ground pepper, appear in the waters off Florida, in the Gulf of Mexico, and in the wider Caribbean March through September. The jellyfish larvae are covered with nematocytes, firing mechanisms that contain long, barbed filaments that can pierce the skin and inject a mixture of toxic substances. Firing is triggered when the larvae are disturbed either through friction, changes in osmotic pressure caused by the transition from salt to freshwater, or even the nematocysts drying out when a diver exits the water. The body's reaction to the injected toxins is often immediate, but it can take up to twenty-four hours.

Jane Gray (Charlotte, NC) was diving off Little Cayman in the month of June. "My first encounter was during a night dive. I noticed a slight stinging around my neck (I was wearing a full wetsuit). The next morning I only had a slight redness and no itching. However, during the next day's dive, I again ran into an area and more stingers. That night I started to develop huge bumps on my neck that began to spread over my face and down my trunk. There was nothing on the island to help the itching, which was unbelievable." Flying back to the States the next day, she immediately paid a call on her dermatologist, and, after skin scrapings, was told that "severe allergic reaction to jellyfish larvae was the probable culprit. Steroids and antihistamines helped, but the itching continued for a week and the red hives over my trunk and face were quite attractive!"

Chapter 1: Dangerous Denizens of the Deep

A few years ago, reader Joan Meskill (Seattle, WA) was literally covered with stings while diving from a Belize live-aboard in the month of April. "I was a new diver at the time. Lucky it happened at the end of the trip — the last two days. It was a long flight home, where I went immediately to the emergency room. I took a course of steroids for five days and had red patches on various parts of my body for months."

How to Avoid Them

Since the larvae are concentrated in shallow water about 10-15 feet deep, make a quick descent once you enter the water and, upon exit, make your shallow water stop around 20 feet instead of 10 feet.

Because the larvae tend to be caught by fabric, then activated by the friction between your skin and the fabric wherever it touches your body, wear a snug wetsuit or dive skin. Wearing a T-shirt (or other loose-fitting garments) will make matters worse, because the shirt can snare the nematocysts and rub them against your skin continuously until you take your shirt off. Also, upon exiting the water, remove your skin, wetsuit, or other clothing (to avoid having a freshwater rinse trigger the nematocyst's firing), and then rinse yourself off immediately.

Jack Hart (Conover, NC) wrote that he has almost eliminated his sea lice problems after observing his divemaster. "He came up under the boat, took his fins off, and let a bunch of air out of his regulator, which moves any larvae out to the sides, then came up and out of the water fast. I tried it and only got a couple of the lice marks on my neck; almost everyone else on the boat that week was covered in them." One reader suggested that, "For exposed skin like the face a good application of viscous lotion or petroleum jelly can do the trick."

If You Do Get the Barb?

Immediately apply a mixture of isopropyl alcohol and vinegar. Lacking that, try pure vinegar or even Windex. Next, apply a hydrocortisone cream/lotion twice a day. Calamine lotion can also be helpful in reducing the itch. As with most allergic skin reactions, a dose of oral antihistamine (e.g., Benadryl, Claritin, Tavist) can help, but factor in how side effects like drowsiness could affect your activities.

Reader Mary Chipman (Singer Island, FL), who is sea-lice-savvy because she lives and deals with them annually in south Florida, says "Safe Sea, sold in most dive shops or online, works as well as anything

16

as a preventive measure. However, the best relief is Tend Skin, which is basically salicylic acid. When you put it on the sea lice sore, there is an intense burning sensation that lasts for a minute or two. Then the itching and pain goes away for hours."

And it's Always No-See-Um Season

Lurking on the beaches of many favorite dive resorts is a disease that can haunt you months after you return home, and even, in the words of one *Undercurrent* subscriber, "seriously ruin your life." Worse yet, the source of the infection is nearly invisible — the ubiquitous no-see-um.

Like most divers, when *Undercurrent* reader Barry Lipman (Brookfield CT) and his wife, Dr. Ingrid Pruss, ventured to Guanaja in 1998, they found no-see-ums an all-night, all-day plague. On a lunch-time beach picnic, Lipman received several hundred bites and finally evacuated to the water to escape the pests. That night he developed a 102°F

One young girl developed a 105°F fever after spending the day as a no-see-um smorgasbord.

fever and discovered that he was covered with little itching bumps. A six-day course of prednisone alleviated his symptoms and allowed him to continue diving, but other guests were not as lucky. One young girl developed a 105°F fever after spending the day as a no-see-um smorgasbord. Given that the voraciousness of Honduras' hordes of no-see-ums is infamous, Lipmans and Pruss tried to take it in stride.

About four months after they returned, however, Pruss developed small, reddish blemishes on her face at exactly the locations of some of the no-see-um bites. The blemishes grew into ulcerated lesions. It took a trip to Curaçao and visits to specialists there before she received an accurate diagnosis. Ingrid Pruss had leishmaniasis.

If you've never heard of leishmaniasis, you're hardly alone. Neither had Lipman nor Pruss, but they were quick studies. They learned that the culprits were indeed minute insects of the genuses Phlebotomus or Lutzomya also often called "sand fleas" or, in the medical literature, "sand flies." Like mosquitoes, gestating female no-see-ums hungry for protein search for a "blood meal," and in the process transmit one of the twenty-plus species of protozoan parasites responsible for the disease. Lipman says he also was told that the fever and rash he developed in Honduras were not the result of leishmaniasis but a reaction to the toxins he received from the bites themselves, and that "multiple no-see-um bites can cause death by kidney failure from their toxins alone, without any other infectious agent involved."

Though Pruss says chemotherapy has gotten her leishmaniasis itself under control, the lesions left behind are another story. One sore refused to heal, and she required hyperbaric chamber treatment to close the wound.

While leishmaniasis affects 12 million people in 88 countries (with 2.5 million new infections annually), most of the high-risk areas are not dive destinations. However, leishmaniasis is now well-entrenched in Honduras, Belize, and other areas in Central America, and appears to be spreading to islands in the Caribbean.

Though leishmaniasis accounts for less than 5 percent of the tropical infections American travelers return with each year, unless the victim consults a physician specializing in tropical medicine, diagnosis is often inaccurate. The disease itself is difficult to cure and victims are prone to recurrences. If you develop persistent sores you fear may be indicative of leishmaniasis, ask for a referral to a tropical medicine specialist or contact the Center for Disease Control (www.cdc.gov), which can help clinicians with biopsies and cultures as well as recommending and furnishing medication.

Chapter 2
Dive Resorts Under Attack

In our thirty-five years of covering dive travel, we have rarely come across threatening incidents. However, two serious events we covered stand out. In the first, which occurred in 1982, the owners of a small resort in Panama, Tom and Joan Moody, were attacked and run off their island. Here's Joan's personal report, with my preface:

Moody's Pidertupo Village, San Blas Islands
Sadly, our final report

Of all the resorts I have visited in our first seven years of publication, Moody's Pidertupo Village was my favorite. Located in the San Blas Islands off the Caribbean coast of Panama, there could be no more idyllic setting. On a tiny three-acre island thick with coconut palms, the Moody family — Tom, Joan and daughter Marijo — built seven thatched-roof huts for guests and a central homey dining area. They provided daily diving trips across calm and clear waters to pristine reefs.

The 365 San Blas Islands are a Panamanian reserve for the Cuna Indians. Only a couple of other tiny tourist establishments exist on the islands. The Indians live as they have lived for centuries, save portable radios, and the whole setting is just superb. At Moody's hearty food, good people, comfortable accommodations, and true peace and quiet were the hallmarks. Frankly, there was no other place quite like it.

Moody's Pidertupo Village is gone now, destroyed by terrorists. The story is tragic. Tom's wife Joan, who communicated regularly with her guests during the off season, has written two newsletters since they were driven from the island nearly a year ago. Her story shows just how strenuous, just how risky, and just how fragile are the lives of those who devote themselves to running remote and distant resorts.

– Ben Davison

"There were six of us on the island on the night of June 20th," Joan reported. "Rex (the new divemaster), his father Bob, and stepmother Agnes, Tom's sister, Peggy, Tom and me. After dinner Tom found his sheets crawling with ants so he wandered over to the office and later fell asleep there.

> *"Others grabbed Tom by his mangled leg and dragged him down the office steps and onto the sand path like a sack of garbage."*

"Around 4 a.m., I was awakened by a familiar Indian voice outside my bedroom calling, 'Mr. Moody, wake up.' I asked what he wanted (I only saw two or three faces) and he said 'gasoline.' When I mumbled that I would have to ask Moody, one of them demanded, 'Moody not here?' I groggily headed out the door toward the office where I knew Tom was sleeping.

"Peggy came out of her house and saw men crouched all around. One grabbed her, knocking her to her knees and holding her at bay by swinging a sword over her head. Tom was already at the office door and I heard him say, 'Oh my God, No.' I spun around to see what was going on. The scene before me will remain imprinted upon my mind forever: so many men . . . so many guns pointing at us . . . the suffocating feeling of utter helplessness . . . some wore masks, others did not. And Tom's saying, 'What is this? You come like banditos in the night, hiding behind your masks and guns'.

"'Moody, you remember our Congresso and we say Moody go . . . now Moody go' . . . A shot rang out knocking Tom backwards about four feet into the office. Seeing Tom writhing on the floor, his flesh and blood splattered everywhere and hearing his screams of anguish and pain, I threw myself over him. It took two or three men to pull me off and they dragged me outside. Meanwhile, others grabbed Tom by his mangled leg and dragged him down the office steps and onto the sand path like a sack of garbage. Kicking and screaming and falling, I broke away from my captor again and again in an effort to get to my Tom.

"My captor cut a piece of our manila clothesline and tied my hands together and began dragging me down the island."

"I never heard the other gunshots over my screams; they were apparently fired into the air. Indians were running here and there, throwing flaming bottles of gasoline onto the thatch roofs of the office, kitchen and clubhouse. Fires were burning everywhere. The barbarians weren't satisfied to have shot Tom; they had to torture him by throwing gasoline all over him and lighting matches in an attempt to burn him alive. Others beat Tom unmercifully with their gun butts over his head, arms and groin. Another savage swung a machete at Tom and at each swing Tom would roll away. My captor cut a piece of our clothesline, tied my hands together and began dragging me down the island toward our Indian employees' house. Some of the Indians then tied a rope around Tom's gutted leg and his neck and hung him from a coconut tree. They then threw gasoline onto the cane walls and bathroom curtains and set them afire. At this point, Tom went unconscious and they left him for dead. His last thoughts were, 'Why fight it any longer, I'm dead anyway.'

"The marauders then set fire to the new blue house while others boarded our launch, *Island Fever*, stealing gear. The Indians had tied Peggy and me up on the beach beyond the employees' house and we could see some of them getting aboard their cayuco. I got untied and one Indian ran back and began to tie me up, so I pretended to faint. Meanwhile, the Indians on the dock had started up our cayuco engine and were coming around the point, so the man attempting to bind my hands ran for his boat. As they were pulling away, Peggy and I got up and hid behind the employees' kitchen.

"After the raiders left Tom for dead, we cut Tom down and began putting out the fires. The buildings had not burned down because we had a heavy downpour around midnight leaving the rain-soaked thatch too wet to burn.

"I had last seen Tom lying on the ground outside the office, and since it was still dark, I almost tripped over him on the path behind our house. I heard his weak voice say, 'Joan come here. I'm fading fast!' I threw myself onto him, crying and gently caressing his bloody face. 'They shot me in the leg' . . . and I touched his bloody shorts asking, 'Not here?' indicating his abdomen. When he replied no, only the leg, I jumped up and began running for the office and my radios screaming, 'God damnit, you're going to live . . . no one dies of a bullet wound in the leg!'

"I hurriedly connected the antennas on both my amateur radios, and threw on the battery switches. When I heard someone talking, I broke in with a MAYDAY call and a ham operator in Florida answered. I begged him to make an overseas telephone call for the MED-DAC helicopter at Howards Air Base. Bob and Rex brought Tom inside the office so we could wash the gasoline off him and bandage the wound. Within ten minutes, I was notified that the helicopter was in the air and would arrive in an hour. It was 4:48 a.m.

"The Indian families living on the island to the west of Pidertupo had heard my screams and seen the fires; some of the men had paddled their cayucos to Rio Sidra to report the incident; two others came to Pidertupo, then returned to their village to report their findings. Boatloads of Indians had gone to the airstrip when the helicopter landed to pick up Tom; they had personally seen the brutalities inflicted upon him by the terrorists. A couple of cayucos filled with men came to our island to speak with me and to inspect the damages; they returned to the village to report their findings.

"Sometime later, an unmarked boat stopped at Pidertupo carrying three Indians. They informed me that they were 'Guardia.' They had guns, but wore no uniforms, and were Indians. After they inspected the damages, one stayed on the work dock while the other two said they were going to Porvenir to report their findings to the Governor. The boat pulled away from the dock with the two Cuna men. An hour later, a flotilla of friendly cayucos from the village landed on the island. They rushed the lone 'Guardia,' confiscating his guns, and transported him to Rio Sidra.

"The next afternoon, ten hours after the attack, we heard the sound of a large helicopter approaching the island. At the same time

the boat from Porvenir with two members of the 'Guardia' pulled up
to the main dock. There was a confrontation between the villagers and
the armed 'Guardia' and both the Cuna 'Guardia' were shot and killed.

"Soon, the Governor pulled up to
our dock and he identified and confirmed that the dead were indeed San
Blas Guardia. As they wore no uniforms nor were there any identifying
markings on their boat, the shooting
was accidental.

"The National Guard helicopter
departed with the dead and injured,
leaving one Cuna guardsman who ap-
pointed fourteen other men to stand
guard.

> "There was a
> confrontation between
> the villagers and the
> armed 'Guardia'
> and both the Cuna
> 'Guardia' were shot
> and killed."

"During the next day, we heard rumblings that the men from Nar-
gana were drinking and gathering on the island of Masargantupo,
(nine miles north of us) and planning a raid on either Pidertupo or
Rio Sidra to avenge the death of the 'Guardia' who were killed. The
Panamanian National Guard said they had no helicopters available but
would send troops the following day. The United States Embassy came
to our aid; American troops in Panama would provide helicopters to
carry Panamanian guardsmen out to Pidertupo.

"A year later, the hate and bitterness have faded, but the pain is still
there. For Tom, the healing will take a long time. The entire muscle of
the calf of his right leg was completely blown away along with most
of the tibia. The end of the barrel of a 20-gauge shotgun was four feet
from Tom's leg when the terrorist pulled the trigger. The biggest fight of
all has been to save his leg; since it had been a very dirty wound (sand,
dirt, leaves and rope fibers) it raged with infection for four weeks. He
underwent five major operations in Panama City. Back in Pittsburgh he
had two major operations, plastic surgery and bone grafts. His leg has
been saved and he is walking with just a slight limp.

"We know that Brigadoon is only supposed to happen once every
hundred years. We found it once and we'll do it again. We are planning to go to the South Pacific this fall to search out another location
to build our next resort. After months of research, it looks as though
we'll spend our time on the hundreds of islands in the Fiji group. The

Moodys will find the location."

The Moodys have never been compensated for their losses. In addition, five days after the attack their license to do business was revoked by the Panamanian government on the charges that guests were "bathing in the nude and smoking marijuana," which Joan steadfastly denies. Having spent a week with the Moodys and hearing their political and social views, we indeed believe her. Joan writes that the accidental killer of the Cuna 'Guardia' was arrested, but that "nothing was ever done about the guerrilla terrorists who brutally attacked us and attempted to kill Tom. To this day they live freely among the tribe."

> *"Throughout the years, we ignored all the little nagging warning signals . . . boats traveling through reefs at night without running lights . . . planes flying low after dark and landing on remote airstrips . . . tales of Columbian Indian shootouts . . . strange yachts passing through."*

The Moodys view the raid not as an isolated attack upon them or their guests, but as part of a much larger scheme. Joan wrote: "Quite obviously, these young attackers had spent time living abroad learning the guerrilla tactics they used. We feel that since it was one of their first operations, they bungled it badly. Molotov cocktails, for example, are not effective unless the flaming bottles of gasoline are smashed against a hard surface, causing them to explode. They simply tossed the burning bottles onto the rain-soaked thatched roofs and the fires we saw blazing were just the gasoline burning off. The marauders were also 'high' on something and were not coherent enough to do a proper job.

"These crimes are not the work of the 'traditional Cuna,' nor condoned by them. It is definitely the handiwork of the terrorist infiltrators.

"All foreigners are now being ousted from San Blas. What is it that they fear we might discover? Throughout the years, we ignored all the little nagging warning signals . . . boats traveling through reefs at night without running lights . . . planes flying low after dark and landing on remote airstrips . . . tales of Columbian Indian shootouts . . . strange yachts passing through. We suspect that economically their new enterprise will bring them much more income than tourism."

In a subsequent letter, Joan writes that she has since viewed a documentary for television entitled *Panama: Another Cuban Crisis?* In which correspondent Matt Quinn investigated rumors of army smuggling and narcotics transfers by Cuban-trained Cunas operating in the San Blas Islands. Joan writes that "We've heard rumors that even though most of the buildings on Pidertupo have been dismantled, the deep-water docks Tom built make a perfect place for unloading illegal cargo."

Tom and Joan did make it to Fiji and built Moody's Namena, an idyllic dive resort on a tiny private island.

As you might expect, Tom Moody is a tough customer. I'll never forget how surprised I was diving off Pidertupo when, at 70 feet, I looked over to see him suspended there, outfitted not with scuba, but only with a snorkel. With an occasional bubble popping from his snorkel, he hovered for a while watching me; then slowly drifted back to the surface. Later, over dinner, where Moody always held court, he said he used to free dive to 100 feet or more. "I was slowed down," he said, "after the doctors removed a piece of my lung."

What's interesting to note is that the Moodys were victims of both Panama and the U.S. Throughout the 1970s and 1980s, Manuel Noriega was the top general and then President of Panama. Evidence shows that U.S. government agencies ignored his drug dealing since he was a "friend" of the U.S. at a time America was concerned about communism advancing in Central America. Because of that, the Moodys received no justice from either government. But Tom and Joan did make it to Fiji and built Moody's Namena, an idyllic dive resort on a tiny private island. Unfortunately, Joan Moody passed away in early 2010.

Divers as Hostages

In 1999, terrorists made international headlines when they invaded a pair of dive resorts in Malaysia, taking guests and resort workers hostage. For more than ten years, the small Pacific Rim island of

Sipadan off Malaysian Borneo had been a favorite of *Undercurrent* readers. Then, it became the most dramatic example of an attractive underwater destination where safety concerns were pushed into the limelight. We got the frightening story firsthand from Ron Holland, founder of Borneo Divers.

Sipadan: Dive Travel Terrorism Dangers

"The raid took place on Easter Sunday around 20:30 hrs. local time. Six armed men infiltrated the western side of the island, near the Police Post and Wildlife Department, first taking one police officer and then two wildlife rangers. They proceeded to Pulau Sipadan Resort, the next place in line, where guests were finishing dinner or just relaxing. The rebels quietly rounded up all the guests and staff that were in the dining hall and ordered them to board two long boats (jongkongs) that were moving just parallel to the beach, keeping pace with the raiders.

"When the raider turned away from them to watch the rest get into the boats, the two Americans scooted off and ran for the forest . . ."

"Sadly, poor Rambo, one of Borneo Diver's staff, was visiting Pulau Sipadan Resort and was also captured. Definitely a case of 'in the wrong place at the wrong time.'

"Harris, Borneo Divers' resort manager on Sipadan, was able to warn all our guests of the situation and lead them into the jungle at the back of the resort to hide after one of our divemasters spotted the armed raiders. He also contacted the police and my partner Clement Lee with his cellphone. The police were on the scene within one hour. It was obvious that this was not a pirate attack and they were not out to just rob. No, these raiders were after people, and as soon as they had hustled their captives onto the two jongkongs, they left without firing a shot. An American couple escaped — it seems the husband refused, along with his wife, to get in the boat because she was a non-swimmer and the boats were lying off the beach and all the captives had to wade out to them. When the raider turned away from them to watch the rest get into the boats, the two Americans scooted off and ran for the forest . . ."

While tourists have been a chosen terrorist target in Bali and Egypt, the idea of a bunch of divers at a remote, quiet resort being abducted and held hostage strikes too close to home. The Abu Sayyaf terrorists who seized the Sipadan divers are one of two separate groups fighting for an independent Islamic nation in the southern Philippines. Both have kidnapped numerous hostages, including schoolchildren.

"After they abducted the divers and loaded them into boats, they drove to Jolo in the southern Philippines and imprisoned their captives in a bamboo cage in the jungle."

After the April 23 raid, the terrorists loaded the abducted divers into boats, they drove to Jolo in the southern Philippines, an hour's ride away, and imprisoned their captives in a bamboo cage in the jungle. Their initial demands were reported to include $2.5 million in ransom, and they threatened to behead two hostages if their demands weren't met. The only two Americans, James and Mary Murphy (Rochester, NY), escaped. The tourists who were abducted were from France, Germany, South Africa, Finland, and Lebanon.

Two Muslim Malaysians were released soon after, however Abu Sayyaf made various demands for the release of several prisoners. Most hostages were released between August and September 2000. The Philippine army launched a major offensive on September 16, 2000, rescuing all remaining hostages except Filipino dive instructor Roland Ullah. He was eventually freed in 2003.

Undercurrent reader Ricky Tuss had been diving Sipadan by boat from the nearby Sea Ventures Dive Resort, about 300 yards off Mabul. He said, "We dived Sipadan the morning after the abduction before we (the guests) knew of the event. I couldn't understand why there were so few dive boats or why the people on the island were staring at us. We did the last dives allowed before Sipadan was shut down for diving. We had two Malaysian gun boats guarding us the next night."

PS: Since the event, all of the cottages and resorts on Sipadan have been closed and it is dived from nearby resorts. It is carefully patrolled by the Malaysian Navy and the number of divers is regulated. There have been no further incidents in the area.

Somali Pirates Hijack Dive Boat

Smaller boats are easier to catch than giant oil tankers, so it was inevitable that Somali pirates would chase after any dive boat that got within range.

In early April 2009, scoundrels seized the *Indian Ocean Explorer*, a 115-foot liveaboard that sails the Aldabra Islands, four remote atolls near the Seychelles and Madagascar, and 700 miles southeast of the infamous Somali coast. (See our review of the boat in August 2006). The boat is often used by scientists to study remote Indian Ocean reefs.

Luckily, the boat's passengers, a group of British divers that had booked the boat with the London-based Aquatours, narrowly missed being kidnapped. They had gone ashore at Assumption Island only hours before the *Explorer* and its seven-man crew, all from the Seychelles, was seized.

The Royal Navy says the boat was to taken to a pirate stronghold north of Mogadishu.

Several months later, we were informed that the Seychelles government paid a ransom for the return of the crew, but the boat remained in pirate hands.

Chapter 3
You Have to Be Crazy to Be a Diver

As a diver, you know that lots of people think you're nuts. After all, who would go down there with all those sharks and scary things? Well, we divers do just that and we know we're not crazy. But are we? Or at least some of us? Could diving-related conditions actually drive you mad? That's a question we've been asking for some time, and this 1992 article, by Dr. Chris Acott with the Hyperbaric Medicine Unit, Royal Adelaide Hospital, Adelaide, South Australia, about Aussie divers states the case.

Does Diving Drive You Crazy?
Psychotic aspects of DCS

During the past ten years, our understanding of decompression sickness (DCS) and its treatment has been gradually changing. Some publications have alluded to the "punch-drunk" diver and the neuropsychological changes occurring with diving and DCS. If there are effects on neuropsychological functioning due to exposure over time to diving risks, they are probably not large (at least in the short term) and probably only affect a few individuals. However, there are numerous anecdotal reports, particularly those associated with commercial abalone divers, which describe acute psychiatric changes.

I have talked with some of the abalone shellers who remain in the boat while the diver is below. They say they could differentiate the depth of the dive by the mood and personality change seen in the abalone diver upon surfacing. These stories were so consistent that one would have to assume that they are true. Acute confusional states were seen with deeper dives, while aggressive, abusive behavior was seen with longer, shallower dives.

Recognizing Symptoms

There is often considerable delay between the onset of the symptoms of DCS and the actual time the diver presents himself for treatment. This delay is frequently attributed to:

- Ignorance of the meaning of the symptoms.
- Overindulgence in alcohol.
- Symptoms blamed on a previous injury.
- Denial (the dive was well within the limits of the tables so the diver could not possibly be bent).
- Guilt (DCS is regarded in some circles as shameful as a sexually transmitted disease).

Failure to recognize that there is something wrong may, in fact, be a manifestation of the disease. Unrealistic, or in some instances, paranoid reaction to the symptoms, may be part of the disease itself. This is sort of a Catch-22. To recognize that one has DCS, one must recognize the symptoms. But a symptom of DCS is that one does not recognize that one has been bent.

The Post DCS Blues and DCS Psychosis

I have observed that most post-treatment patients go through a depressive phase, and that divers diagnosed as having cerebral DCS have a degree of psychosis, manifesting itself mainly by paranoid behavior. The following case histories will demonstrate this.

Case 1: The Abusive Instructor

This 32-year-old diving instructor came to our department on September 27, 1989, after having been flown in from Darwin Hospital in a pressurized aircraft. He was agitated, irritable, slow and vague. He had poor short-term memory. He was unstable on his feet.

The previous April he began working in the Maldives. He usually dived twice a day, six days a week. The first dive in the morning was to 20 or 30 meters for 50 to 60 minutes. The second dive was about three hours later and could be to 20m. He used a Beuchat computer.

Occasionally, he had the afternoon off. He drank heavily. He played hard. The staff at the resort noticed a slow personality change. He became aggressive and abusive, not only toward the staff, but also to the guests. He was told to stop drinking, which he did a month prior to his departure from the island. His last dive was on the morning of the 14th of September. He does not know how he finished the dive. On ascent, he became extremely confused. He remembered falling over in the boat. He was put on a flight to Australia that day. His confusion worsened. He disembarked at Singapore and stayed there for a week. His girlfriend in Darwin reported receiving several distressing phone calls. She said his conversation was bizarre, vague and extremely slow. He finally arrived in Australia on the 22nd of September.

Unable to fill in his customs declaration, he was strip searched by officials, as they suspected drugs. His girlfriend took him to Darwin Hospital where he was admitted to the psychiatric ward. They were unable to diagnose the problem, as his behavior was unlike anything they had seen. When they finally found out that he had been a diving instructor, they contacted us and he was flown to Adelaide that day.

He received ten hyperbaric treatments. He improved after each treatment, but he was not quite right. On the 10th of October, he had an acute paranoid psychotic reaction. At a major psychiatric hospital, he underwent a series of investigations and they concluded that he had a "neuropsychological profile that one would expect from a person suffering from hypoxia: probable cause, DCS."

Follow-up revealed a pleasant fellow, off all medications and able to return to work. He still had a moderate degree of memory deficit.

Case 2: The Paranoid Father

This 31-year-old male made a dive to 20 meters with a "slow" rapid ascent. When he surfaced, his symptoms were consistent with a cerebral arterial gas embolism or cerebral DCS. He was told never to dive again. He waited for two years and then did four dives over two days. None was deeper than 15 meters. The bottom times were conservative and there were no rapid ascents. He surfaced from his last dive (to 10m) with symptoms similar to his episode two years earlier. He went home, deciding to sweat it out. He slept that night with his bed on blocks to elevate his feet. In the morning, his symptoms were worse. He contacted us. The diagnosis was cerebral DCS.

Divers diagnosed as having cerebral DCS have a degree of psychosis, manifesting itself mainly by paranoid behavior.

He was extremely aggressive and abusive with paranoid overtones. He made remarks like "What are the police divers doing here? Are they after me?" He later said that he could not stop these odd feelings. He had a headache and was very unsteady. There was a short-term memory loss.

His treatment was successful, to a degree. Follow-up revealed a different person from the one who had been admitted. He was a gentle, caring father. He admitted to having had paranoid feelings, and also to having been extremely depressed. He said these feelings took about a month to disappear. He still complains of short-term memory loss and of being "slower" than he was before this episode. He will not be diving again.

Case 3: The Depressed Swede

This Swedish tourist was treated at Townsville. She had been diagnosed as having had cerebral DCS. Although successfully treated clinically, she admitted to not feeling her normal self. She was still slightly depressed, and said that this had gradually gotten better over the past couple of months. The interview revealed that she had extreme paranoid feelings during treatment and just after. At that time, she did not like being alone because space creatures were going to get her. These creatures had been in a book that she had been reading before she went diving.

Conclusion:

Clinically closest to what I have described here is puerperal psychosis, a brief psychological disturbance, typically one of depression, with confusion and thought disorders. Recovery takes time.

To be bent and not recognize it may in fact be an important diagnostic tool for cerebral DCS. The symptoms of DCS, which are obvious to us, may not be of importance to the diver because the various pathological processes alter perception. Reluctance to seek treatment may actually be part of the disease process due to specific Central Nervous System (CNS) deficits. Indeed, aggressive, abnormal and paranoid behaviors indicate significant CNS involvement.

One year later, another medical expert shared with us the chilling story of a diver whose decompression sickness was misdiagnosed, with near-disastrous results. Here is a report from Paul Hard, M.D.

DCS Masquerading as Psychiatric Illness

Decompression sickness is among the most difficult medical conditions to diagnose. Essentially, wherever bubbles form determines the location of the pathology. It has been elusive to MRI, CT scanning, and for the most part, electrophysiological testing.

The Jo Ellen Smith Hyperbaric Medicine and Diving Unit (New Orleans, LA) treated a 34-year-old man who had gone on a scuba diving trip to Lake Powell, Arizona. He experienced a regulator malfunction at 30 feet, panicked and surfaced rapidly, after taking a deep breath and holding it.

On the surface he felt extremely fatigued. Over the course of the following week, his neurologic impairment became progressively worse, with difficulty walking, talking, and writing. He also lost his memory and fine motor control to the extent that he could no longer play the piano after twenty-five years of piano playing. The patient saw a number of physicians who were unable to pinpoint the cause of his problems until he happened upon a friend of mine who was a physician in New Mexico.

During a phone call it was ascertained that the patient had central nervous system DCS until proven otherwise and needed hyperbaric treatment. He was treated three times in Albuquerque; however, no change was noted. Subsequent neuropsychological testing resulted in grossly abnormal findings and the patient was told that his problem was psychiatric.

After considering suicide, he was admitted to a psychiatric hospital and, through a bizarre twist of events, taken to jail and eventually committed for thirty days to a second psychiatric institution. At this point, the patient's parents contacted me.

After evaluating the patient, central nervous system decompression sickness was diagnosed. A nuclear medicine brain scan showed decreased blood supply to the patient's frontal lobes. He was placed in a hyperbaric oxygen chamber for a single hyperbaric dive and upon exit the scan was repeated, showing filling in of all of these damaged areas. The patient's brain cells were living, but just in need of blood supply and adequate oxygen to work.

A series of hyperbaric oxygen treatments was initiated. During the next six weeks he steadily regained all of his neurological functioning. His final scan was normal. All his abnormal tests reverted to normal and his neuropsychological exam showed him to have risen twenty IQ points on the test. This was a startling result.

The patient returned to his normal junior high school teaching job, resumed playing the piano, recorded an album, and formed his own band.

As the above reports indicate, divers deny they have the bends; they ignore the symptoms, report them too late or not at all. Before we discuss more cases of "crazy divers," here's a definitive article by Bret Gilliam we published more than a decade ago that stimulated lots of positive discussion in the dive community.

Getting the Bends out of the Closet
The problem of denial

Decompression sickness (DCS) or the "bends" is a statistical inevitability in diving. It has no conscience and rarely abides by any set rules. Yet, too many sport divers absolutely deny the possibility that they might have been bent, even though their symptoms are clear to others and should be clear to them. Regardless, they steadfastly refuse further evaluation or even basic surface oxygen.

The Bends Stigma

For many divers, there is a stigma attached to announcing that one may be experiencing bends symptoms. Yet any delay in reporting symptoms and seeking treatment only leads to a poorer prognosis for recovery.

Why would any intelligent adult ignore symptoms with the knowledge that DCS manifestations are getting worse with time? Because divers have come to believe that they, personally, have erred if they get DCS. They can expect to be blamed for bad profiles, criticized for screwing up, blamed for drinking a beer or exercising, or get labeled a "bad diver." Rather than report seemingly insignificant symptoms and get immediate treatment, too many divers would rather dodge embarrassment by hanging on to their pride until the pain gets too great. Such a delay can mean that greater and perhaps permanent damage, once preventable, will occur.

> *Too many sport divers absolutely deny the possibility that they might have been bent.*

It's time to stop pointing fingers and using antiquated analogies ("He screwed up and got bent, the idiot!") or continued reluctance to report symptoms will prevail.

With few exceptions, it is no one's fault that he got bent; a diver can follow his dive plan precisely by the book and still get hit. Likewise, a deliberately high risk dive profile may not produce symptoms. Although we can identify certain factors predisposing divers to DCS, it is still impossible to explain the exact physiological mechanisms that allow one diver to be bent while his partner escapes unscathed.

Where Bends is Seen as Normal

In a 1991 DAN Workshop held at Duke University, it was reported that the overall incidence of DCS for commercial divers was approximately 1 in 1000 dives. For sport divers it was 1 in 10,000 dives, while the scientific diving community rated an extremely low 1 in 100,000 dives.

With these rather startling multipliers of ten, it would be tempting to conclude that the scientific diving group is 100 times safer than the commercial diving group. Rather, diving "attitude" seems to be the reason for the difference.

Most scientific diving projects are planned from inception to eliminate as much risk as possible. This is accomplished by strict training and supervision and conservative dive profiles. At the other end of the spectrum, the commercial diving community must deal with a job performance/task completion goal motivated by economics. They are steadfast in their opinion that immediate evaluation and treatment are an acceptable alternative to a lesser incidence rate.

Of course, no bends hit is a good one. Terry Overland of Ocean-eering International made this point: "While most sport and scientific dive operations would like to reach zero percent DCS incidence, in commercial diving this is simply unrealistic. We accept that if we give a worker a hammer, he will eventually hit his thumb, and when he does we'll treat it. Our protocols allow us to treat DCS effectively enough that Type I hits are essentially manageable. We feel that this is a more responsible outlook than attempting to unrealistically eliminate the malady. Our divers feel that our system works, and their butts are on the firing line."

If DCS is promptly reported and evaluated with ensuing on-site treatment, then the prognosis for complete resolution is often excellent. The attitude of many chamber operators is "No matter what the problem, if reported and treated quickly, we can clean the diver up."

Oxygen is the Key

Type I DCS (mild symptoms, pain only) affords less risk than Type II DCS (serious symptoms, central nervous system involvement), but in either presentation, aggressive oxygen therapy and prompt recompression have produced nearly a 98 percent success record. A significant percentage of symptomatic DCS patients may be relieved following a 30-45 minute period breathing 100 percent oxygen, if delivered by demand valve/mask immediately upon experiencing symptoms.

During the year I was in charge of diving operations aboard the *Ocean Spirit*, I observed nearly a dozen cases of symptomatic DCS (1 in 12,000) clear completely following demand system oxygen during transit to our chamber on the ship. We were successful in encouraging divers to report any symptoms and had a 100 percent resolution rate on every DCS case we treated.

It's time divers woke up to the fact that bends is an injury like any other and common sense dictates its treatment. The encouragement of prompt reporting with no associated peer or professional blame will vastly improve the safety of a sport infamous for symptom denial.

Now that we have taken bends out of the closet, let's move on to people who were diagnosed as having decompression sickness, only to learn that they really were crazy.

Crazy Divers?

Craziness, it seems, can mimic decompression illness, say researchers at Brigham Young University. They uncovered two cases in which acute psychosis mimicked the bends.

In the first case, a 39-year-old diver was searching a river bottom for a drowning victim at 30 feet for 45 minutes.

Upon arriving home he complained of severe headache, hip and joint pain, then became uncommunicative and had difficulty recalling events. He went to a local hospital, where his brain CT, EEG, and laboratory tests were normal. His neuropsychological tests, however, were abnormal — for example, he could not remember his wife's name.

Within 12 hours of diving he experienced delusions and hallucinations: e.g., the television told him to go visit President Clinton.

Suspecting DCS, doctors treated him in a chamber, but he showed no improvement. After doctors interviewed him further, he recalled finding a decomposed body that came apart in his hands — an event that apparently spawned psychosis.

In the second case, a 22-year-old California diver made several dives to 85 ft. for up to 30 minutes. Within 12 hours of diving he experienced delusions and hallucinations: e.g., the television told him to go visit President Clinton. Testing showed impaired attention, verbal memory impairments, and a distorted thought process. Toxicological and neurological tests were normal. And he had no pain. Still, the symptoms after diving suggested DCS, so he was treated in the chamber, but there were no changes in cognitive impairments.

After further interviewing, the diagnosis was psychosis secondary to schizophrenia.[1]

---

1 RO Hopkins, LK Weavers, *Acute Psychosis Presenting as Decompression Illness.*, Psychology Dept., Brigham Young University, Provo, Utah; Department of Hyperbaric Medicine, LDS Hospital, SLC, Utah; Undersea & Hyperbaric Medicine, Volume 27, 2000 Supplement.

Even rational divers can be affected by the underwater environment itself. Here's a piece by Paul Bernstein that originally appeared in the now defunct Human Behavior Magazine *that we carried in 1979.*

Deep Trouble: How diving affects simple task performance

Two divers are learning to buddy breathe, sharing one regulator between them. Suddenly, they realize they're sinking. Why? They were concentrating so hard on learning to breathe that they forgot to kick.

A commercial welder has been working for years on land, but when he starts to weld on a pipe underwater he finds himself doing things in the wrong order, forgetting how parts fit together — mental tasks that would seem to have nothing to do with the problems of the new environment.

A human being faces significant problems when underwater. The cues he normally relies on are missing. One's sense of balance disappears. It's impossible to tell where sounds are coming from. He can't communicate, see clearly or distinguish colors well. He's in a strange environment carrying only a tenuous life-support system. But should that affect his ability to do simple arithmetic? To perform on simple abstract tests? His memory of what was observed? His concentration? Or the ability to make decisions?

Yes, says kinesiologist Glen Egstrom of UCLA. In a series of studies, Egstrom set out to measure just how much divers are affected by their surroundings when it comes to performing mental tasks.

In one study, groups of experienced and novice divers were given sentence-comprehension tests ("B here precedes A:AB. True or False?") and diving questions involving calculations — pressures, remaining bottom time and so on. They were to solve them in their heads or with whatever scratch pads they could manage underwater. They were tested both in a 15-foot tank with observation ports and in the ocean at a depth of 18 to 20 feet. They were given the tests both before and after completing a pipe-assembly task.

For the sentence-comprehension tests, locale didn't make much difference; percentage scores were in the 90s for each group. But on the diving questions, there was a striking difference between performance in the tank and in the ocean, and between novices and experienced

Diving Can Make You Crazy

A 31-year-old male walked into a Louisiana hospital emergency room agitated, with delusions, paranoia, and complex visual hallucinations. Tests found some brain abnormalities, but physicians couldn't pinpoint the cause. He reported that two days previously, while scuba diving, he had made a breath-holding ascent from 45 ft. to 15 ft., so the doctors consulted Louisiana State University hyperbaric medicine specialists, who recommended recompression treatments. That resolved his psychosis.

(Glover, Van Meter, LeGros and Barratt, Health Science Center, LSU, New Orleans. UHMS Abstracts, 2004.

divers. Before the pipe assembly task, novices scored an average 87 in the tank, but only 52 percent in the ocean. Scores after the test were 60 in the tank, 57 in the ocean. Experienced divers did much better: 90 in the tank pre-test, 77 post-test. In addition, the novices registered radical changes in heart and respiration rate when in the ocean, with no apparent connection to the tasks they were performing, which was attributed to either heightened anxiety or heightened arousal.

Another study, based on memorizing short passages about subjects related to diving, showed that the water temperature when the diver first learned the material had a significant effect on his ability to report that material once he surfaced. Like the drunken student who can remember what he or she learned better when drunk than when sober, a diver who learns material underwater can apparently remember it better underwater than on the surface. Thus, divers can be excused for their reputation as storytellers.

Divers' reports about what happened to them while working underwater often are at odds with the facts as monitored by a television camera. Egstrom once found a 15 to 20 percent loss of information in divers underwater compared to what divers on the surface had observed of the same conditions.

It's not just environment; there's a definite psychological factor involved. To demonstrate that, Egstrom set up a fake pressure chamber. When subjects thought they were diving to 60 feet (based on a rigged gauge and hissing air to simulate pressurization and depressurization) they showed significantly higher anxiety scores and heart rates than a control group performing the same tasks outside. They performed their tasks correctly but took more time to do them; they were also less aware of other things around them, perhaps because they were focusing all their attention on the immediate task at hand.

Besides nitrogen narcosis, other factors contribute to what Egstrom calls "cognitive disruption," or not being as alert as usual. There's a cold factor, a kind of sensory deprivation, weightlessness and even a plain old aversion to water in some people. And, notes Egstrom, "there's stress, which is compounded if you take water and make it cold water; or water and fill it with animals, some of which have teeth. And while some people really like it in the water, others don't, but choose to operate in the water anyway." They really like it, but their performance would tend to indicate otherwise.

Many effects can be overcome with training, but until the diver

Who are More Afraid, Who Take the Risks: Men? . . . or Women?

Clinical psychology graduate student Edith Hoffman from Miami's Barry University conducted a study in the early 90s to determine whether male or female divers exhibit greater risk-taking behavior. For the seventy-eight divers, Hoffman developed a scale that assessed risks divers take in the maintenance of their scuba equipment, with their physical health and mental well-being, and in adherence to diving rules. As you would imagine, the men were bigger risk takers.

Thirty-six percent of the male divers had dived alone, where only eight percent of the women had dived without a buddy.

Forty-three percent of the men admitted to diving with a hangover, compared to five percent of female divers.

Both female and male divers succumbed to peer pressure when they were hesitant to make a dive. The female divers led with forty-six percent, followed by the male divers with thirty-three percent.

adapts to the new environment, he may have to concentrate as much as 50 percent more than an experienced diver on what he is doing, therefore blocking out surrounding factors that can be important.

For instance, Egstrom notes that new divers often cannot spot abalone or scallops, even if the instructor points them out. "Part of it is that they're having stress interference. They aren't able to focus their observational powers on this thing, because they have other things on their minds — they're worried about being able to stay with their buddy, and how deep they are, and how much air they've got in their tank."

This inability to concentrate on more than one subject at a time may be responsible for the "avalanching effect" that often causes novice mishaps. "In a study of surf entries and exits, we noticed that if you trace back with people who have relatively serious problems, usually it starts off with one small thing, where they begin to concentrate on that one thing, and meanwhile the world around them goes to hell in a hand basket. The waves crash on their heads, knock them over, roll them up on the beach. It's rare that there's any single catastrophic thing that brings on the trouble. It's usually a series of events, each one feeding on the error from the last."

Arthur Bachrach, chair of the Behavioral Sciences Department at the Naval Medical Research Institute in Washington, DC, and a colleague of Egstrom's, notes that many of the 150 sport-diving deaths a year can be attributed to panic.

But people panic on the surface too. Is diving panic any different from, say, panic on the freeway? "I think the strange environment contributes," says Bachrach. "We find people training for scuba do fine in the pool, and then when they go out into the sea, they panic. Those four walls of the pool are no longer there, and they're suddenly faced with this vast void; and it's not necessarily a diminished situation but an enhanced one in terms of the role of the stimuli — there are so many more than there were in the pool. The diminishment of senses, and the fact that the individual is losing a lot of his abilities, is coupled with the enhancement of more things happening around him."

As a result of these findings, diver training has begun to emphasize the psychological factors. Diving instructors are finding that if we want to dive in the ocean, we'll have to learn in the ocean.

If there's one lesson humanity has learned since emerging from the sea eons ago, it's that we can't go home again — at least not without a great deal of mental preparation.

Attitude can have profound and adverse effects, both in and out of the water, as indicated in a study we summarized in 1996.

Those Who Go Down in Caves

Psychological tests provide a rough gauge of who will be successful and who will fail in high-risk cave diving activities, says Milledge Murphey, a professor in the University of Florida's College of Health and Human Performance.

"In this extreme high-risk group of cave divers, there seem to be certain types that do not do well, and others that do quite well. The majority of successful cave divers are introverted. Scuba divers are mostly extroverts," he said.

Cave diving is the only sport where death is an absolute result of performance failure.

Since 1963, 430 cave divers have been killed in Florida. "Cave diving is the only sport where death is an absolute result of performance failure," he said. "It must be done right or there's no tomorrow."

With its high-tech equipment and precise set of instructions, cave diving requires someone with a mind set for details. Many of the people the sport attracts work in technical professions.

Research on cave divers, acrobatic pilots, sky divers and other participants in high-risk sports shows that they are serious, professional people who enjoy technical precision, not brash risk-takers who jeopardize their lives for a good time.

Cave diving, like other high-risk sports, has become increasingly popular, probably in part because of people's desire for greater risk-taking in their lives, Murphey said. "Many people in advanced cultures crave more excitement in their mundane lives than going to work, coming home and watching television. They seem to want to look back toward the gladiator days when people truly lived on the edge."

Another reason for cave diving's growing participation is rapid advances in the technology of the equipment, allowing people with relatively little experience to make deeper and longer dives into caves, he said.

Cave divers, like other participants in high-risk sports, often seek sensations of vertigo, according to Murphey. "It's a little like floating outside of a space capsule in outer space. The environment of an underwater cave is so hostile that there's no possibility of being able to surface if you have an equipment malfunction or technical problem."

All the training, redundant equipment, and special safety procedures in the world can be negated by one factor: panic. Our 2004 report explored the anatomy of panic, and recounted some sad cases where panic proved deadly.

Why Divers Die: The True
Cause of Death — Panic, Not Drowning

Throughout the years, *Undercurrent* has emphasized that panic is the diver's worst enemy. It makes us forget our training and act illogically. A panic attack is intense fear or discomfort, often accompanied by feelings of imminent danger or impending doom, and an urge to escape. It's the old "fight or flight" instinct that's hardwired into all of us.

A study of panic in recreational scuba divers conducted by David F. Colvard, M.D. and Lynn Y. Colvard, Ph.D., found that 15 percent of survey respondents who reported panicking while diving had made a rapid or uncontrolled ascent. Five percent of them reported symptoms of DCS, and many who embolized are not alive to respond.

You don't have to dive deep to risk an embolism; with full lungs, a rise of just a few feet can be enough to cause an embolism.

One Divers Alert Network's report on sport diving fatalities includes the case of a 43-year-old who had difficulty equalizing, panicked and aborted the dive after going no deeper than 28 feet. She made a rapid ascent, complained of difficulty breathing, and later died of an air embolism.

Panic is more common than most divers think — and more than most training agencies care to acknowledge. More than half the scuba divers in a national survey reported experiencing panic or near-panic behavior, according to research by Dr. William Morgan at the University of Wisconsin-Madison. The incidence of panic was higher in women (64 percent) than men (50 percent). Morgan notes that panic responses can occur when a diver is suddenly exposed to an unanticipated stressor, such as running out of air — a problem that's almost always avoidable. A well-trained diver knows she can always get a couple of extra breaths from an "empty" tank as she ascends and the ambient pressure decreases. Even a partially-inflated BCD can provide an emergency breath or two. Of course, divers must keep their wits about them in the first place.

> *A well-trained diver knows she can always get a couple of extra breaths from an "empty" tank as she ascends and the ambient pressure decreases.*

In his book *Medical Examination of Sport Scuba Divers*, Alfred Bove wrote, "Panic, or ineffective behavior in the emergency situation when fear is present, is the single biggest killer of sport divers." But panic is often overlooked as a cause of death underwater. Instead drowning is listed as the medical cause.

A panicky diver can be dangerous to others as well as himself, a result that people who eschew buddy diving like to emphasize. While taking a deep diving course on a 130 ft. wreck, a 33-year-old ran out of air and began to breathe from his buddy's octopus. For some reason he panicked and began descending, dragging his buddy down too. (Panic can also cause disorientation.) The buddy broke free, made an emergency ascent, and was transported to a local hospital where he recovered. The 33-year-old's body was found two days later.

A 57-year-old diver went to 80 ft. Within 15 minutes, he was out of air and pulled his buddy's regulator from his mouth. The buddy tried unsuccessfully to share air with him, but the panicked diver took off for the surface, where he passed out and didn't respond to treatment.

Diving "rust" can lead to panic. A 55-year-old rescue diver who had not been underwater for two years made a wreck dive to 74 ft. for 24 minutes. At the safety stop, his mask flooded and he panicked and ascended rapidly to the surface. While climbing the boat ladder, he collapsed and could not be resuscitated. Air embolism was the killer.

As Dr. Morgan pointed out, panic attacks are not restricted to novices. Divers with many years of experience can panic for no apparent reason. Affected divers often spit out their regulators, even though they have air left. Similarly, firefighters are sometimes discovered following a fire with their full face masks removed, even though air remains in their tanks. In studies, some anxious firefighters wearing respirators will remove their full face masks (hence air supply) if they experience respiratory distress.

A typical case: A 30-year-old technical diver with extensive experience made a cave dive to 100 feet using nitrox. Her dive buddies saw her twitch during her ascent, but she did not appear to have a seizure. She then dropped the regulator from her mouth and wouldn't take an alternate gas source. Her dive buddies, who skipped 22 minutes of decompression time, brought her to the surface. She had drowned.

Some serious divers speculate whether regulator manufacturers should be including neck straps to help keep a lost mouthpiece from floating too far away. Often, technical and cave divers mount the primary regulator on a long hose, looped around the torso, which can easily be unwound and donated to an out-of-air buddy. A necklace keeps the octopus handy, hanging just below the chin. It also prevents the regulator from dangling in the sand or dragging across a reef.

In almost every case, panic is the culmination of a series of events, each increasing stress to the point where it becomes unmanageable. Being alert to signs of increasing stress, both before and during the dive, can help a diver deal with what's causing stress and solve those problems before they build to a panic situation. The more confidence you develop in the water, the more likely you are to deal successfully with unanticipated stressors. For instance, knowing you can make a free ascent from your diving depth could make it a lot easier to deal with an out-of-air situation.

A key to avoiding panic is to recognize our comfort zones, and to exceed them only when we're ready. Managed stress is a good thing — it heightens our perceptions and mental acuity, and adds excitement to what otherwise is usually a pretty placid sport. When we place ourselves into situations we're not ready for, that's when stress turns from friend to foe.

While the effect of pressure or being underwater can affect the mental state, there are those who bring an altered state with them to the dive boat. Here's one study we commented on in 2003.

Who You Callin' Hostile?

Sport divers are a mellow bunch. At least that is what researchers in South Africa found after studying anxiety and hostility among military and recreational divers.

Both navy and recreational divers tend to have lower anxiety than the average population. Lower anxiety is "important for divers, since divers with low anxiety scores tend to have higher performance scores than divers with high anxiety scores." Anxiety levels were lower among older divers but were unaffected by diving experience. The researchers noted, however, that a little anxiety is helpful in keeping divers focused and cautious.

When it comes to hostility, the gap widens between sport divers and military divers. Navy divers had a stronger urge to act out their hostility and a pronounced tendency to be critical of others. While military divers are trained for hostile times, the researchers postulated that the military may attract enlistees who recognize "a venue where they can externalize their hostility without resulting in antisocial behavior." Having passed the navy's diving course — one of the most demanding — divers may have developed a superior self-image that makes them more critical of others.

This hostile trait is found among other naval personnel, but not among civilian divers, suggesting that increased hostility is due to the subjects' military affiliation rather than their diving interests.

What's it all mean? Well, you can expect your fellow divers to keep their cool, but if you're on a dive boat with an ex-Navy Seal, you may want to watch your step.

Well, so sport divers might be mellow, but add a fifth of rum to the mix and things can change, as we reported in 2002.

Drunks Aboard Your Boat: When Jerks Spoil the Fun

The misuse of alcohol creates all sorts of problems for divers. Alcohol dehydrates, and dehydration is strongly suspected of impeding offgassing efficiency. The adverse effects of alcohol on mental ability, motor skills, judgment and impulse control are very well documented.

The problem on a dive boat is not just that a drunk diver will go diving, but that a hung over, severely dehydrated diver may get into trouble the next day. Even if we stop worrying about people diving drunk or hung over, we can worry about how their behavior can affect others. An injured diver on a liveaboard may mean that diving is over for everyone. More likely, however, is this scenario, where a bunch of drunks just make for a miserable trip, as *Undercurrent* subscriber Dean Knudsons (Golden Valley, MN) reported about his 2002 Blackbeard cruise in the Bahamas.

"One urinated on the first mate in the middle of the first night and another screamed at the cook."

"Discount prices attract a variety of clients to Blackbeard's Cruises, and not all are frugal and unassuming (or even divers). On board were five members of a construction crew who had received the trip as a Christmas bonus from their boss.

"They spent the average day wrapped in blankets sleeping on the deck, only to arise at 3 p.m. and begin drinking beer, continuing to 4 a.m. each night, much to the dismay of the passengers who took the trip to dive. Several of the men were hung over and irritable from 7 a.m. to 3 p.m., often refusing to move from their topside sleeping spots even to allow the crew to handle lines, or to allow passengers to navigate from one end of the boat to the other. One urinated on the first mate in the middle of the first night and another screamed at the cook (the captain's wife) in the middle of the night.

"The captain actually warned them in a public announcement that he had permission to abandon them in Bimini. This did calm them, but they still managed to drink an astonishing quantity of alcohol. The shouting, screaming, profane language and stereo blasting made it difficult for the diving passengers to sleep, despite repeated polite requests for them to drink quietly. I was surprised to learn that this was their second Blackbeard trip.

"They had taken precautions to bring a large quantity of their own alcohol, since they had consumed all the alcohol available on the boat by the midpoint of their previous trip."

Divers at dedicated dive resorts can face similar problems. At Belize's Turneffe Island Lodge in January, Sue Ann and Howard Hackworth ran into three jerks who "were a pain in the *@!*.

"They were very hung over when they went diving at the Blue Hole and promptly drank beer when they surfaced (while we were in the water on two dives, they consumed the beer the other divers had ordered for the trip back). They kept dropping below the dive limits even with two divemasters with them — the divemasters had to physically pull them back up twice.

"The third time the divemasters gave up and took us all up for our safety stop. They drank heavily all the time and the folks at the resort finally told them they couldn't dive if they were drinking. They thought this was ridiculous — they chose to drink instead of dive pretty much from that point on. They would only do the middle dive and then drink all afternoon.

"One guy was a divemaster (he had no buoyancy control and was always running into everyone and kicking coral). His wife kept having runaway ascents. When we went for a night dive he told the divemaster she didn't need her own light — crazy!"

Of course, the problem with boats and dedicated resorts is that you have nowhere else to go. If jerks are causing problems and management doesn't act, you're stuck. In at least one case — a week called "Cayman Madness" — partying and diving is pushed heavily in the dive community through advertising and magazine articles. Subscriber William Hall (Oak Harbor, WA) writes about one October Madness during which: "There were cheerleading and drinking contests and lots of other party-type things." In situations like this, of course, there's no control over who goes diving the next day. However, one wonders whether such a week ought to garner headlines in diving magazines that are purported to be watching out for our safety.

Finally, one can counter all this diver craziness with a mellower approach to diving, as we reported to Undercurrent *readers way back in 1989. The article, by Robert Applebaum, originally appeared in the* New Age Journal. *Turns out renowned underwater photographer Amos Nachoum and a few other divers know how to find peace below the surface.*

Deep Meditation: Spacing Out at Sixty Feet

When Amos Nachoum plummets beneath the ocean's surface these days, he is not always searching for exotic sea life. Nachoum's quest often is to explore the inner workings of his own psyche.

"For me, meditation is more powerful in the water," he explains. "I usually drop down 40 or 50 feet and sit on the reef or hover in the water. It's just like being in the womb."

Nachoum is not the only diver getting off his zafu and meditating underwater. A small but dedicated number of fellow explorers have made the same discovery; when it comes to clearing the mind and gaining personal insight, they say, the ocean's weightlessness, virtual silence, and diffused light make it a near-perfect environment. Says Marian Rivman, a New York sport diver and meditator: "The peace and energy that I might feel after an hour of meditating on land I can accomplish in just ten minutes underwater."

Some veteran divers question the wisdom of "spacing out" underwater. They note that a self-induced trance could dull a diver's response time in an emergency, make it difficult to communicate with a diving partner, and hinder the monitoring of air consumption and depth.

Nachoum, who often dives and meditates alone at night,

> *"For me, meditation is more powerful in the water, I usually drop down 40 or 50 feet and sit on the reef or hover in the water. It's just like being in the womb."*

acknowledges that he is courting danger, but says that after years of diving he knows what he's doing. Rivman is more cautious. "Never go into a state of meditation without first planning it beforehand with your buddy on the surface," she advises.

Such precautions seem particularly wise in light of the profound experiences many underwater meditators report. Although no scientific studies have explored why the dream-like alpha state may be intensified while diving, several researchers hypothesize that the reduction of sensory input allows divers to concentrate more fully on their inner experiences. In essence, they say, the ocean becomes the ultimate flotation tank.

John Turner, a physiologist and flotation tank researcher at the Medical College of Ohio, points out that the ocean's silent, buoyant environment, coupled with the diver's insulating wetsuit, eliminates a great deal of distracting sensory stimulation. "When that sensory input is decreased," Turner says, "our body and thoughts become more prominent. That helps us to develop a greater focus on ourselves." Turner also theorizes that the rhythmic, echoing sound of the diver's air regulator acts as a form of biofeedback, relaxing a diver as he or she becomes keenly aware of breathing.

Nitrogen narcosis, the stupor-like condition that occurs underwater as blood nitrogen levels rise, also may contribute to the meditator's underwater euphoria, according to Bruce Bassett, a San Antonio, TX, dive physiologist. Most divers notice the "rapture of the deep" beginning at 80 to 100 feet, he says, but nitrogen levels increase to a certain degree at lesser depths as well.

Rivman, however, has a more philosophical theory about the appeal of deep-water meditation: "The ocean is one big hug, and there is a great sense of trust," she says. "You know that it will always catch you — you will never fall. I feel the quintessential underwater, a cell in a vast universe."

Chapter 4
Unconventional Wisdom

As an independent, subscriber-supported publication that doesn't accept advertising, *Undercurrent* has been able to delve into some diving controversies and "alternate" viewpoints that other dive media won't touch. It's been our pleasure to provide a platform for some of the dive community's most notorious gadflies and rugged individualists to challenge some of the sport's golden rules, such as recreational dive limits. Here's Bret Gilliam's expert opinion, from 1992:

The Myths of Nitrogen Narcosis
As told by the deepest diver ever

Due to the adoption of the 130-foot recreational diving limit, much discussion of narcosis theory has been conducted "underground" by diving professionals without a public forum of information exchange. With the willingness of *Undercurrent* to tackle more controversial issues, we have a forum that goes beyond simple condemnation of any diving practice that does not apply a "lowest common denominator" standard.

Some early diving accounts by none other than Jacques Cousteau relate instances of near total incapacitation at depths of only 150 feet; they cite the supposed "Martini's Law" and the classic "Rapture of the Deep," where the increased partial pressure of nitrogen turns compressed air into an intoxicating gas.

In reality, well-trained and well-equipped divers with adequate experience at depth are often far less severely affected and impaired. Narcosis certainly must be dealt with responsibly, but many texts suggest levels of impairment that are highly exaggerated. I can attest to this from extensive personal experience, having made more than 2,000 dives below 300 fsw. In fact, in February of 1990 in Roatan, Honduras, I set a new depth record on air of 452 fsw.

In reality, experienced deep divers "adapt" to narcosis. Divers who regularly face deep exposures exhibit a tolerance to depth that far exceeds that of the diver who has not become adapted. This adaptation is best achieved by gradually working up to increasing depths over several days. I also have found that facial immersion breathing prior to significantly deep dives institutes the "diving response," thus lowering the diver's heart and respiratory rates.

Furthermore, for deep diving, using a regulator that can comfortably deliver adequate volumes upon demand is particularly important. Many so-called "professional models" will fall sadly short of performance expectations below 200 feet. Surprisingly, exhalation resistance may be a more important factor in breathing control than inhalation ease. In fact, studies have shown that the most significant fatigue factor in underwater breathing tests is exhalation detriments. Slow, deep ventilations with minimal exertion will keep CO_2 down and delay the onset and diminish the severity of narcosis.

The Power of Suggestion

Many factors contribute to narcosis: hard work or heavy swimming that elevates carbon dioxide levels; cold, alcohol use or a hangover; fatigue; anxiety; motion sickness medications; side effects of some medications used to manage other conditions; lack of an "up" reference such as in bottomless blue water or in severely reduced visibility; and increased oxygen and, obviously, nitrogen partial pressure.

Way back in 1965, psychiatrist Dr. Gilbert Milner and professional diver Tom Mount reported a study of three groups (each with four students) who received identical dive training with the following exceptions:

- Group One was taught that divers will get narcosis at 130 fsw. The instructor emphasized the high probability of narcosis with severe symptoms.

- Group Two was taught that narcosis exists, and that its symptoms can occur beginning at 100 fsw. Its likelihood was not emphasized.

- Group Three received three hours of lecture on symptoms, risk, danger and known research. They were told that divers with strong will power could

I had no significant nitrogen narcosis impairment at 452 fsw for an exposure of approximately 4.5 minutes

mentally prepare themselves and greatly reduce the effects of narcosis.

Prior to the actual test, all students were taken on a 50-foot dive. In the initial dives to 130 fsw, all those in Group One indicated that they experienced minor to average narcosis problems, while those in Groups Two and Three indicated few noticeable effects.

At 180 fsw test depth, two divers from Group One dropped out because they experienced severe narcosis problems. Although all Group Two divers were affected, they still functioned at about a 50 percent level. Group Three divers indicated minor impairment.

At 200 fsw, the rest of the Group One divers and two of the Group Two divers dropped out.

At 240 fsw, one diver from Group Two and one from Group Three dropped out; the balance indicated some impairments but felt that they were not severe. Thus, it appears that conditioning divers to expect narcosis impairment at 130 fsw led to actual impairment.

From my own experience, I had no significant impairment at 452 fsw for an exposure of approximately 4.5 minutes. I admit, however, that this is the extreme end of adaptation: I had dived every week for more than a year, never taking more than a six-day layoff. Furthermore, my 627 dives during this period included 103 dives below 300 fsw.

Overcoming Impairment

Individuals vary widely in their susceptibility to narcosis, but eventually, almost all divers will become impaired. Initially, divers will notice a reduced ability to read fine gradations in a watch, for example, combined with an increased awareness of or sensitivity to noises, such as the sounds of inhalation and exhalation. Short-term memory and time perception can also be affected. The deep diver may experience lightheadedness, slowed mental activity, overconfidence, numbness and tingling in lips, face and feet, levity or tendency to laughter, perceptual narrowing, and diminished tolerance to stress. Deep divers need to be constantly aware of their own limitations and not hesitate to abort a dive if their impairment becomes unreasonable.

With experience, divers can learn to overcome or control these deficits to some extent. But the danger should never be underestimated. A diver unaware of his depth, bottom time, or remaining air volume is about to become a statistic!

The deep diver also has to be attentive to impairments in companion divers. Scores of experienced deep divers have used the "Gilliam narcosis hand signals" to assess their buddies. If one diver flashes a one-finger signal, the companion diver is expected to answer with a two-finger signal. A two-finger signal would be answered with three fingers. If a companion diver cannot respond quickly and correctly to the signal, sufficient impairment can be presumed and the dive should be aborted.

Although narcosis is eliminated with ascent, many divers experience some degree of amnesia about their performance. For instance, commercial divers have reported that they had completed their work successfully only to learn later that the work had not been accomplished at all! Typically, less experienced deep divers will not remember their greatest depth or bottom time even though it is recorded on their computers.

Therefore, experience is vital before attempting progressively deeper dives. Needless to say, before penetrating below sport diving depth, the diver should seek training from a competent, deep-diving instructor at a deep-diving training center.

Australian Bob Halstead, then the owner/captain of the highly regarded Papua New Guinea dive boat Telita, *weighed in on deep diving a year later.*

Deep Diving and the Meaning of Life
When 200 feet is a risk, but not dangerous

The *Telita* departed Garove Island at 1900 hours, bound for Ravieng. I found myself alone on watch. The moon rose, and I moved to the bow to savor the glorious New Guinea night. Undisturbed by even a sigh of wind, the seas were flat and glowing with a pearly light, and the surface parted, sparkling with luminescence and crying a submissive hiss.

Over the past three weeks I had, together with my wife Dinah and a few competent and adventurous divers, made some incredible dives. We had collectively made 143 dives ranging between 155 and 225 feet, along with many others to modest depths. Had we not made the deep dives, we would have missed sights and encounters that have enriched our lives.

> *"Danger" depends on how well the person making the dive copes with the risk.*

I sat alone on the bow of *Telita* thinking of the good humor, intelligence, skills and discipline that the divers demonstrated in flawlessly performing difficult and high risk dives without incident. Were these dives dangerous?

Two were. And I'll tell you about them later. But first, let me be rational. This will upset some people. Obedience or fantasy seems to be more popular these days, but when things get too irrational I feel insecure and go all wobbly. Which is, of course, why I am forever making comments about irrational behavior such as taking giant stride entries from the side of the boat, jumping into the water with air in the BC, wearing a snorkel when scuba diving, diving with a buddy, and acting as if the Queensland, Australia, government diving regulations have anything to do with making life healthier and safer. Of course, my rationality is also the reason we never start a cruise on a Friday.

Risk is Not Danger

The words "Risk" and "Danger" are often deliberately misused. This is a bureaucratic technique to make the simple seem confusing, thus to justify taking control. "Risk" is something inherent in a dive and it is the same for all divers.

"Danger" depends on how well the person making the dive copes with the risk. A dive to 25 feet in clear, calm water is low risk, but it would be dangerous if the person attempting it did not understand the consequences of breath holding on ascent.

Understanding the real risks is the most important factor in safe diving. A safe diver knows when not to dive — the diver assesses the risks and decides he or she does not have the education or experience to overcome them. If the diver is unable to do this, then the dive is dangerous and injury is likely.

A safe dive is one where it is unlikely (but not impossible) that injury will occur. If a "safe" dive turns out to be dangerous, one must ask if the problem could have been foreseen — should it have been assessed as a possible risk — or was it so totally outrageous that anyone considering it would have been thought paranoid?

Safety is never absolute. Stuff happens. Recently some unfortunate people were sitting, they thought safely, in their living rooms when an aircraft landed on their heads.

The Right Stuff for Diving Deep

Some people have the right stuff for diving and some do not. Some people will never be safe divers, while others will be able to make high risk dives and never run into trouble. Safety rules rarely work. Rules are for the guidance of the wise — and the observance of fools.

The deep diving rule implies that it is the risk assumed that needs limiting . . . "no deeper than 130 feet." What should be limited is the danger. And that depends on the individual diver. Which is the most dangerous situation? A qualified advanced diver, with nine dives, at 100 feet? Or me, with 6,000, at 150 feet? Or Bret Gilliam, with more than 12,000 dives and the world record to 452 feet, at 200 feet? Yes, limits do exist. But they are personal. Not absolute.

What I Find Deep

Some people dive deep just to see if they can do it, but every deep dive we made was to see something that could not be seen in shallow water. I and my companions assumed the higher risk for a secondary purpose, not because of the risk itself. And it was worth the extra care needed to perform the dives.

The highlights were a series of dives on the wreck of the *S'Jacob*, a WWII armed cargo carrier found a couple of years ago. The wreck is upright, 325 feet long, totally intact (it still has its propeller) and has never been fished, let alone dived. It's an oasis of life in the middle of a plain 182 feet to the bottom and miles from anywhere.

In the best conditions with clear water and a slight current to bring the fish and soft corals to life, the experience is mind-blowing. The last time I dived it, I was alone at 160 feet preparing to unshackle our mooring line when a pair of manta rays came and danced around me, skimming the bridge and soaring around the funnel, scattering clouds of baitfish that were then set upon by a school of jacks. Did I have complete control? Of my air, depth, time, location, schedule, camera . . . yes. Of my emotions . . . no!

The last time I dived it I was alone at 160 feet preparing to unshackle our mooring line when a pair of manta rays came and danced around me.

You know what I am talking about. The joy brought tears to my eyes. Moments like these make life worthwhile. I went back, and so did Dinah and my friends, and we all came back safely. We dove it again and again. We hear about the glories of nature, and most people experience them via the television screen. But that is not how I want to live my life. I want to be there, and I have and I will.

Certain exquisite fish cannot be found in shallow water. So I have been taking my camera to 200 feet, usually by myself, to photograph sand tilefish, anthias and dartfish that only a handful of people has ever seen in their natural habitat. They are beautiful animals and I am fascinated by their hidden lives. Taking photographs at these depths is difficult. It is dark, and the fish are often spooked by the necessary light I use to be able to focus. Technically, it is my greatest challenge, but my skills are improving and the satisfaction I get when I see the rare successful result is enormous.

I would like to go even deeper, but I have reached my personal limit. If I do not feel right on the way down I will stop, check myself out, and if necessary stay in shallow water. I am not happy unless my head is totally clear, my breathing and buoyancy are in perfect control, and I feel good about the dive.

A Bad Example?

Soon, someone will criticize me for "encouraging deep diving" or "setting a bad example." But that's nonsense. I do not go around saying that diving is fun and all the family can join in. As soon as people mention that they are afraid of the water, sharks, being alone, or they have ear problems, or that they are not really interested but their spouse wants them to learn, or they are weak swimmers, or that they are nervous or worry about currents or whatever, I tell them straight away: take up golf.

Too many people diving do not have the right stuff. They give the rest of us a bad name, are excuses for imbecilic regulations restricting what we can do, and mess up the dive sites.

The only people I encourage to dive are those who tell me they have an unsatisfied inexorable desire to experience the underwater world. All the top divers I know are the same — you could not keep us out of the water if you tried. So it is with deep diving.

Divers should stick to what they are happy doing. But if you have that undeniable urge to see what lurks in deeper depths, and you are willing to study and practice to overcome the higher risks involved, then you are going to do it anyway. It is better if you take advantage of the knowledge and experience of those who have done it successfully, instead of playing Russian roulette, learning by trial and error.

I am not going to encourage you, but I will certainly tell you what I have learned about diving safely (and you won't find any of that stuff in the standard diving text books).

As for "setting a bad example," this is one of the nuttiest arguments ever — yet we hear it all the time. It assumes that others have no minds of their own, which is possibly a valid assumption, but the speakers should realize they have to be included in the "others." Why should people with merit and ability be prevented from doing anything that those with less drive and talent are incapable of doing? For sure, it is the cry of the life haters — the jealous and the mediocre.

I rejoice in seeing skilled or clever people do things that I will never be able to do. I do not get bitter and twisted about it. I do not have the skill to walk to the North Pole, but I am thrilled that someone has done it. I am also glad that someone has climbed Mt. Everest, flown to the moon and, for that matter, designed the Gardner diesel and written a Ninth Symphony, even if it is not me. After all, the first persons to successfully climb Mt. Everest or sail single-handed round the world did not get accused of setting a bad example (even though many have perished trying to emulate them since). No, they got knighted!

Some of the criticism that divers have to put up with comes from people concerned with the cost to the public of the rescue and treatment of distressed divers. Since recompression facilities are expensive, this almost sounds reasonable. But the figures for an Australian chamber show that the great majority of the case load is not bent divers — but attempted suicides with carbon monoxide poisoning.

I was to subsequently suffer a month of unrelenting pain, neuritis and muscular atrophy, and ended up with a weak left arm that will take a year to get back to normal.

Now, I admit to making dangerous dives — two shallow dives to the top of a sea mount in 40 feet of clear, calm water. The mount was carpeted with olive brown anemone-like critters, about four inches across. I was wearing a dive skin and did not think I could damage the anemones if I touched them, so made myself comfortable to take some fish photos. I noticed with surprise that I was getting stung through the dive skin — but the stings were not painful and I have good tolerance to marine stings, so I ignored it.

I was to subsequently suffer a month of unrelenting pain, neuritis and muscular atrophy, and ended up with a weak left arm that will take a year to get back to normal.

The critters were corallimorpharians. They capture small creatures by enclosing them inside their bodies by forming a sphere with small opening on top. If a fish swims inside, the sphere closes and the fish is doomed. When disturbed they are able to produce fine white filaments that are loaded with giant nematocysts. They are what got me. The effect is rather like big sand fly bites — except more serious symptoms can occur. The dive was dangerous because I did not understand the risks of that particular dive site. Now I know — and so do you — do not touch corallimorpharians.

The Joy of It All

My life would be a sad one without Nature, even if she stings sometimes, and no other endeavour could bring me closer to Nature than diving does. I also have the feeling that if I do not see these deep fish in this life, I am not going to get another chance. I say "Life, be in it!" and to the fullness of your ability, not to some arbitrary limit.

So I am not going to tell you to dive to 200 feet or even 50 feet. But, how about studying and testing yourself to discover who you are, what you want to do, and what you can do? Perhaps that is the meaning of life.

Nitrox is so common around the world these days, it's hard to believe that in the early 90s many U.S. dive industry leaders closed ranks against the innovation — even though it had already proven very popular in Europe and many foreign diving destinations. We dug into this controversy in our January 1993 issue.

Getting Down and Dirty
Mud wrestling over nitrox

Who'd-a thunk that the notion that divers can dive more safely by using nitrox — a gas with 32 percent oxygen and 68 percent nitrogen — would have started a mud wrestling match in the diving industry that's on the verge of busting into a bare-knuckled fist fight.

In one corner, we have *Skin Diver Magazine*, the Cayman Dive Operators Association, and PADI, among others. They argue that, for recreational divers, nitrox is not safe — that it leads to deeper and more risky diving. They believe that the motive for promoting nitrox is the almighty buck, since it's being promoted by those who expect to make money from training, sales of equipment, and the sale of nitrox, itself.

In the other corner are 100 nitrox stations, two nitrox training agencies, NAUI and NASDS, and a bunch of technical divers who argue that the safety record of nitrox is nearly perfect and that the conservative, knee-jerk reaction by the opposition is designed to protect their own turf.

Letters, faxes and editorials are flying about, and claims from both sides suffer from hyperbole. One claim is that nitrox has been banned throughout the Caribbean, which isn't true. However, the Cayman Dive Operators Association has banned nitrox — which means you're not going to use it on a Bob Soto boat. (God forbid you should be able to extend your bottom time by 30 minutes.) But, nitrox is available to trained divers from a Cayman gas supply house.

The Cayman Dive Operators Association, speaking through the

voice of the Cayman hyperbaric chamber, has stated that they would not treat a bent diver who had been using nitrox. That's pretty ridiculous. No reputable or ethical medical facility could refuse treatment. Dr. Bill Hamilton, President of Hamilton Research and noted physiologist, told us, "I hate lawsuits, but if treatment is refused to any injured diver using nitrox, I'll be an expert witness if asked."

Using Nitrox

Nitrox, like compressed air, requires training in its use. And, the gas needs to be analyzed to determine the correct mixture.

Neither compressed air nor nitrox is a perfect diving gas. It is possible to be bent on both. It is possible to embolize on both. In July alone, eleven American divers died. Eight were using air. Three were using a mixed gas of some sort, but only one was trained and certified in its use.

When using compressed air, narcosis can be a problem. When using nitrox, oxygen toxicity can be a problem, so depths must be limited to 130 fsw. However, within the constraints of 130 fsw, nitrox is safer than compressed air because it reduces the amount of nitrogen absorbed into the diver's body.

Nitrox may not be a gas that everyone either needs or wants to use. But it is a new option that a trained diver can consider for use down to 130 fsw.

While the mud wrestling continues, nitrox diving will expand, nitrox computers will be developed and sold, and more and more divers will use. In the long run, divers are going to do what they want to do, anyhow.

-Ben Davison

Then, gradually, all the opponents changed their minds. Once the industry accepted nitrox, it became considered something of a miracle gas. People claimed all sorts of benefits, from less fatigue to more warmth, even increased libidos. Starting in 2003, we looked at these claims with our usual jaundiced eye, and here are some of the results.

Are We Warmer Diving with Nitrox?
Probably not

Nitrox offers a number of benefits for divers, but one that's generated some controversy is the notion that breathing nitrox keeps us warmer underwater.

First, no one can argue with an individual's personal experience. If someone claims to feel warmer when diving nitrox, then it is difficult to argue with that. However, many other factors influence warmth, such as whether the diver has just eaten, the level of insulation worn, and the old "psychological factors," which can influence us all.

Humans cool about four times faster in water than in air of the same temperature. Body temperature remains stable only in water that's about 95° F. When we get colder, the main physiological response is peripheral vasoconstriction to reroute the blood away from the cold skin. We also increase heat production via shivering and burning energy metabolically. In extreme cold, both cold and pain receptors are stimulated, which leads to metabolic changes in skeletal, muscle and liver cells; in that situation, we would increase our consumption of oxygen (O_2) and production of carbon dioxide (CO_2).

Various studies using nitrous oxide (N_2O) as an analog for nitrogen narcosis have demonstrated a narcosis-induced decrease in the shivering response. Due to the inhibitory effect of narcosis on shivering, divers are predisposed to heat loss when diving with compressed air or other gases with a high partial pressure of nitrogen.

Both intermittent and prolonged exposure to hyperoxia (high PO_2) have been shown to suppress the metabolic response to cold in animals, but that reaction hasn't been observed in humans immersed in cold water.

Experiments conducted with N_2O in humans have revealed that sub-anesthetic levels of narcosis increase thermal comfort during mild hypothermia. Divers perceive their body temperature to be higher than when in identical conditions without narcosis. In other words, if you are narced, you may feel warmer, but you're not.

Does one feel warmer when diving nitrox? There is no clear reason why that should be the case, and there seem to be no published studies of nitrox's effect on thermoregulation. One could speculate, however, that if a diver claims to feel less narcosis with nitrox, then the shivering response might not be as blunted by narcosis, so he would maintain heat production. Future research will, no doubt, look more closely at these nonthermal factors and their interactions with each other.

Diving with a closed circuit rebreather — now that does indeed reduce the heat loss because the breathing gas is recirculated.

– A version of this article, by Lynn Taylor, Ph.D., appeared in *Dive New Zealand*.

Four years later, in 2007 we explored an even steamier subject:

Have a Little Nitrox, M'Dear

Last October, we quoted an *Undercurrent* reader who'd discovered an unusual benefit of nitrox. After she and her husband made two dives with a 32 percent blend, "something amazing happened," said Karen Decker (Oxnard, CA). "We went back to the room and had sex. Yep, that's right, sex. Something that had never happened before the nap before that day." Decker reported that she and her husband "actually had the energy to engage in this extracurricular activity each day after diving. We've been enjoying nitrox ever since!"

That article brought several comments, including this from a subscriber who requested anonymity. "I love diving; however, I found the drastic diminution of my sexual responsiveness after a day of diving on air to be an intolerable side effect. I proposed to my husband that I dive only every other day and see if that helped.

"He was not similarly affected; regular air or nitrox, he was always in full, happy vacation condition. He is a physician and said that he thought nitrox might fix the problem. The change was immediate.

"We have experimented with one tank of nitrox and one of air when nitrox is in short supply. This also seems fine. For many of us, the whole vacation is not about diving only. No one said a word about this in the nitrox classroom, but discreet inquiries on my part have revealed that this is not a new discovery."

Al Ankus, an *Undercurrent* subscriber and pharmacist in Chicago, IL, offers an explanation. He told us that nitric oxide (a by-product of nitrox inhalation) serves as a neurotransmitter between nerve cells. Production of nitric oxide "also plays a role in development and maintenance of erection by stimulating the smooth muscle cells surrounding the blood vessels supplying the corpus cavernosum (region of erectile tissue that contains most of the blood in the penis during erection). Through relaxation of these muscles, more blood can flow in." By the way, adds our friendly pharmacist, "Nitric oxide is the main ingredient of sildenafel — commonly known as . . . Viagra."

Ern Campbell, MD, who runs the Scubadoc blog, told us that while there are good anecdotal reports, there still isn't any hard evidence. He speculates, with tongue in cheek, that perhaps vigorous sex and Cialis before diving might decrease the risk of decompression illness, citing research showing that, while fitness above a basic level made little difference, a bout of intense exercise (amorous or otherwise, he says) twenty hours before a simulated dive in a pressure chamber dramatically reduced nitrogen bubble formation. The researchers believe that the exercise eliminates microbubbles that seed the formation of larger bubbles in the blood.

Other studies suggest that these microbubbles are attached to the walls of blood vessels. Exercise is known to stimulate the release of nitric oxide (NO), which not only dilates blood vessels but changes their surface properties, making them more slippery.

Obviously, there's a need for more research in this subject. As soon as we find a research team willing to take it on, we'll put out a call for volunteers.

Over the years, we've examined several other widely accepted dive shibboleths, such as this article by Larry Clinton in 2003.

The Skinny on Wetsuit Shrinkage
Or is the problem really calories?

"Hey, it looks like your wet suit shrunk over the winter." That gag is so old it's become a diving cliché. But, like most clichés, it contains a grain of truth.

An article in the *Journal of The South Pacific Underwater Medicine Society* recently said: "Divers often complain that wetsuits shrink with age. Certainly, as the air cells in the material collapse as a result of neoprene aging, the suit may become stiffer and therefore less easy to don and less comfortable to wear, but mainly the 'shrinkage' is due to the diver's configuration changing with age!"

Plenty of divers put on the pounds, especially with all those vacation calories. However, two experts at RBX Industries (formerly Rubatex), the largest manufacturer of closed cell Neoprene in North America, take the problem of shrinkage more seriously.

As divers know, wet suits are made from closed cell synthetic rubber (known by the DuPont trade name Neoprene), which consists of thousands of tiny cells, each containing bubbles of insulating nitrogen. Roger Schmidt, manager of marketing and technical services for RBX, confirmed that over time the gas bubbles can escape through the cell walls. Two conditions escalate that process in opposite ways. On one hand, exposure to heat, such as intense sunshine, can expand the bubbles so some can actually rupture the cell walls. On the other hand, repeated exposure to pressure encountered underwater compresses the bubbles to the point where they can permeate walls and escape.

Jeff Ryken, national sales manager for RBX's Laminates Group, puts it this way: "Imagine a bundle of balloons. If the inside ones burst, the outside circumference will retract." Besides retracting, the fabric loses elasticity. Schmidt adds that shrinkage of just 5 percent could make a difference of four inches in a 72-inch long suit — or two inches in a 36-inch waist. He adds that linings such as nylon and metallic compounds do not affect shrinkage, one way or another.

If like Seinfeld's George Costanza, you have a problem with shrinkage, how can you select the right suit? The problem is, not all Neoprene is created equal. Different formulations with variations in cell sizes and cell wall thickness provide varying resistance to heat and pressure. Since RBX began losing market share to Asian firms, their emphasis has switched to lighter, more stretchable wet suits, which are cheaper to manufacture and ship, and more comfortable to wear.

But, the cheaper suits are more likely to shrink. "The consumer buys a suit in the store, not in the water," Ryken points out, adding that professional diver grade suits are more durable, and thus less subject to shrinkage.

However, there are no industry standards for professional diving grade Neoprene. Moreover, it's nearly impossible for a consumer to identify the grade of Neoprene when examining a wet suit in the store. Ryken suggests that anyone shopping for a suit should ask the dealer a few questions: "Is this suit appropriate for repetitive deep dives? Have you been using it, and, if so, what has your experience been? Have you had any complaints about this model?" A custom suit maker might be able to select different grades of Neoprene for different needs.

To prevent shrinkage, Ryken says to dry your suit in a dive locker or in a dryer at low temperatures rather than in direct sunlight. Besides overheating the foam cells, sunlight will fade any fabric, even a black wet suit. Now, whether your wet suit did shrink or you're putting on pounds, you can do something about it. The seams can be split and pieces added to give you more room. Your local dive store can probably help you out because some people make a living expanding wet suits. They can take measurements and ship the suit out for alternations. Since each job is custom, prices vary depending on the thickness of the original suit and what needs to be done. Letting a suit out is

If your suit still doesn't fit . . . well, you can always consider moving up to an EXXL like the fellow in this ad

more expensive than taking one in, because additional fabric must be purchased. One company even installed a zippered panel in the stomach of a wetsuit for a diver who swore he was going to shed the extra pounds soon.

Now, let's suppose that your wetsuit does fit. And you've made an hour-long dive and you just can't hold your bladder any longer. Well if you don't hold it in, here's a dive operator who may not let you back on your boat.

New Rules: Pee in Your Wetsuit and You Won't Dive on My Boat

If you're diving with Scuba Shack in Kihei, Maui, you had better hold your water. As we reported in 2007, they don't "allow" divers to pee in their wetsuits while in the water, or even on the boat (well, only the British do that, or so we've been told).

Undercurrent subscriber George Entwisle (Cashiers, NC) dived with the company last January, and recalls that during the first dive briefing, his boat captain told his group of ten there would be no peeing in wetsuits in or out of the water. When someone replied it was common practice in diving, especially due to the need to stay hydrated between dives, the captain said with great emphasis, "that's disgusting. Do you know how many germs and bacteria can breed in your wetsuit?"

"At first, we all thought she was joking, but to our amazement, she was dead serious," says Entwisle. The second dive on each trip was a shallow one with bottom time of 60 to 70 minutes. "The only way not to pee was to stay unhydrated."

Entwisle's group had booked three days of diving, and dived the second day. But a distrustful captain told the divemaster to give the group a dive briefing before getting on the boat, and if anyone made any negative remarks about the "no peeing" rule, the entire group would be taken off the boat. Fed up, Entwisle and friends bailed out on the third day and dived with Ed Robinson's Diving, which had a more "relaxed" view on peeing in wetsuits.

According to Scuba Shack owner Charley Neal, his captain did not make the comments about the bacteria, but he stands by the no-peeing rule. "The thought of putting on a rubber suit, filling it with pee, swimming in it for an hour, coming back on the boat, letting the urine run out onto our carpet and the deck where other guests are barefoot, letting the sunshine bake that pee into one's skin, and then putting that same stinky rubber suit back on to do the whole thing again, well, yes, to me that is not only disgusting, it is gross and sick. Why would you use hand sanitizer yet think it is OK to soak your body in urine for up to four hours?"

Neal says he refunded the Entwisle's group and promptly filled their vacancies, due to his company's good reputation. "I have the highest rated dive operation ever in the State of Hawaii, because of quality and safety." Part of that, he says, is because that he also doesn't allow smoking on his boat. "Why? Because it is what's best for the majority of my guests, and yes, I think that, too, is disgusting."

After we published this story, we had, you might say, a steady stream of comments:

Dear Ben: As a physician and diving instructor, I feel compelled to address some of Mr. Neal's "esthetic" points. Urine is sterile. If it were not, we would all have urinary, kidney, bladder and prostate infections. Sure, urine has waste products, especially ammonia, but not bacteria. While Mr. Neal may not like urine on his skin, he can be assured that he is not promoting bacterial proliferation in his wetsuit. The exchange of water in his wetsuit while diving has a diluting effect on the volume of urine in his suit. So the idea of dumping urine onto the carpet and the deck is not going to lead to infections. In fact, it is theoretically more unhealthy to spit in your mask and rinse it off in a community rinse bucket, although this, too, is unlikely to lead to sickness. The human mouth harbors more numerous and more toxic bacteria than the urinary tract. Divers are a "spitting" group — we spit when we climb on board, when we have something in our regulators to clear out, and so on. Perhaps this habit needs to be banned as well! So I will continue to use hand sanitizers when appropriate, because shaking hands is far riskier behavior than peeing in your wetsuit.

– Steve Werlin, Dillon Beach, CA

Ben: Scuba Shack can make the rule and customers can agree, but when the urge to pee hits, all rules are off. Most dive boat operators don't put carpet in areas where salt water (and all the plant and animal organisms that come with it), as well as urine, will be. That Scuba Shack has chosen to do this is surprising. The thought of walking on carpet that has baked in detritus is not pleasant, and I would be surprised if you could smell trace urine over the stench that must come from everything else embedded in the carpet.

– Michael Jones, Gilroy, CA

Dear Ben: I was in Fiji for four weeks of diving and had my own wetsuit but was concerned about peeing in it. So each morning, I had a little coffee, a small juice and no water. I was diving almost every day plus hiking and exercising, but I went easy on the water. At my last stay in Wakaya, I got up in the middle of the night and passed out, hitting the deck. The next day, after diving and little water intake, I went down again. Wakaya flew me back to the U.S. I did every doctor test possible, and I am the healthiest man on earth. I called DAN, and DAN's doctor said without delay, "Dehydration." Now I drink tons of water, when diving or not. I feel much healthier, but I pee a lot. I took all my wetsuits to an alteration shop and had Velcro put in the right places. Now I drink juice and coffee at breakfast and water, water, water.

– Craig Condron, Spokane, WA

Ben: I have dived with Captain Charley several times, and have never found this rule to be unavoidable. There are other options for "relieving" oneself. Captain Charley provides a working head, and Captain Valerie gives clear instructions how to use it after she tells everyone about the no-peeing rule. Perhaps "once underwater, the urge to urinate increases," but still, if a full-grown man in fit condition to dive can't hold it in for the seventy minutes he is underwater, then perhaps he ought to see his doctor. Second, every captain has the right to make his or her own policies regarding their boat. Captain Charley stated his reasons for enforcing the no-peeing rule, and provided an alternative. His rule seems reasonable. You have given readers the completely wrong idea about Scuba Shack.

– Jenna Jackson, Mountain View, CA

Ben: In a wilderness first aid class, the instructor, while discussing irrigation of severe wounds, referenced the Army's field medicine advocacy of using urine to flush wounds if no other sterile fluid is available. The idea of peeing into a chest wound sounds gross, but if the wound must be flushed and there is no other reliable sterile fluid, pee on it. There is a natural seepage of seawater through even the best wesuits. A few minutes of active finning will flush out nearly all of the pee. There

69

is no way to generate a puddle of urine on his pristine decks. If Scuba Shack has decent rinse facilities, there should be no problem with odor. Best advice to Charley Neal: Stop endangering your clients with dehydration or the risk of a burst bladder.

– **Peter A. Silvia, Falls Church, VA**

Dear Ben: I had to laugh at the ignorance of the Scuba Shack staff. As the president of my daughter's preschool, I had to deal with the safe handling of toddlers' pee and poop. We parents agreed in an open meeting that urine was sterile, while handling poop needed training and caution. For the first thirty years of my diving, I worried about peeing. When I became a father and "Mr. Mom" and changed thousands of diapers, the subject became a lot less important. To answer Captain Valerie's question: "Do you know how many germs and bacteria can breed in your wetsuit?" I believe that it depends on the sanitation of the local Maui seawater reduced by the action of the pee. So give up your "no peeing" rule or place prominent notice of this silly rule on your Web site. Because this is an uncommon rule, by not stating it before people commit their resources to come dive with Scuba Shack, you make yourself vulnerable to damages that a customer might incur in a last-minute cancellation.

– **Steve Chaikin, Whitmore Lake, MI**

Chaikin also e-mailed his comments to Scuba Shack owner Charley Neal, and forwarded us Neal's reply, which we have considerably edited:

Dude, it stinks. Pee stinks. If you would like to come use a wetsuit that a plethora of people have pissed in, we have a list of shops that have them for your use. I'm not on the list. I don't pee in my cars, my pants, my beds, on my carpets and rugs, my hot tub, my swimming pool, my wetsuit. You, feel free. You just can't come out with us and piss yourself. Sorry, we run with a clean crowd.

– **Captain Charley Neal, Kihei, HI**

Well, even though Captain Charley has established a silly rule, we did years ago run an article establishing the protocol for wetsuit whizzing.

Warming up your Wetsuit
Protocol for the socially conscious

A while back we discovered a piece in the *San Diego Divers' Log* entitled "To Piddle or Not to Piddle." We've always had a warm spot in our wetsuit for Southern California divers, and now we know why. We've taken the liberty to expand their brief tome, adding a few drops of our own fluid thoughts

To many new divers, it may come as quite a shock when a fellow diver suggests that the solution to a full bladder while dressed in a wet suit is simply to empty the bladder – that is, while one is underwater. But, it doesn't take long for the novice to realize that trekking back to the shore, undressing, relieving himself and returning to the water is excessive. Furthermore, when a cold diver learns that by not controlling his bladder underwater, he can in fact cut his chill, he tends to give in to his impulse and warm up a bit. It's not uncommon for old timers to load up with coffee, tea, soups and other liquids prior to a dive to ensure a high rate of urine production to keep warm.

Of course, newbies can't expect encouragement from dive shops for peeing in a rented wetsuit. Many shopkeepers who rent wetsuits often advise against the practice, claiming that the effect is only temporary and that the diver actually loses some of his body heat, which had been stored as urine. But the facts provide a different argument.

First, liquid has a much greater heat capacity than does its equivalent volume of gas.

Second, the volume of urine produced is controlled by the level of antidiuretic hormone (ADH) secreted into the bloodstream. The more ADH produced, the less urine.

Third, a cold environment has an effect similar to that of ingesting alcohol. The body inhibits the production of ADH and more urine is produced. Most divers wonder why they feel the urge so often when diving. A lower level of ADH is the answer.

Fourth, the body must burn up enough energy to maintain a constant body temperature in a cold environment. The more mass that must be heated to prevent chilling, the more energy required.

Therefore, when one urinates under water, he is reducing his mass by the amount of expelled urine. This in turn results in having to expend *less energy* to keep his body warm.

And, the warm urine has a temporary warming effect on the exterior of the body.

So, if you want a little extra warmth, respond to the urge. However, let us suggest that you follow a few basic rules:

- One should not urinate in his wetsuit while on board a dive boat. This is especially true if he is wearing only a wet suit top, and truer yet if the beaver tail is not fastened. New York divers may have their own standard of acceptable behavior.

- One should not urinate underwater in the presence of marine biologists. The resultant thermocline will only cause their hearts to flutter as they believe they have discovered new substrata hot water vents, and within seconds they will no doubt embolize while dreaming of grants from NOAA for further study.

- One should not force urination. The resultant jaw pressure can cause one to bite off the nubs on the regulator mouth piece.

- One should not urinate in the presence of a professional photographer. If the thermocline is visible to the naked eye, it most certainly will be captured in the photo, which may someday appear on the pages of *National Geographic Magazine*.

- Cut your chill at the beginning and midpoint of a dive, not the end, to give the sea water ample opportunity to dilute the urine. Pulling off a smelly suit in public is an unacceptable social behavior, no matter how solid your friendship with your buddy.

- Do not eat asparagus prior to a dive. If your olfactory glands are not sufficiently sensitive to understand this, ask around until you find a friend who will share such private information.

- One should not urinate in the presence of a damsel fish. Damsels nip at any intrusion; if they are nipping at your knees and you spring a warm water intrusion on them, they will change targets quicker than a cowboy with a cattle prod.

Chapter 5
Diving Poets? Well . . .

Years ago, we announced a limerick contest and eighty diving poets answered the call, cluttering our desks with nearly five hundred limericks, poems, and even stories. Limericks have notoriety because most are naughty, but naughtiness no way describes the defiling prose of the derelict divers who sent us their missives. Several submissions, however clever, were just too gross to adorn the pages of a publication even so irreverent as *Undercurrent*. So, if you are offended by off-color limericks, please read no further. If we get letters denouncing them, we will presume that the letter writers derived some pleasure from reading those limericks they denounced.

Of those who submitted limericks, many writers seemed to be intrigued with diving behind their buddies, while others were more into passing gas. For example:

A lovely young diver named Nancy,
Wore a bikini bottom quite chancy,
The fish of Bonaire
Watched her derriere,
And the sea fans all tickled her fancy.

Howard Fischer, Hillside, NJ.

Chapter 5: Diving Poets.

There once dove a man from Madras,
Who tended to suffer from gas.
For when he did sink,
The gas — it would shrink,
But on ascent, oh what a blast!

Dr. John Barclay, Port Moody, B.C.

The owner of a wet suit named Gotty,
Came into our shop quite haughty.
"The suit seems just fine,
But I sure have a time,
When down deep I have to go potty."

Nancy Osterheim, Superior, WI

Several divers created their own words just to get a rhyme.

A diver in upper New York,
Bobbed 'round in the lakes like a cork.
But the water's so cold,
Up there I am told,
He came up with a frozen gazork.

Jim and Vivian Roberts, Pacific Grove, CA

There once was a diver so fickle,
He let his air slow to a trickle.
He made a panicked descent,
Proceeded to get bent,
And turned his squash into a pickle.

Dr. Howard Grossbard, Brookline, MA

Could it be that these divers may have been carrying a squash and a gazork in their goody bags? Or, did we miss something? Now, some divers just took classic old limericks and rewrote them for diving.

There's a Cockroach in My Regulator!

One day a Monterey daughter,
Did scuba down under the water.
She later turned up
The mom of a pup,
And they say t'was an otter that got her.

Jim and Vivian Roberts, Pacific Grove, CA

A lobster hunter named Shefty,
Saw a bug in a hole that was hefty.
He reached in to feel,
Disturbed a large eel,
And now he is known as Lefty.

Rich Myberg, New York, NY

Many divers focused on diver safety, preferring less serious topics for their levity.

Let us dwell on the fate of poor Joan,
Who always went diving alone.
She ran out of luck,
When in a cave she got stuck,
With no buddy to take her back home.

Elliot Blum, Far Rockaway, NY

A nervous new diver named Kent,
Made a deep and too rapid descent
He saw some things beautific
Then a moray, Horrific!
Screamed loudly, rose quickly, and bent.

Y. Resun, Los Angeles, CA

Chapter 5: Diving Poets.

Now, without rhyme or reason, we give you the winners. Our second choice:

> At a depth not too great as it's reckoned,
> Diver Dan met his girl and love beckoned.
> And so, glove in glove,
> Exhaling their love,
> They screwed up at one foot per second.

C. Dorworth, Lancaster, PA

The winner.

> There was a young man from Bonaire;
> Often narc'd in the dark, I declare.
> He found, when imbibing,
> Then deeply night diving,
> He frequently ran out of air.

Barry Lambert, Vail, CO

Thanks for your patience. If limerick-writing frustrated you, consider these words of Howard Fischer from Hillside, NJ:

> A diver who's nicknamed "the Fish"
> This contest, to win, was his wish.
> He knew limericks rhymed
> Almost all of the time,
> But he couldn't for the life of him
>   think of anything that rhymed with
>   spontaneous pneumothorax,
>   or even mediastinal emphysema, for that matter . . .

Chapter 6
Two Divers, Diving Together

The idea that two divers should pair up and look out for each other has become a cardinal rule. It's taught in class, it's demanded at resorts, and it's expected of everyone, or so it seems.

Yet, the buddy system is fraught with problems, as *Undercurrent* has reported over the years. While there are endless cases in which a buddy has truly helped out his fellow diver, in other cases buddies only got in the way.

Today, many dive operations tell you to buddy up, but do nothing to enforce it. The idea that two photographers diving together will aid each other if one gets in trouble, ignores the fact that a photographer can spend five minutes concentrating on a single shot; more than enough time for a buddy alongside to run out of air, die of a heart attack, or just get swept away.

But, we all pay lip service to buddy diving and professionals know that if you don't tell people to buddy dive and there's an accident, the plaintiffs in a law suit will have you for lunch for not following accepted procedure.

Buddy diving is no panacea.

In our first article, author Cathy Cush looks at the psychological dilemmas in buddy diving.

The Underwater Power Struggle
Hidden Risks in Buddy Diving

It was one of those nights: warm, clear, moonlit. Romantic. It would have been a perfect dive with a buddy who was more than a friend — with the exception of a few minor details.

At the end of my dive the lights on the dive boat were so far away they didn't look much bigger than the stars in the sky. Worse, we were fighting a current that threatened to carry us to Portugal. The swim back to the boat seemed endless. The mate pulled me up the ladder and stripped me of my gear. I didn't have the strength to take off my wetsuit. I barely had the energy to tell myself, "I know better than this."

And I did know better. Although it was my first night dive, I had been diving long enough to know that it's much easier to come back to the anchor line at the end of a dive than to fight the kind of current we had just plowed through. And if I hadn't known better, there was an instructor on board who suggested that, considering the conditions, I stick close to the anchor line.

Then there was my buddy . . . .He wasn't going to stick near any anchor line, and he let me know that if I planned to do so, I'd find myself down there in the dark by myself. So instead, I was lying in the cabin below, nauseous from overexertion.

At least I wasn't — or I'm not — alone. Often one member of a buddy team will wind up in some dubious situation under the leadership of the more aggressive buddy. It doesn't just happen to women, and it doesn't just happen among buddies who are romantically involved. Human nature being what it is, it probably happens fairly frequently. For the most part the outcome is no worse than a longer-than-planned surface swim or a similar inconvenience. But at least one member of the buddy team may feel uncomfortable about the dive.

Observes Beverly, Massachusetts-based psychologist Dr. Samuel Migdole, himself a diver, "If you go along and all of a sudden you find yourself at a depth or in a cave where you don't want to be, you're a good candidate for panic."

What You Do Above, You Do Below

Not surprisingly, an individual's behavior as a diver will generally be consistent with his or her behavior in other areas of life, notes Dr.

Michael H. Smith, a diver and an organizational psychologist at California State University's Hayward campus. He says a leader in "real life" will most likely take the lead underwater, while a follower will probably go along for the ride — above or below water. "They're both legitimate forms of behaving in the world. You need both. Most people, he adds, are not entirely passive or aggressive, but instead fall into gray areas.

Smith believes that buddy teams get together unconsciously, like their topside counterparts, because opposites do attract. Generally, this is for the good of both. "Two passive people will have a hard time making decisions," Smith observes, "while two aggressive people will be fighting over turf. So pairs tend to be complementary."

Diving complicates the issue. The leader of the buddy team may not necessarily be the more skilled diver. He or she might be more of a daredevil. Sometimes that diver will propose a dive, or make a decision while underwater, that the other buddy feels may be beyond his limits or knows is unsafe. In that case, many divers will speak up and correct the situation. But a lot won't. They'll just go along with the dive, albeit uncomfortably.

When a primarily passive person follows another into a potentially dangerous situation, a number of factors may be at play. "To some degree," says Smith, "it is a denial of death. It's a way of saying: 'This is not going to happen'."

Philadelphia psychiatrist Dr. John Worthington offers another possible interpretation. "It's almost like gambling. They need the thrill." Often, says Worthington, the more passive partner will go along just to save face — especially if the more aggressive partner happens to be female."

Walt Hendrick, NAUI's national training director, believes group dynamics play a major role. "Look at what happens with automobiles. Why do people push [the limits]? Why do they drink and drive? They know better. You're right with them and you're having a good time."

Why Not Speak Up?

For some people, Smith notes, it is easier to deal with a potentially risky situation than it is to deal with the certainty of a confrontation with the other diver.

Migdole agrees. "People tend not to say the way they feel. They get into a situation they don't like and they just go along with it. Most people don't make waves — for the same reason they won't send food back in a restaurant." They want other people to like them. But, Migdole concedes, there is a difference between settling for an overdone steak and drifting off to Portugal in a killer current. Maybe if divers start thinking about it, he adds, we'll see some changes in behavior.

> Regarding husband-wife buddy teams, there is a latent power struggle there that's never really resolved.

There is also a difference between dealing with a waiter whom one is not likely to see again, and confronting a dive buddy who might be a good friend, a spouse, a lover — or a total stranger.

Buddy teams who have an intimate relationship have the most potential for complications. Regarding husband-wife buddy teams Smith says, "In my opinion, there is a latent power struggle there that's never really resolved." Says Migdole, "If they can't be honest about their diving fears, that will be indicative of their general relationship." The healthier the relationship between the two, the better their ability to deal with each other in problem-solving and the less likely they will be to find themselves in the sort of scenario described at the outset of this article.

Bringing Your Baggage

When friends dive together, Smith observes, "these issues will have been worked out, the repercussions will be less." But even friendships aren't without their "extra baggage," psychiatrist Worthington points out. "There are all sorts of possibilities that come into a buddy system if there are other relationships involved. If you dove together for a while, you would complement each other, but it would also bring up human deficits like dependency," he notes.

What about strangers buddying up at the dive site? On the one hand, they bring no preconceived notions of their relationship, no power struggle to the buddy team. On the other, they have no knowledge of each other's abilities, limits, fears.

The answer to dealing with a first-time buddy is the same the experts offer in relation to a closer companion: Communicate.

"Most of the time people who are diving together don't talk enough," says Dennis Graver, NAUI's director of special projects. "You have to coordinate and feel comfortable going with each other into the circumstances you're going into." What is needed, he says, is "a little bit of assertiveness and a whole lot of communication."

The worst situation, according to Graver, is when both divers are about to do something that neither feels comfortable about, but both feel an obligation to the other diver. "Because neither of you said anything, you both did it. Later you find out neither of you wanted to."

> *The worst situation is when both divers are about to do something that neither feels comfortable about, but both feel an obligation to the other diver.*

Just Say No?

Saying "no" isn't easy. Hendricks observes that, "it goes right back to that human trait. It takes a lot of guts to say 'no,' when you're on a boat and about to make a dive that absolutely goes beyond the limits of safe sport diving." Migdole adds, "If you've got issues like identity and self-esteem wrapped up in it, it's going to be very difficult for a less assertive person to say 'no,' and harder for a more assertive person to take 'no'."

A few things make it easier to decline a dive. One is to plan the dive in advance. "It's much easier before you go to a dive site," notes Migdole, "to say, `Gee, I don't really feel comfortable with that'."

Building self-confidence is another key, according to Migdole. "If you feel comfortable, you're much more likely to put a limit on what you'll do. It's harder to be pushed when you're sure of yourself."

Still, it's tough to change human nature, especially when the behavior represents a lifetime of reacting to situations in a certain way. And most of the time, it's probably not necessary, as long as the diver is aware of his or her behavior, and stays within limits of comfort and capability. If extreme passivity becomes a problem in diving, if a diver consistently finds himself led into situations that are truly beyond his or her limits, then the same is probably true in other walks of life. If such diving behavior leads to a close call, some form of professional therapy or assertiveness training may be in order.

What can be worse for an experienced diver than having a boat crew assign you to dive with a neophyte who shouldn't be diving in the first place? There's no better formula to ruin a dive. One diver wrote that in Key West, Florida, "I got buddied inappropriately with a diver without enough weight and spent the whole dive shallow (because she couldn't overcome buoyancy) pulling her down. It was a wasted dive, wasted money, and there was no attempt by the operator to compensate."

Aussie Bob Halstead doesn't like that kind of pairing any more than we do. Here's his take on it, which we published in 2001.

Line Dancing and the Buddy System
Why experienced divers should go alone

I recently saw a TV promotion for a country music festival. A special attraction was a horse, line dancing in step with a family all togged up in cowpoke gear. Viewers were meant to be astonished at how smart the horse was and rush off to see this phenomenal animal perform. To me the horse looked quite ordinary, perhaps a bit bored. I wondered just how smart the line dancers were.

Divers are usually quite smart simply because they have to pass a sort of intelligence test to get certified. That is correct I think, isn't it PADI? . . . NAUI? . . . Hello, where are you?

Well, I might as well go the "Full Monty" here and offend everybody. I do not know whether it is because I am 6'2" and have a clearer view of the world, but I do tend to see things differently.

My latest complaint is that a very silly diving practice has risen from the dead — buddying inexperienced divers with experienced divers. The argument is that inexperienced divers are vulnerable (true) and they therefore will be much safer paired with experienced divers (doubtful). This ignores three things:

First, this makes the dive less safe for the experienced diver.

Second, it becomes a form of instruction, by using an experienced diver, not an instructor.

And third, it assumes human nature is different from what it actually is.

In other words, they're dreamin'! I know the uneven buddy system does not work because I have tried it. Either the experienced diver has to sacrifice a dive to care for the inexperienced diver, or he leads a too advanced dive for his novice buddy.

Each dive is incredibly valuable. You spend a lot of time, effort and money to get to dive, and even then nature can deliver rough seas and poor visibility. The thought of finally getting to the dive site and having to babysit a beginner — well, it's an unnatural act.

The theory assumes that people behave in good and unselfish ways. Like I said, they're dreamin'! We train instructors and divemasters to teach and look after beginners. It is their job, a tough and skillful one at that. They get paid to do it, as they jolly well should. This is no place for amateurs.

I am no admirer of the buddy system. It is a big mistake — along with insisting on no-decompression diving — that we make in diver

Thanks for Draining the Lake

Diver David Gant and his buddy went diving in Tennessee's Nickjack Lake in August 1992, slipping past a chain-link fence blocking a cave entrance. To hell with the barrier. They were in search of dinner — enormous catfish that grow up to eight feet long and weigh 200 pounds.

Trouble is, Gant got separated from his diving partner and 1,200 feet into the cave, he ran out of air.

Gant held onto a stalactite and treaded water with his fin, breathing air trapped in the 8-inch space between the water and the top of the cave. His buddy escaped the cave and notified authorities.

While the air in the pocket was running out, Gant hung on. The Tennessee Valley Authority, which operates the lake's dam, dropped the water level three feet, flushing the cave with fresh air. Sixteen hours after beginning his dive, Gant was dragged out, weak and nauseated, but in good condition.

No charges will be filed, although the whole experience means a mighty tab for us taxpayers.

training. We should have ditched it years ago and instead promoted self-sufficient diving and surface support. Alas, too late now. The legal risks are too great for instructor organizations to make the changes.

> *I am no admirer of the buddy system. It is a big mistake — along with insisting on no-decompression diving — that we make in diver training.*

Nevertheless, if you are going to buddy, it is essential that your buddy be of equal standard and interest.

I first defined buddy diving many years ago as follows: "The buddy system occurs when two divers of similar interest and equal experience and ability share a dive, continuously monitor each other throughout the entry, the dive and exit, and remain within such distance that they could render immediate assistance to each other if required." I am flattered that several authors have borrowed my definition.

Many dive operators seem to think that just by putting two divers together they create a buddy system. A little thought will expose this stupidity. After observing some near-catastrophic so-called buddy dives, I put my own theory into practice and paired inexperienced divers with other inexperienced divers. It worked like a charm. The divers did not dive deep. They did not stray far from the boat. They did not have unrealistic expectations about their buddy's ability to rescue them. And they surfaced from the dive proud of their own achievements and eager to gain more experience.

I also allowed experienced divers to dive solo, though this does not mean diving alone because we always provided excellent surface lookouts and rescue capability. Solo diving is extraordinarily popular with experienced divers, especially photographers, since it allows close experiences with many wild marine animals that would swim away if confronted with pairs or groups of divers. In fact, only solo divers ever had close contact with wild dugongs while I was running our boats.

When Mike Ball was operating all his boats some years ago, he offered qualified but inexperienced divers the opportunity to buddy dive with a qualified divemaster or instructor. That was their job. If you came alone, the crew would help you meet with like-minded divers on board. If you were experienced and had a redundant spare air supply (such as a pony bottle) with an independent regulator, you could solo dive. This service was dedicated to giving divers the best possible experience commensurate with their ability and interest. It provided choice instead of treating everyone at the lowest common denominator. And it promoted excellence rather than mediocrity. Mike Ball is a smart operator. I do not think you will ever find him line dancing, with or without a horse.

Your Liability as a Buddy:
What the courts have said

"Always dive with a buddy" — probably one of the first things you learned in your beginning scuba course. If you get in trouble, your buddy's job is to rescue you. But what if he doesn't? Can you, or your estate, sue?

Despite a paucity of judicial decisions, the question is more than hypothetical. Legal actions against buddies by divers or their heirs have been filed and sometimes settled for large, although undisclosed amounts. Courts have shown a willingness to entertain such claims. So, is there anything you can do to ensure that putting on a wetsuit doesn't lead to finding yourself on the wrong side of a lawsuit?

As is true in any tort or negligence action, to recover against a dive buddy, a plaintiff must prove: (1) duty, (2) breach of that duty, (3) proximate cause (which means the injury was a direct consequence of the buddy's actions or omissions) and (4) damages.

Judges who have faced the issue conclude the buddy relationship itself establishes a legal duty. Litigation experts such as Robert K. Jenner (Silver Spring, MD) caution that by agreeing to be a buddy, you take on a variety of roles: responsibility for (1) checking and monitoring equipment before and throughout the dive, (2) creating and diving a safe plan, (3) sharing air if needed, (4) staying close, (5) untangling a partner caught in debris and (6) getting both of you to the surface in case of an emergency. As a buddy, the person suing must prove that your negligence caused his injury.

Rasmussen v. Bendotti, the first reported appellate opinion directly pertaining to buddy diving, was decided in August 2001. Although negligent, Eugene Bendotti escaped responsibility for his buddy's death

— who happened to be his wife. Her children from a previous marriage brought an action against their stepfather of five years.

Bendotti did neither a self nor buddy equipment check before their fourth dive of the day. As a result, he didn't notice until he was in the water that his power inflator was not connected to his BC. He immediately surfaced. However, his wife, perhaps while ascending herself, got caught in a rope at 40 feet and was unable to disentangle herself and drowned.

Using a legal doctrine that relaxes the required standard of care for an individual faced with an emergency, Bendotti denied accountability. Yet the Washington court explained that this protection is not available to a person who, like Bendotti, created the dangerous situation himself. Therefore, the finding that he breached his duty was "inescapable."

While responsible, Bendotti avoided liability because the connection between his mistake and his wife being trapped was "too attenuated." Expert witness Jon Hardy, a widely published scuba professional, made three points: (1) no relationship existed between the error and Bonny Jo Bendotti's entanglement, (2) the loss of buddy contact could not be tied to her death and (3) the proximate cause of her death was that she was not carrying a knife.

Further, the judges noted it was unknown how Mrs. Bendotti became entangled, why she was unable to free herself and whether a non-negligent buddy could have saved her. The unknowns were inadequate to establish proximate cause.

Other lawsuits have reached similar results. For example, in 1998 Tai Wilkerson, an experienced diver who had previously been as deep as 415 feet, died searching for the Spanish ship *Juno* and its millions in treasure off the Virginia coast. At 170 feet, Wilkerson was attaching a tether to the anchor line when his buddy, Mike Fantone, noticed his partner was entangled in another line.

"He was really breathing hard, oh Lord, and struggling with the line," Fantone said. After untangling Wilkerson, Fantone signaled to his friend to calm down, then noticed his regulator had come out of his mouth. Fantone replaced it. "He tried to take a couple of more breaths. But right after that, I looked in his eyes, and they got all dilated, and he stopped breathing. After that, the only thing left to do was to send him to the surface." There was no time to worry about the hazards of ascent without decompression, and after sending Wilkerson up, Fantone ignored the risk to his own life. Despite attempts by crew members to revive Wilkerson, and the arrival of the Coast Guard, he died en route to the hospital.

His widow sued Fantone, among others, claiming they were negligent. The Norfolk medical examiner determined that Wilkerson, a 41-year-old airplane pilot in excellent health, had suffered a heart attack. When, without explanation, the plaintiff subsequently dropped her legal action, defendants'attorneys asserted the dismissal proved their clients were blameless. There was no settlement and no money changed hands.

Opinions from related cases may shed more light. For example, in *In re Adventure Bound Sports*, a trio "formed a dangerous, three-person buddy team in which one diver was to separate from the other two, contrary to PADI procedures." As their own defective plan was "a significant contributing factor to their deaths," the damage award received by the decedents' estates against the *MV Seahorse's* owner and charterer was reduced by the percentage of fault attributed to their negligence.

Similarly, in *Lyon v. Ranger III*, a federal case decided under maritime law, the court found that Thomas Lyon surfaced way beyond the statutory maximum distance from his dive flag and contributed, along with his two partners, to their "seriously flawed" plan. In Massachusetts waters, another boat struck and killed Lyon. As a result, he was found 45 percent responsible for his own death.

The court suggested that, because Lyon didn't control the others, and was required to do more to protect himself, his "negligence vis-à-vis his own safety . . . exceeds theirs." Moreover, the judges concluded that even if they were wrong about decedent's own responsibility, the negligence of the other divers should be attributed to Lyon because of the "common control of the diving plan."

Suing Buddies

The scarcity of reported cases against buddies is not surprising. Most buddies simply don't have enough money to justify the costs of bringing suit. Generally, course providers, boat operators, shop owners and equipment manufacturers have the "deep pockets," making them more likely targets. In addition, buddies are usually just that

— friends or even relatives of the injured or deceased diver — people you wouldn't expect to sue. (Of course, there can be exceptions when children or an estate steps in.) Courts may also reject these cases based on the legal theory of assumption of the risk (e.g., by participating in certain ventures you accept responsibility for known hazards typically associated with such endeavors).

Thus, in *Dao v. Shipway*, an unpublished decision, a California judge granted summary judgment to a buddy because the friends were "engaged in a voluntary, active sport with inherent risks" of which the victim was aware. Although Doug Shipway (1) had been diving with his partner for years knowing he was not certified, (2) provided him tanks, (3) failed to follow the buddy system and (4) did not go back under water to search and waited an hour to call for emergency assistance, he was not responsible for his buddy's death.

Another explanation is that lawyers are reluctant to take these cases. "Juries just don't want to hold buddies liable," says Alton J. Hall, Jr., an attorney who specializes in diving litigation. This is especially true if the buddy tried to do anything to help, "no matter how stupid."

Rick Lesser, an attorney whose practice consists of diver negligence cases, warns that although the definitive list of buddy legal obligations has yet to be written and there are few cases so far, in today's litigious society, negligent divers run the risk of being sued. He says the best thing you can do to protect yourself if you agree to be a buddy, is "to be a buddy." While uncertainty about the probability of someone filing a buddy lawsuit exists, everyone seems to agree that gross negligence, or egregious violations of the standard of care, mean you could be facing a large verdict. What can divers do?

- When you agree to be a buddy, you must act as a reasonably prudent, certified diver. Be conscientious yourself and choose your buddy carefully.

- If you find yourself on a boat being pressured to accept a partner you neither know nor want, don't give in. Vessel operators may push to make sure everyone is paired because, as a federal court in Hawaii explained in *Tancredi v. Dive Makai Charters*, "it is a breach of the standard of care in the recreational dive industry for a dive charter company to conduct a dive without assigning 'buddy' teams."

Similarly, in *Kuntz v. Windjammer "Barefoot" Cruises, Ltd.*, although the deceased was negligent in drinking and taking drugs the night before the accident, the court held the cruise line liable for her death because if their employee "had instituted and maintained a partner system during the deep dive, as required by the practice and standards of the scuba-diving instructors and [NAUI] . . . this mishap would not have occurred."

> *If you find yourself on a boat being pressured to accept a partner you neither know nor want, don't give in.*

Notably, however, in *Madison v. Superior Court*, a broadly worded release relieved an instructor and training course from liability for their "failure to follow the 'buddy system' rule." Possibly signing such a waiver would convince a boat operator to allow you to dive solo. If not, it could be a serious mistake to agree to the buddy he gives you. Your moral and legal responsibility to a stranger will probably be the same as to a close friend or even a family member, but a person who doesn't know you is much more likely to sue if something goes wrong.

- Recognize that a buddy who is not competent endangers your life as well as your bank account. In one survey of approximately 200 divers, 15 percent of the respondents said their greatest fear was a bad buddy. "Indeed, some experienced divers, unwilling to assume the responsibility and potential liability, have turned to solo diving. And some folks say most people are really solo divers — "they are just in the same ocean at the same time." For example, one study recently reported in *Undercurrent* revealed that in 80 of 100 fatal cases, the victim was not with another diver at the time of the accident. However, in only 21 of these was the diver deliberately solo.

- If you truly want protection, purchase personal liability insurance. Before you take that step, check your homeowner's policy. It might provide coverage. Apparently homeowner insurance policies are used to paying settlements. But a cautionary note: people with insurance are more likely to be sued. In other words, by having coverage, you become a deep pocket.

Phyllis Coleman, Professor of Law, Nova Southeastern University, Ft. Lauderdale, Fl., is the coauthor of Sports Law: Cases and Materials. *Disclaimer: diving liability laws are constantly evolving, and vary from one jurisdiction to another. If you're concerned about this issue, you should consult with a qualified attorney.*

While the debate may never end about buddy diving, here is one article that shows a need we had never considered for a buddy . . . until this incident happened to a very good friend.

A Woman's Frightening Underwater Experience

Through the years, we have received reports of dive guides molesting women divers. These were not Cayman Cowboy sorts of incidents, making off color wise cracks on the dive boat or trying to pick up the women after the dive, but far more serious and dangerous incidents. Here is one that we printed in the 80s.

Safely back home and lodged in the routine of daily life for a week, I look back on a confusing and humiliating underwater experience. I think my feelings and hindsight are worth sharing, especially with women who dive, and with men who dive with women.

In retrospect, two things stand out from my certification week, which now have profound impact on me.

First, I felt that in diving I had found a world separate from the world above, where frustration and hassle are the norms. Underwater, I thought, was an environment that possessed the challenge of danger but was free of fear of fellow man.

Second, I remember feeling a need to depend only on myself in gearing-up and assuming the responsibilities of diving. I remember the words of my instructor, a female: "Why are you struggling so? Let your husband do that for you." Somehow it didn't seem right to me. I wanted to be independent.

Since certification, I have been on a dozen or more warm water dives. Until last week, my feelings about diving taking me away from it all held to be true.

When the dive boat came to pick us up at our beautiful, secluded beach in Akumal, on Mexico's Caribbean coast, I was filled with the usual sense of excitement and anxiety. It had been nearly a year since my last dive, and because I was diving with a type of vest I had not used before, I was more anxious than usual. The divers included my husband, *The highly attentive guide helped me adjust my weight belt and BC straps and then gear up. It didn't occur to me that he paid no attention to the two male divers.*

a good friend who is a very experienced diver, myself and our guide, whom I had met at the dive shop. Since I felt a need to hide my anxiety from my friends and to be independent, I was relieved when the highly attentive guide helped me adjust my weight belt and BC straps and then gear up. It didn't occur to me that he paid no attention to the two male divers. After descending to 25 feet, the guide, never taking his eyes off me, spent about three minutes adjusting my straps and making me feel comfortable. I was unaware that the straps needed adjustment, so I was grateful. We completed a very pleasant dive.

The next day the boat arrived to pick us up again. Once more, the guide took me under his wing. Once underwater, I was hardly aware that anyone was diving except for the two of us. Soon the guide, by swimming rapidly, had left behind my husband and our friend, both photographers. At 25 feet deep we stopped for adjustments. This time I began to realize my naiveté. My straps didn't need any adjustments, and although I kept saying in sign language, "I'm OK," he kept swimming around me, pushing and pulling the straps and me.

At last we resumed the dive. My guide swam quickly, and I followed with all my might, although I was working too hard to enjoy the dive. Soon, we outdistanced my husband and his buddy. And then, close to the end of the dive, my nightmare began. I signaled that my air was at 700 psi. In a very macho way he signaled me to come to him. I held out my pressure gauge. He shook his head "no" and grabbed for the crotch strap of my vest, but his hands landed elsewhere. I signaled again "I'm OK," but he had other plans. At first I thought to myself that we were only in 30 feet of water and I should simply go up. Then I thought, "Where is the boat? I can't see the boat. I'm scared. Don't panic."

As his hands worked in and out of my bathing suit bottom — occasionally pulling on a strap — I stared in horror, uncertain about what to do, uncertain about my diving skills, afraid to struggle to get away.

Close to the end of the dive, my nightmare began.

Fears of embolism and bends shot through my mind as I felt a captive victim. Then for a moment my panic subsided. I kicked him away and started to swim upwards. He signaled, "You OK?" and followed me to the surface. My heart began to flutter when the boat was nowhere in sight — and I really needed the boat. We bobbed in 3-foot waves, a mile from the shoreline. My guide waved his arms, glancing at me from time to time, but I couldn't look at him. I worried more and more. Finally, ten minutes later, he spied the boat. Onboard, my husband spied us.

Later, during what should have been a pleasant beach picnic, I was in a state of confusion and hurt. After a while I shared the experience with my husband; we both struggled with what to do. Expose the guide, end the picnic, and return to the hotel? Pretend as if nothing happened? Chalk it up to a learning experience and try to enjoy the picnic? Seek advice from our friend and risk ruining his day? I decided to accept the support of my husband and set the experience aside for the day.

It wasn't until the next day that I could share the experience with our friends. And, I reported — too gently, I suppose — the guide's actions to the dive shop owner who listened but registered no response. We didn't dive again, and the incident is now over. Today, I'm more tuned in to the subtleties of the behavior of some men than ever before. I've not lost my general trust of men. I've just become aware of what I've been unaware – above and below sea level. As for diving, I'll put my trust in my husband and friends, people I'm used to diving with.

This incident occurred more than twenty years ago. If it were to happen today, I belive the divers and her trusted friends' response would be much tougher.

Rodney Dangerfield made a living getting no respect. But a diver should at least expect a little respect from his fellow divers, especially his buddy, who in the next article is the one who should be embarrassed, not the writer of the article.

Beyond Embarrassment:
The musings of an occasional diver

A sailing friend of mine once said that 90 percent of what sailors do is to look good for other sailors.

Probably the same comment could be made about divers. Embarrassment is commonly defined as "experiencing a state of self-conscious distress," but I prefer the vernacular syllables right there within the word itself: "bar(e) ass."

As an occasional diver, "bare ass" is something I too often experience. I dive six to twelve times a year on tropical vacations. And like anything else, after a six- to twelve-month layoff, I am a "rusty diver." I am not unsafe. I have thirteen years' experience, and am very conservative. But some things that happen can often make me the butt of diver jokes.

Preparation and Gear

I like to use dive gear for as long as it is serviceable, which can be forever with proper maintenance. (I don't dive enough to warrant a major expensive changeover.) All my dive gear is at least ten-years-old, and some of it closer to fifteen. I did splurge on a new mask for my last trip, but the thirteen-year-old mask worked better than the new one. I am about to inherit a second-generation wetsuit top from the same buddy who gave me his original (I cut the arms off that one because there were unpatchable elbow holes in the dried out Neoprene). I used a horse collar BC, if you remember those, well into the 90s. My gauge console is jury-rigged. I pack my gear in an ugly, twenty-year-old suitcase without wheels. (No one will steal that at the Miami airport). I get a lot of comments from people. "Does that top still keep you warm?" "What's the suitcase for?"

Though I check my gear before I leave, occasionally age does show. The last time out, the zipper on my wet top stuck. It took some thought to remember over which shoulder the regulator should fall (it helped to watch someone else hook us his regulator first), then it took a couple of false starts before I got my mine attached to the tank correctly. Everyone is helpful, but heads shake. I even learned of a magic substance to unstick the zipper: spit.

The Diving Frame of Mind

I accept that I am rusty. To counter this, I review the basics before a trip and even listen to DAN's diving medicine review tapes. I ask the guides for a little extra watchfulness.

Unfortunately, after they look at my gear, this often garners an unhelpful response: "Do you have a log?" (No.) "Listen to the lecture for the people being certified" (don't hold your breath, here is how to clear your mask). "Can you handle the first dive?" Granted, there are safety concerns being expressed. Yet, I feel like it is the third grade again.

The Pace and the Race

My life is swift with a serious job, a family and numerous other responsibilities. When I vacation, I want to slow down, to leave the rush of life behind, and have no need to accomplish or justify anything.

Yet many of us turn vacations into quasi-duties filled with schedules and intentions. Everything a diver does can be subsumed under the phrase, "do it slowly." Yet, I find the pace frequently set by dive operators and other divers more like my work pace.

Everyone rushes to the boat. They're eager to leave the dock. The pace does slow during the ride, but once there, it is like Marines landing at Iwo Jima, "everyone in, move it, move it." What is the rush? And once in, it is full bore around the site. The philosophy seems to be: "cover the most territory." And the trip home is often a race across the waves. Pile out, unload the boat, pay the bill. Go.

On a trip to the Grenadines, my dive buddy and I had our own sail boat (the two of us!). No herd, slow down, take your time. After a few dives, I heard "Are you usually the last off the dive boat?" And even when I rushed, it never was quick enough. I started sounding like my four-year-old, "I'm trying, I'm trying."

Going Down and Coming Up

A big problem is remembering how much weight I need. It never seems to be the right amount ("You look about X pounds"). I let the air out of my BC and watch everyone else descend while I keep bobbing, with the water barely over my head, getting sick from the surge.

I fin down like a wounded fish. On Bequia, the guide was concerned and guided me down. Thanks. The price: "How long have you been diving?" "Thirteen years." More head-shaking.

Surfacing, I have a terrible fear of the open water swim to the boat. I'm an average swimmer, and fatigue somewhat easily. On occasion, a current has made this a reality. On one dive, after slugging against a current and being asked twice, from the boat, whether I was okay, I decided to pack it in. The guide swam the distance in five seconds and hauled me on board. Everyone had a chance for a few wisecracks. Fortunately for my ego, someone else had been bitten in the ear by a turtle.

On another occasion, while drifting toward Africa, I did have five minutes of near-panic. The current was swift, the boat was lost in the swells and the guide was searching in the wrong area. I clamped onto my buddy and, at his encouragement, listened to stories about how we could survive for two days! We were picked up twenty minutes later, and as expected, my "near panic" received a full (and reasonably

They Need More than Buddies

When I was an instructor for Lahaina Divers on Maui, I once took out our boat with two guys in their 20s for their resort course near Lahaina Harbor. In shallow water, they easily handled their mask clearing and regulator exercises, so I motioned them to follow me toward the reef and swarming fish.

I swam a short ways and looked back, but they were both just kneeling and looking at me. I motioned again, and they waved back, but stayed put. After several tries to get them to swim around and enjoy the dive, it was apparent they were going nowhere. They didn't seem frightened, but they wouldn't budge.

Eventually, I took them back up the line, helped them into the boat and out of their gear. "So, how come you guys didn't follow me?" I asked. "Didn't you want to swim around and explore the reef?"

One looked back at me in amazement. "How could we?" he asked. "We don't know how to swim."

– Lucia Christopher

gentle) airing.

Years ago, after a dive in Hawaii, I had a pain in my toe. A couple days later, still worried, I confessed the pain to my buddy, and wondered out loud whether I had been bent. When the pain returned after the next dive, I learned that my fin was too tight. We both got a laugh, he more than I.

Moral

On my next vacation I will probably repeat some of the above lapses and gaffes, or create some new ones. Nevertheless, as I age, and harbor a degree of success and maturity, embarrassment is less of an issue. I now chuckle openly at myself, apologize if necessary, and try to correct the problem. Most important, I can ask for, without embarrassment, a little bit of help. The price used to be high; it decreases each year.

There are worse fates than appearing bare assed before your buddies. And no matter what they say, I'm still going diving.

Michael H. Smith, PhD., is a psychotherapist and a consultant in organizational management and development in Oakland, CA. Much of his commentary comes after reflecting upon his diving with his frequent, always ready to go-go-go buddy, Ben Davison.

Chapter 7
Deeds of Derring-Do

There was once a day in dive travel when getting there was half the fun, as the old adage goes. Today, flights are crowded and airports unfriendly, but in the 70s and 80s, getting to most Caribbean islands meant flying LIAT (Leave Island Any Time). Flights in Indonesia, Fiji or PNG were in tiny planes, and never on time. If you missed a plane or it had mechanical problems, it might be a day or three before you could catch another flight.

In 1990 a bunch of friends and I chartered a liveaboard in Papua New Guinea. I had to get there from Spain, where I was attending an international Greenpeace meeting as a consultant. I had a 15-hour layover in Singapore, then a connection to Port Moresby, and on to Madang, where I would join the liveaboard.

When I arrived at the Singapore Airport with my ticket in hand, I was advised my flight had been canceled, and I was to be rerouted through Tokyo, which would not get me to Port Moresby until 12 hours after the boat departed. There were no earlier flights. On the verge of panic, I learned the plane was still going to Port Moresby, only it had now been chartered by UN officials who were flying from the Hague. I pleaded with the private travel organizer for the UN to get me on the plane. No way, she said. I explained that if I missed the flight, I would miss a ten-day cruise. She said there were security issues. After all, this was a UN mission. I told her she could inspect my bags and I would fly naked, if necessary. She laughed, pulled me aside, and said if I gave her $500 cash she'd find me a seat. I got to PNG in time.

Of course, this is why we always advise liveaboard divers to arrive a day ahead of time if your boat won't be stopping at islands with airports. So, many wise travelers no longer face that drama. Still, there are other kinds of adventures, and here's one we published in 1991 by Joe Bark, M.D., a frequent contributor to *Undercurrent*.

Getting There is Not Half the Fun

These notes are going down as I'm sitting in the Roatan, Honduras airport, my hands still shaking. The Bluegrass Dive Club was returning from a week-long dive trip to Guanaja aboard a DC-3, one of the world's most dependable aircraft, in service more than 50 years.

On the way to Roatan rain started, and we had really rough bumps as we approached the island. The pilot anticipated a problem landing, so he made one low pass over the landing strip to check it out. On the second pass, he decided to go for it. I saw the start of the runway beneath the plane — and then more and more runway as the plane stayed airborne. There was not a sound from the passengers, as each of us glued his or her nose to a window, hoping soon to hear the familiar "clump, clump" of the landing gear grabbing tarmac. The pilot touched down again, but only for a second and we again became airborne. We bounced again, but the runway was running out. "Touch down . . . Touchdown!," I silently screamed.

We touched. I saw the parallel white stripes zip past. We were out of runway. I pulled in my gut and held my breath. Several people yelled "Oh Shit!" as the pilot tried to make an emergency maneuver, but the plane skidded and rocked. Carry-on bags and other objects became briefcase-sized bullets flying everywhere inside the plane. There were booms and crashes. The seats buckled and several broke loose. There was a flash somewhere up front, no fire that I could see, but some dust or smoke. And then we stopped. The airstrip ended at the sea and someone shouted that we might be sinking, a possibility I hadn't considered. I moved quickly to extricate myself while one of the passengers who had been sitting in front of me literally flew over the seats behind him and headed for the door two seats behind me. We kicked that emergency door open and a ferocious rain poured in. The plane had come to rest on the huge erosion control boulders at the end of the Roatan runway, its nose in the sea.

I climbed out, taking my carry-on which contained the Tandy computer upon which I'm writing this, and leapt for the nearest rock, then went back to help the others get out of the plane. The airport rescue squadron arrived, sirens blaring, and we quickly formed a line in the water to pass folks up to the runway. A Honduran woman, nearly 60 years old, stood in the cold rain in her nightgown, soaked to the skin, pulling the people we passed to her up the hill from the water. She had come over instantly from the tiny village adjacent to the runway and met us almost as the door opened.

Even at such a moment, after we knew everyone was safe, there was time for a little humor. Lexington Police Officer Debbie Wagner, who had completed her 99th dive in Guanaja, remarked as she stepped into the water outside the plane: "I'll tell you one thing. This is going into my log book as my 100th dive!"

Not the kind of dive anyone would like to log, but there are worse. It's good to keep in mind the old adage, "The sea is a cruel mistress," with rapidly changing conditions that can turn a pleasant dive into a life-threatening disaster.

Australia's Lonergan Trial:
Learning how to count heads

One of the most terrifying dive experiences imaginable is being left behind by a dive boat. *Undercurrent* has reported on several such incidents over the years, but the best known was the incident that became the inspiration for the film *Open Water*, which was based on the January 1998 tragedy where Thomas and Eileen Lonergan from Baton Rouge, LA, disappeared after the day boat *Outer Edge* left the Great Barrier Reef for Cairns while the couple was still diving. (In fact, the filmmakers were subscribers to *Undercurrent* and learned of the story by reading our article).

The couple was not missed for two days, when the boat crew finally noticed that some of their gear was still on board. They tried to contact them at their hotel, but learned they had not returned. That's when the unsuccessful search began.

Despite claims from some members of the Aussie dive industry that the couple may have faked their own deaths, an inquest concluded that the divers had drowned or been killed by sharks. Here's the story of the trial.

The skipper of the dive boat *Outer Edge*, charged with manslaughter after leaving behind two American divers on Queensland's Great Barrier Reef, was found innocent by an Australian court. The missing pair went unnoticed until the crew found some of their belongings two days later.

None of the three crew members could remember who was in charge of the diver's log book or who had done the head counts.

The remains of the Americans, Tom and Eileen Lonergan of Baton Rouge, LA, have never been found, although a fin, BC, wetsuit hood, and tank belonging to the couple were found, and a slate washed ashore with a message in Eileen's handwriting with their names, address, and phone number, and a request for help because they had been abandoned.

During the trial, the defense argued that it was possible the couple had faked their deaths and feigned their disappearance.

A journalist attending the trial told *Undercurrent* that he visited the site of the Lonergans' disappearance and noted that the two-story tower of a day-boat mooring 2.3 nautical miles away could be seen from the surface of the water, leading to speculation about whether they would have swum toward it. Also, several other boats overnighted in the area, and their lights would have been visible. The weather was good and the seas were calm and flat, people reported.

The skipper of the charter boat *Quicksilver* told the court that he heard an American accent among his 288 supposedly Italian passengers during a dive trip to the same area the day after the Lonergans disappeared. He said the boat count was three more at the end of the day, but he did not investigate.

During the trial, the defense presented nine witnesses who claimed they had seen the Lonergans in Queensland during the days following their disappearance. Because newspapers and television broadcasts carried photos of the couple, they were recognizable.

Some people theorized that the couple wanted to commit suicide. Six months before the couple vanished, Tom Lonergan wrote: "I feel as though my life is complete and I'm ready to die." Just 16 days before they disappeared, Eileen Lonergan wrote that her husband had a death wish.

The prosecution theorized that after being left at sea and surviving at least overnight, they succumbed to shark attacks. No one has heard from the couple nor have their bank accounts been touched.

No matter what happened to the Lonergans, boat captain Jack Nairn said as a new owner of the boat, he accepted responsibility for leaving them behind, but he had delegated responsibility for diver safety to the experienced crew he inherited with the boat.

He laid the blame for a failed head count at the feet of divemasters George Pyrihow and Kathy Traverso, who had told him all divers were accounted for, Nairn said.

Pyrihow claimed he had informed Nairn he could find only 24 of

The Lost Art

Life was never like this. If you dived from a boat, you were expected to be able to get back to it and end your dive at the boat ladder. If you were diving from a small boat without a separate tender and failed to surface right at the boat, you would have to swim for it or wait, drifting around for 30 minutes or so, shark bait, until all the other divers were on board before the boat could pick you up. If it could still find you.

On our boats we had a rescue tender, but if you were picked up away from the main boat, we considered that to be a rescue, and we used to charge for rescues. A crew member would take the tender and pick you up. To be assured of survival, it was wise to carry $5 in your BC pocket.

Nowadays most diving seems to be from big boats with multiple tenders. The art of underwater navigation appears forgotten. Divers surface all over the ocean, inflate their safety sausages and get picked up — and no one charges anything. It is a pity, because the rescue fee had multiple benefits, including keeping the crew alert to surfacing divers, since the cash went to the crew member who effected the rescue.

– Bob Halstead from *Dive Log Australasia, 2005*

the 26 passengers during a head count after the final dive of the day and was told to add two swimmers who were in the water. Nairn denied any such conversation had taken place and said he would have ordered a recount if there were a discrepancy.

None of the three crew members could remember who was in charge of the log book or who performed the head counts following the first two dives of the day. But all testified it was standard practice to assume a head count had been done if the boat's engines were started. They were, and the *Outer Edge* returned to shore without the Lonergans.

After the death of the two Americans — and most observers believe they did die at sea — the state of Queensland issued regulations for dive operations. They instruct operators on how to conduct head counts and maintain lookouts. They also provide advice about the strenuous nature of diving and snorkeling, and its potential to worsen existing medical conditions. In the past four years, 13 scuba-diving deaths involving six tourists were recorded in Queensland. Twenty people have died snorkeling, all but two of them tourists. Unfit and elderly Westerners are more likely to die than Asian tourists.

Ironically, in September, two Japanese divers spent nearly five hours lost off the Great Barrier Reef after they became disoriented during a dive on Ribbon Reef, 150 km. northeast of Cairns. Unlike the Lonergans, these divers left their boat behind. After being located on choppy seas by a rescue helicopter, the brother and sister pair were cold and shaken when they returned to their liveaboard, the *Reef Explorer*, the same boat that was in the news a year ago when passengers had to tie up a skipper who was trying to ground the boat on a reef. The woman hid her face and refused to make comments to reporters, because, according to Wayne Inglis, *Reef Explorer* spokesman, she believed she "lost face in making a mistake."

The Lonergan deaths led dive boats worldwide to tighten up their headcount procedures, but not all. We still get several reports a year of dive boats overlooking divers in the water.

But let's move on. While it may not be as deeply frightening as being lost at sea, being underwater during one of the most destructive tsunamis ever ranks right up there as a pants wetter.

Viewing the Tsunami from Below
Divers caught in startling currents

As divers and travelers, we are routinely confronted with a wide range of dangers we usually negotiate with relative ease. But a tsunami isn't an expected danger on any diver's list. Hence, when a tsunami destroyed the coast of Thailand on December 26, 2005, surprised divers, like everyone else, were caught unaware. Here are stories from divers who were underwater when the giant wave rolled over them.

In the Maldives

Greg and Deirdre Stegman, retired diving instructors from Queensland, Australia, were a half a mile off Faru Island, diving at 60 feet when they were suddenly sucked down to 90 feet in a one-second underwater terror ride. They clawed at the reef to save their lives. "We would have gone down another 30 to 60 feet if we had not held on to the reef," Mr. Stegman said. They were clueless as to why this was happening.

Two British divers were instantly forced down to 125 feet by wild crosscurrents when the tsunami rolled over.

On the boat ride out, they had noticed the currents were particularly strong that morning, which was unusual. Once they were in the water (along with six other experienced divers from France, Switzerland, and the UK) the current reversed directions, sweeping all the divers along for seven to eight minutes at a tumultuous five knots. After a five-minute lull, the ripping current reversed and sucked them back in the other direction. Mr. Stegman said the diving party somehow managed to keep together by holding on to their diving buddies. "Every now and again we'd see the other divers come past us and they'd disappear again."

Their dive boat had miraculously remained intact, and once the waves had passed, the driver was able to take them back to the shore.

British divers Matthew Oliver and Emma Simcox were instantly forced down to 125 feet by wild crosscurrents when the tsunami rolled over them on a dive off Hakuraa, the Maldives' most southerly island. They eventually managed an emergency ascent, sharing air, and returned to Hakuraa, only to find their beach bungalow destroyed and their few remaining possessions gone.

"There was debris everywhere — rubbish, bottles, trees, lamps from bungalows. The roof had been ripped off the restaurant, and there was a boat in the trees. People were covered in blood. The husband of one injured woman told me that his wife had been dragged underwater and had her skin ripped off by broken glass and coral," they said. A Pakistani Navy destroyer eventually rescued the couple.

George Chinn, a student from Cuckfield, England, was down 50 feet off the coastline of Meru (an hour from Male) when the main 30-foot wall of water surged over him. He was forced to cling to the reef as the powerful surge threatened to drag him out to sea. He surfaced to wood and life jackets floating in the water. "The whole thing lasted only a few minutes, but it was not until we got back to the island that we realized the scale of what had happened."

A divemaster on the liveaboard *Manthiri* reported that their boat met the wave at Vaavu Atoll with no damage. He described the wave as being like nothing he had ever seen in his lifetime. "When the wave flowed in, the tiny islands were consumed and when it ebbed, the reefs, normally several meters under the water, were naked and visible."

In Thailand

Canadians Gobeil and Francois had traveled to the island of Koh Phi Phi, where they were training to become dive instructors. They were boarding the dive boat with eight others when, without warning, the first wave reared up in front of them.

"The water at the pier is 60 feet deep, so there was no warning," she said. "The wave just came up. It was 30 feet high. My boyfriend yelled to me to run, but I froze." She managed to hold on to the railing of the pier until the metal broke loose in her hands. Tossed around like a rag doll in a washing machine, she popped to the surface three times while in the wave as it carried her up the side of a mountain. Then she crashed through a bamboo hut full of people who were then washed away alongside her. Eventually, she ended up on the roof of the dive operation's compressor shed about 400 feet away.

Her partner, Francois, suffered severe cuts after he was flung through debris of trees, furniture, and construction up the side of another mountain, landing next to several dead Thai children in a schoolyard. Eventually, Gobeil and Francois found each other, and after spending the night in the jungle they were airlifted by helicopter to Phuket.

In Sri Lanka

When Warren and Julie Lavender surfaced from their first-ever certified scuba dive the day after Christmas, they pulled off their masks, looked at each other and said, "That sucked." Then Warren threw up. The dive had sucked because the water was choppy on the surface, the current was hellaciously strong below, and,

"Gee; I could really learn to hate this sport."

for some reason, the fish were all hiding in crevices. The Lavenders were happy to climb back into the dive boat for the half-hour return trip to the beach, where glorious Alka Seltzer awaited.

However, on the way back, Julie noticed something weird in the water. Somebody's wallet, she said, pointing at it. Then came a chair. Then a coconut tree.

Then Warren noticed something worse — a horrified look on the captain's face. He spun around to see that the beach wasn't there anymore. That's when they knew something was very, very wrong. "That beach had to be 150 meters wide, and it was just . . . gone. So were the docks." Waves were crashing straight into the hotels, some of which caved in like sandcastles, he reported.

The Lavenders had unknowingly scuba-dived through a tsunami. It was now hammering their vacation spot, the resort town of Beruwala on the western coast of Sri Lanka, gobbling up homes and boats and people, pulling them all back into the Indian Ocean and then flinging them back at the town again and again, killing hundreds.

Suddenly, it all made sense to the novice divers, the way they'd had to fight the torrential current at the bottom — like a "hurricane underwater," was how Warren described it. Sixty feet below the surface, his mask was ripped off. It was all they could do to hold on to coral to avoid being sucked away. Warren said, "I remember thinking, 'Gee; I could really learn to hate this sport.'"

And if You're Diving in a Tsunami?

Ironic as it seems, the safest place to be in a tsunami may well be in the ocean itself. It may be safer still to be beneath the surface: as divers we've all experienced how, on a rough day on the dive boat, it's much more comfortable once you're down below the surface of the water. And a tsunami at sea doesn't reach great heights; the immense waves don't form till the tsunami starts to reach shallow water and roll up against the ocean floor.

What most of the underwater tsunami stories had in common was that this was no time for coral conservation; grabbing on to a reef kept several divers from being sucked down to more dangerous depths. And, as with all underwater emergencies, the most critical factor was remaining calm enough to make the right choices.

These stories were compiled from e-mails, first-hand accounts, AP wire stories, and other sources. The Lavenders' story was taken from an article by Rick Reilly, Sports Illustrated. *The following is taken in part from an article by Gillian Flaccuss.*

Caught in Open Water

Open Water filmmakers Chris Kentis and Laura Lau were among those caught up in the killer tsunami in Phuket, Thailand. Kentis was returning to his hotel in Phuket after running morning errands when he saw the huge wave headed toward him.

"I heard people yelling, 'Run, run!'" said Kentis. "I looked behind me and I thought, 'This is what happens in a movie when there's a tidal wave.' You could hear the rumbling and this wave was coming right at us." Fleeing to his upper story hotel room, Kentis discovered his wife Lau and their seven-year-old daughter were not there. They were in a second-floor Internet café, trapped by a telephone booth lodged in the stairwell.

Lau and her daughter escaped by lowering a bamboo ladder over the balcony, then hiked in waist-deep water back to the hotel. They collected their luggage, then, afraid another massive wave might follow, hiked several miles into the mountains. From there, they took two minicabs to Phuket's east coast, which Kentis said seemed almost unaffected by the tsunami. "When we got there, it was all people on yachts having a good time. It was just surreal," Kentis said. "Two hours later, our kids were swimming in this beautiful hotel pool. And we're ordering food."

As the tsunami shows us, nature can be tough on divers in strange ways. What to do when a tsunami strikes is not a skill taught in any diving course. Nor is what to do in a lightning storm.

When Lightning Strikes During a Dive

An average of seventy people are killed by lightning every year in the U.S. About nine of those deaths take place in or near the water, in boats, or on docks. Florida gets more lightning strikes than any other state, and in July 2007 diver Stephen Wilson, 36, died when lightning struck his tank. He was diving from a small boat with three friends during a severe thunderstorm near Deerfield Beach, 40 miles north of Miami. Wilson surfaced 30 feet from the boat when the lightning bolt struck his tank and electrocuted him.

The problem for divers is that water is a good conductor of electricity, and lightning's electrical current can be carried for significant distances. Lightning tends to strike the highest thing around, and on the water the boat and everyone in it are prime targets for lightning bolts. Diving underwater may not be an option because lightning can be even more deadly when its electricity flows through the waves.

Underwater caves can be especially dangerous locations. In May 2008 Marc Laukien was diving in Florida's Madison Blue Springs, touching a cave wall with his hand, when he suddenly felt a strong electric shock through his entire arm. "We completed the dive without further incident, but when we reached the basin, it became clear there was a huge thunderstorm above us," he wrote online at RebreatherWorld.com.

"Staying in the water wasn't a good idea, and neither was getting out really, given that we had lots of metal on our backs. Since the thunderstorm could last a long time, we got out of the water, and after dropping our gear, made a run for the bathhouse."

If you're in a boat during a storm, says David Sawatzky, M.D., a medical columnist for the Canadian magazine *DIVER*, says the best method is to huddle in the middle of the boat as far as possible from water, electrical equipment, radios and anything metal. Lower the antenna and anything else sticking up on the boat. If there is a lightning protection system on the boat, don't touch it. And don't climb to the top of the boat to enjoy the lightning show.

Divers consider day boats and liveaboards their "mother ships," and homes away from home. Imagine the terror when disaster strikes a fully loaded dive boat.

Dive Boat Explosion Kills Four

Just eight days after taking their wedding vows, Tim and Victoria Simpson from Blue Bell, PA, were sitting side-by-side on the bow of a St. Lucia dive boat, donning their gear. Just as the crew of the Sandals' Halcyon resort boat began to lift anchor, the boat exploded, hurling its passengers 30 feet into the air, peppering them with fiberglass shards, and then bursting into a ball of flame.

Four people died in the October 19, 1997 explosion. An American, Paul George, from Long Island, NY, died after being transported to a Miami hospital. A Swiss woman and two St. Lucian diving instructors also were killed by the blast. The seven survivors, including the newlyweds, had fractures, back injuries, burns, and embedded fiberglass slivers.

> *"I was up in the air looking down at the water, thinking, 'Make sure you go down feet first.'"*

Though rumors abound that the Sandals' explosion stemmed from tourist business turf wars on this Caribbean island, two separate investigations have concluded that the accident was due to flawed boat design or boat maintenance. The St. Lucia Police Superintendent announced: "our forensic people have gone over every inch of the debris, and there is absolutely no trace of any explosive substance on the Sandals boat." Witnesses to the explosion reported seeing a line of fire extending out from the site of the explosion, suggesting a fuel leak.

Still, skeptics abound. Though it was the first incident to claim lives or involve dive operators, the blast was the fourth on St. Lucian tourist boats in the last 14 months. There have been many reports of severed fuel lines and engine tampering. So far, they have been confined to the fishing and sailing charter section of Rodney Bay Marina. Most incidents involved the boats of one particular charter operator.

Police and government efforts seem designed to sever any perceived connection between the Sandals explosion and the other bombings.

Most fingers are pointing at Sandals and the U.S. manufacturer of Sea Scip boats. The St. Lucia Police Commissioner called the explosion "an incident which could have been avoided with adequate maintenance," and said their investigation suggests that the explosion was caused by under deck gasoline leakage that had gone undetected before being ignited by electrical short-circuiting.

A Sandals spokesperson countered by labeling the statement an "overreaction" and insisted that the boat-maintenance program at their twelve Caribbean resorts is widely known to be among the most comprehensive and thorough anywhere in the Caribbean. Citing its own internal investigation pointing to a design flaw by the manufacturer, Sandals has concluded that a ruptured fuel line under the sealed deck on that hot, still day had filled the hull with fumes. When the captain tried to start the bilge pump, the fumes ignited, pushing up the deck of the boat and catapulting the passengers into the air.

Neither Tim nor Victoria Simpson thought it was sabotage, reported the *Philadelphia Inquirer*. Tim said he became concerned when he noticed smoke seeping out of a porthole near the boat's engine. That was the last thing he remembers; he thinks he hit his head against a tank and blacked out during the explosion.

Victoria saw "fire coming out of the engine. In that split second, I remember being thrust into the air and there was this intense sound. I was up in the air looking down at the water, thinking, 'Make sure you go down feet first.' I felt for my legs and my arms and made sure I could move them and wasn't paralyzed."

Undercurrent contacted Sea Scip, the boat manufacturer in Arkansas, and spoke with Fred Herman, who said he was unaware that any of his boats were in St. Lucia and that no Sea Scip boats had exploded. The following day, the number was no longer in service the telephone company confirmed it had been disconnected at the request of Sea Scip.

Here's a chilling first-hand account of a Bahamian liveaboard that went aground with two dozen passengers aboard.

Women First, please

My Orlando, Florida, dive club booked passage the last week of September (1992) on the *Crown Islander*, homeport Freeport, Bahamas. While the brochure expounded on the luxurious accommodations for 32 passengers on the 135 foot craft, our trip carried only 24 passengers — 16 members of my dive club, one Californian, and seven Norwegians. After we got settled, the divemasters briefed us on the boat, casually explaining where the life jackets and life rafts were, and what to do if the ship alarm sounded.

By late afternoon the first day, we were anchored 25 miles from Freeport for an unexciting checkout dive. When night fell, even though the sea was getting rougher, some of us hearty souls plunged into the darkness with lights and glow-sticks for our dive. While we were on the bottom, the seas became rougher still, making climbing back onto the boat a real challenge. After showering, we went to the sun deck for a couple of beers to discuss the diving. With the boat rocking from side to side, a few chairs actually tipped over.

About 11:30 p.m., I climbed into my top bunk. Because the ship was really rolling, I couldn't sleep. Although lower deck windows had been bolted shut to prevent water from entering from large waves, water was striking my second deck cabin window. At 12:30 a.m., I heard the engines start. The captain had decided to pull anchor and move to the leeward side of the island. But, they were unable to free the hook from the reef. At 1:00 a.m., they shut the engines down and assigned the night watch, deciding to simply ride the rough seas out until morning. I finally fell asleep.

Earthquake Diving

At the end of a night dive at Indonesia's Raja Ampat islands in 2005, subscribers Allan and Barbara Jones (Anaheim, CA) were returning to the ship when they felt a loud and heavy vibration. "It was as if a very large freighter was passing overhead," they told *Undercurrent*. The vibration increased in intensity until "we had to wrap our arms around our chests to keep our internals from vibrating." The 7.3 earthquake lasted about 20 seconds, and passengers on the boat felt as if it were slipping its anchor. The quake's epicenter was 200 miles away, said the Joneses, but since water transmits energy much more efficiently than air, "it seemed we were over the source."

About an hour later, I was shocked to full consciousness by an impact that almost threw me to the ceiling of my cabin. Then another impact. I heard the divemaster yell "get to the sun deck!," and then the alarm sounded. Heading for the top deck, I careened off the walls from more impacts. On deck, life jackets were being passed out to the passengers, some still in their night clothes. It was pitch dark, no moon, and I had no idea where we were. More impacts. We counted off, to make sure that everybody was there. Life rafts were being inflated and sent overboard. Then the order came down "Abandon ship, women first."

Passengers tried to climb from the stern dive platform into the life rafts, but the seas were angry. A divemaster pinched his foot in one of the dive ladders. We climbed over the railing and waited for the word to drop 10-12 feet. I hit the opening in the life raft and people already in the raft pulled me out of the way so the next person would not land on me.

We 16 were packed so tight in the 20 person life raft that three people were on top of me. Looking through the opening, seeing the

Underwater Suicide

In Croatia in 2002, a scuba diver was found dead at the bottom of a cave at 180 feet, with a knife protruding from his chest. After his body was retrieved, an autopsy found that the death was due to both drowning and the penetrating knife wound.

Officials believed at first it was a homicide and arrested two suspects. However, the "blood stains" on their clothing proved to be paint, and they passed a polygraph test. A forensic analysis of the profile of the diver's last dive stored in his computer and other findings led officials to conclude the diver committed suicide, most likely because he ran out of air and wanted to avoid the agony of drowning.

However, drowning, once underway, is considered a peaceful way to pass. Not so for a knife wound.

– *Nadan M. Petri, Undersea and Hyperbaric Medicine Department,*
Naval Medical Institute, Split, Crotia

waves breaking and the raft drifting under the hull of the ship, I knew that if something happened there was no way I was going to get out of here. I would drown. The last person who entered was one of the Norwegians. He promptly tied the opening shut, against the screams of the others. He didn't understand English. He didn't know his knots; he had tied a knot that he couldn't untie.

They finally let go of the lines holding the rafts to the ship. We were adrift in rolling seas. Yet, in no more than a couple of minutes, I felt something hard under the bottom of the raft. We were on land. There, 30-40 yards offshore, was the now brightly lit ship. The anchor had let go, and the ship had drifted ashore and grounded, without anybody noticing.

We headed inland in search of a telephone. After about a mile, we came upon a house and called taxis. At 6:00 a.m., twenty wet, sand-coated people with nothing but the clothes on our backs showed up at the Bahamas Princess Casino and Resort.

We spent the next three days at the resort getting our clothes and gear off the boat. Several months later, refunds arrived for our failed trip.

– **William D. Turman, Oviedo, FL**

The *Wave Dancer* Tragedy: Twenty Deaths
Belize releases its final report

The tragic loss of twenty lives on October 8, 2001, when Peter Hughes' *Wave Dancer* capsized while moored in Big Creek, Belize, during Hurricane Iris, will long be remembered by divers.

Both the *Wave Dancer* and the *Belize Aggressor* sought shelter from the hurricane by motoring a mile upstream to the Port of Big Creek, about 75 miles south of Belize City. During the night, the full force of Hurricane Iris' 150 mph winds struck the port. The *Wave Dancer* broke away from its moorings, colliding with the *Aggressor* before capsizing. Seventeen divers from a Richmond, Virginia, dive club and three crew members died, while three guests and five crew members survived.

In January, more than three years after the accident, the International Merchant Marine Registry of Belize (IMMARBE) published findings of their official investigation. The report was delayed, they said, in part because the *Wave Dancer's* insurers commenced legal proceedings against the *Belize Aggressor* alleging that the collision between the two vessels was the fault of the *Aggressor.*

While some of the circumstances of the accident remain a mystery, a few key points of the report follow.

A Horrifying Scene

The chilling accounts of the survivors and the report's findings evoke a terrifying picture of the disaster: "Due to the very short time between the vessel breaking free from the dock and rolling over, those guests who were still in the salon were thrown from the starboard to the port side. Due to the element of surprise, disorientation and flooding coupled with a sensation of entrapment, death as

> *Neither the Captain nor 2nd Captain had significant experience sailing in Belizean waters during a hurricane season.*

the result of asphyxiation due to drowning would have ensued in less than two minutes."

Divemaster Bart Stanley noted that guests in the salon "were thrown violently." Many of the deceased had head injuries. Stanley was trapped, but thanks to his knowledge of the boat, he swam out, exiting from the "starboard exit door facing the wheelhouse." He dived back down to try to open the salon door, but couldn't. Head diving instructor Thomas Baechtold stated that after the vessel capsized, he "came out near the propellers, which were moving. I was blown out of the water by a tornado-like gust onto the mangrove," about 100 meters.

When 2nd Captain Wouters felt the mooring rope break, he raced to the wheelhouse and tried to gain control of the ship. "The vessel was free and out of control. I made a futile attempt to obtain some sort of control with the engines, but to no avail. . . I then felt that we had gone aground and had heeled to port, which accelerated into capsizing the vessel. I found myself . . . still in the wheelhouse under water. I swam through the wheelhouse door."

After the boat rolled over, the life rafts were afloat but still attached to the boat. Captain Philip Martin ordered several people into the life rafts and pushed them clear of the boat. He then swam across the 400-ft. channel to the *Aggressor*, took their tender, and returned to the *Wave Dancer*. Meanwhile, 2nd Captain Wouters, who was on a life raft, started banging on the hull and yelling to get a response from anyone trapped inside. He quickly helped three survivors into the life raft.

Report Findings

The report noted that the *Wave Dancer* was adequately manned with a qualified crew, though neither the Captain nor 2nd Captain had significant experience sailing in Belizean waters during hurricane season. Hughes had hired Martin in February 2001, then promoted him to captain in May. This was the first commercial vessel he had commanded.

On Friday, October 5, Captain Martin received clear instructions by phone and e-mail from Peter Hughes Diving to monitor the storm. The *Wave Dancer* departed port the following day, October 6, and headed for Lighthouse Reef. The report finds that Martin failed to follow the boat's hurricane plan, which required him to contact the shore managers and monitor the storm.

According to the report, "neither the Captain nor the 2nd Captain listened to the local Belize radio stations themselves and were apparently satisfied with receiving morsels of such information from their catering staff."

The next day, Sunday, October 7, with Hurricane Iris headed toward Belize, Martin decided to remain at Lighthouse Reef, a decision based on his mistaken belief that Iris' landfall was still projected for the northern Yucatan. Wouters said he told Martin "it was best to go to Belize City immediately. I attempted to persuade him that we could drop off the passengers at a hotel and we could take the boat to an area deep in the mangrove with just a skeleton crew. He rejected the idea. I returned twice more. Each time the discussion became more heated until we were both shouting. This is the argument I believe several other people heard."

The report faults Martin's decision, noting that his passengers should have had the opportunity to get off the boat, part of the boat's hurricane plan. Martin had polled the guests, but the report notes that their view "could not have been based on any better knowledge of the weather situation than that which the Captain and/or 2nd Captain possessed . . . furthermore, voting by guests is nothing more than an indication of their preferences, but no means by which a Captain arrives at his decision with regard to safety matters."

With the storm approaching, the only alternative was to steam to Big Creek, where he tied the boat alongside the *Aggressor*. The guests remained on board at Big Creek rather than seeking shelter on shore. While the hurricane plan stated "where possible disembark guests," the report says that the decision "was a considered one . . . in our view, both remaining onboard the *Wave Dancer* as well as moving to the shore entailed risks . . ." But none of the local residents who took refuge in the local bank building was injured.

Hughes was insured for only $5 million, and after raising the Wave Dancer, less than $4 million was distributed among the relatives of the twenty dead.

The report also dismisses the rumors that there had been excessive drinking by passengers or crew. But it does note that Martin failed to supply guests with, among other things, flashlights, and to instruct them to remain with life jackets and remain on the floor in accordance with the plan." And, "despite the extreme weather conditions, the Captain failed to order the engines to be started and for the wheelhouse to be manned either by himself or the 2nd Captain."

The report raises questions about how the boat was positioned when moored, with the bow extending 30 feet past the dock, "exposing the section of the vessel to the hurricane winds," and how the mix of nylon and polypropylene mooring lines may have contributed to the disaster. (Because polypropylene stretches more than nylon, the nylon alone had to bear the entire strain, which suggests that the polypropylene was useless.) However, it concluded that the extreme weather conditions and "tornado-like gusts" prevailing at storm's peak were the chief causes of the loss of the *Wave Dancer*.

Recommendations

The report issued a list of recommendations intended to prevent future tragedies:

- Passenger-carrying recreational craft operating in Belizean waters should return to port whenever a hurricane watch is issued;

- Every liveaboard passenger vessel operating in Belize should have at least one navigating officer with experience navigating Belizean waters;

- Vessels not use mixed mooring ropes, opting instead for all polypropylene or all nylon;

- Belizean nationals serving on live-aboard passenger vessels have written employment contracts to provide the right to disembark in case of a hurricane as well as providing insurance if there is death or injury. (Belizean crew members on *Wave Dancer* had no contracts and were allegedly told they would lose their jobs if they disembarked before the storm. One crew member did opt to leave and survived the storm.)

P.S.: Divers Alert Network (DAN) insurance covered none of the deceased divers. The tragedy was not a diving accident. Hughes' company was insured for only $5 million, and after raising the *Wave Dancer*, less than $4 million was distributed among the relatives of the twenty dead.

Making New Friends at Forty Feet: A Horror Story

When we were kids we used to sit around the campfire, spinning "true" yarns about scary events we would swear had happened to us. We hadn't heard many diving stories worth repeating around the campfire until we came across this piece, written by John Burgess for Alabama's *Opp News*. We can't attest to the veracity of the tale, but we can attest to the chills it produced.

* * *

Our oldest son, David, has gotten into the world of scuba diving. He related this true story that was told to him by his diving instructor some weeks back.

Like boys will, Dave asked the instructor what was the most frightening thing that he has ever had happen to him while he was diving. Without hesitating the instructor said that it was an incident that occurred many years ago when the sport of diving was still in its infancy and he was among the few certified divers in this part of the country.

Of course, everyone knew that he put on air tanks and descended into the far depths of water, and most of them thought he was crazy.

Anyhow, this didn't deter them in the slightest when a man in a Volkswagen went plunging off an embankment at a hydro electric dam near his home, and sank in some 40 feet of water. In fact, he said they had him and his gear on the scene only minutes after the mishap had occurred. Shortly he found himself swimming down through the murky waters of the lake unable to see more than a few inches in front of his face.

He screamed into his mouthpiece, nearly losing it, and he thrashed around like a 175 lb. fish on a tight line.

Miraculously, though, he went almost directly to the car and touched the top with his hand. Using his hands as his eyes he swam around the car until he found an open window, and shoved his head and arms into the car to see if he could locate the man's body.

Suddenly, 40 feet beneath the surface of a muddy lake, locked in almost pitch blackness, a hand shot out of nowhere and clamped in a steel-like vise on his wrist.

He said nothing that has ever happened to him before or since has ever come even halfway as close to frightening him as badly as did that hand.

He went into an absolute and instant panic, something that divers, especially experienced ones, are conditioned not to do no matter what happens. He screamed into his mouthpiece, nearly losing it, and he thrashed around like a 175 lb. fish on a tight line, but nothing he did would dislodge him from that steel grip that held his arm.

Finally, from sheer exhaustion, he stopped fighting and cautiously reached down with his other hand and felt the hand and arm of another human.

Slowly, carefully, he pulled himself further into the car until he suddenly broke into a chamber of air that had been trapped inside at the top, and there was the driver of the car with his head in the air pocket, still alive but in a state of absolute, total shock.

So bad was the man's state of mind that it took some minutes to get him to release his grip and to understand that he could go safely to the surface with the diver by both of them using the diver's regulator.

The diver was kind of the town hero for several weeks after, but even this didn't stop months of horrible nightmares for him. Nightmares, he said, in which a cold clammy hand would suddenly shoot out of the blackness and clamp onto his wrist like a steel band refusing to let go no matter what he did.

Chapter 8
Skullduggery on the High Seas

A lot of strange adventures can happen on the high seas. Divers often face bizarre situations not only when diving but even when collecting their baggage. And, then there is the dive shop owner found guilty in a Rhode Island civil court of killing his wife underwater; the Ponzi scheme that sucked in more investors than an old scow of a liveaboard was worth; divers arrested for tracking down underwater treasures, including illegal abalones. Let's kick off with a simple tale of two divers having their suitcase with clean underwear switched with one stuffed with ganja — and the absurd hassles that followed.

Another Packing Peril

My husband and I were flying on Air Jamaica from Chicago to Barbados to go diving in October 2002, with a two-hour layover in Jamaica. Before boarding our flight in Montego Bay to continue to Barbados, an Air Jamaica representative said our tag had fallen off a piece of our checked luggage. He wanted us to identify the untagged bag, which we did. He gave us a new tag, and we boarded the plane.

After we got to Barbados and were sitting on the resort shuttle, a Barbados customs officer stopped us and said we were missing a piece of luggage. We told him we had all our luggage, but he wanted us to come with him. He took us to a room where a green suitcase was sitting on a table. We said it wasn't ours, but he asked if they could open "our" piece of luggage. We said go ahead, but repeated that it wasn't ours. He cut off the locks and opened it. Inside were six bricks of marijuana. I almost fainted.

They took us into a small room where an official looked through the marijuana. They kept referring to the luggage as ours. A narcotics officer asked us questions, and a police officer commented that the marijuana could have come from Chicago. We said this had to have happened in Jamaica where one of our tags had "fallen off" — that tag was now on this green luggage.

He cut off the locks and opened it. Inside were six bricks of marijuana. I almost fainted.

They didn't tell us what was going on, but said we had to go to the police station. I was so afraid, I called the U.S. Embassy, so the officials then said that after we went to the station to give statements, they would take us to the resort. It was 10:00 p.m. We had been up since 4:00 a.m. and had been in custody for four hours, much of the time in a locked room watching them process the marijuana. We were afraid, hungry, and exhausted.

The police station was a pigsty. They put us in separate rooms, and for the next two hours took and retook our statements. They didn't have a computer, so everything was handwritten. We got to our resort at 1:00 a.m. While we considered catching the next flight back to Chicago, we decided to stay and are glad we did because the diving was great. We didn't hear from the police or customs again.

We asked local Bajans about Air Jamaica, and several said that Air Jamaica is frequently used for drug smuggling. One person told us that he stitches closed the outside pockets on his luggage because an Air Jamaica employee will slip drugs into an outside pocket and at the next airport another Air Jamaica employee will take it out.

However, this hasn't stopped us from flying Air Jamaica. We are using the two first-class tickets they gave us for this ordeal and heading to St. Lucia at the end of March.

– Katie Moyle, Appleton, Wis.

Back in 1990, we had a reviewer aboard the Bottom Time, *a liveaboard boat out of Fort Lauderdale that visited the Cay Sal Banks in the Bahamas. His experience included a bit more than just diving:*

Drugs at Sea

All in all, the diving was a kinder and gentler experience, and basically what I had expected in the laid-back Caribbean. But, dear reader, there's more.

You see, I'll not remember this trip for the diving, but rather for the discovery we made — and the captain's decision about that discovery. It's a story within a story.

Toward the end of the cruise, floating somewhere in the westernmost reaches of the Bahamas, but with neither a speck of land nor a single boat in sight, one of the passengers spotted an orange floating object. He pointed it out to the captain, who turned the boat. Once alongside, we scooped in what proved to be a padlocked rubber bag.

It might have been Juan Valdez's coffee, but another slit of the package produced a white, powdery substance.

Judging from the rust on the lock, it appeared the bag had been in the water for only a few days. With a diver's knife, our captain sliced open the bag. Inside were 48 individually wrapped, waterproof bricks, lettered "Columbia." It might have been Juan Valdez's coffee, but another slit of the package produced a white, powdery substance, which the experts among us determined had to be 100 percent pure cocaine. More than 100 pounds of the stuff! With a street value into the millions.

What would be your response? I scanned the horizon to see if anyone was in sight. I pictured Miami Vice's Don Johnson racing up in a speedboat to nab us. Or worse! What if the original toot owners zipped over the horizon? Would they have thanked us generously for the find, tipping us with a couple of bricks for our trouble? I doubt it. Would they have boarded and raised hell? Perhaps. Either way, I wasn't interested in meeting them.

To a person, we realized we had a dilemma. Someone suggested we radio the Coast Guard. But, would open radio transmission attract the guys who wrapped the package? And, what if we did reach the Coast Guard safely? Would we spend the rest of the trip waiting for them, explaining ourselves and miss the remaining diving? A loud hoot to that.

Perhaps the best alternative was to cut open the bag and sink the stuff. What about the toxicity, warned an amateur ecologist? Would we wipe out the reefs? Mutate the reproductive systems of groupers? Would 48 turtles eat 48 packages and die? Who knew?

So, here we have a captain and crew and passengers, at times laughing their butts off, at times concerned, at times trying to figure out what to do, but getting kind of antsy about it all — especially since we were missing some diving.

Well, the law of the sea puts the captain square in command of his vessel, fully in charge of any issue that pops up. And, up had popped the orange bag. It was the captain's call. The crew huddled, and then concluded to reseal the snow in plastic trash bags. Once done, the captain steamed off, arriving eventually at a small, nondescript, unnamed, and uninhabited cay, (of which there are nearly 700 in the Bahamas). The captain and his crew boarded the Zodiac and took the stuff ashore. They returned to tell us that they had buried it where it would never be found again. I gather that the captain, wishing to assume full responsibility for the incident, as would any good captain, did not wish any of us innocent bystanders to witness the final disposition. Good fellow, the captain. I suppose eventually the tropical rains and all those little bugs will destroy the evidence, but then again those water proof bags are pretty tough.

We departed, not knowing the name of this isolated, lonely Bahamian cay, nor having the faintest idea of its location. And I trust that goes for the captain and the crew as well.

* * *

After our reviewer's report, we decided to find out what a diver should do if he finds floating contraband. Both the Drug Enforcement Administration and the U.S. Coast Guard says to inform authorities.

Lt. Commander Jeff Karonis, Coast Guard public affairs officer, says this happens three to four times a month. "It's highly unlikely, but not impossible," he says, "that the original smugglers will be monitoring the radio or still be in the area. What was found was probably part of a drop of perhaps a ton or so of cocaine that drifted off."

Should this happen to you, he says, "notify the Coast Guard that you found some packages that we may want. If you're in our waters we will come out, take the drugs and inspect the vessel, a procedure that should take no more than an hour."

John Fernandes, DEA public affairs officer, says to request non-emergency assistance. "If they ask what sort of assistance, just tell them it can't be dealt with on the air. That should stimulate them enough without alerting anyone else. Throughout the Bahamas and the northern Caribbean," he says, "there are several helicopters in operation and someone will be along soon."

Another option, says Fernandes, is to keep the stuff on board, "but to notify some authority that you have a package with smaller packages on board and make that note in the ship's log." That puts you on record as having notified an authority. When you dock, Fernandes says, "make sure that the first thing that you do is tell an authority that you have drugs on board that you found at sea and tell them who was notified."

If you are in the waters of a Caribbean country, says Karonis, "you should still call us. We may still arrange to pick the stuff up." All radio calls, he says, are recorded, so if you have to go through foreign customs, he says, "a call will indicate that you did report it and are not smugglers."

In any case, the authorities want the boodle. Fernandes said that the packaging might provide some indication of exactly where it came from and who was involved. Furthermore, Fernandes mentioned, "just sinking the stuff doesn't guarantee that it will stay sunk." The point is to get it out of circulation.

So reporting such a find is not likely to alert the Medellin Cartel, nor is it likely to disrupt a dive vacation — unless the Coast Guard shows up unexpectedly and you have 100 pounds of nose candy on board. That will spoil your trip.

Exploding Tank Yields $150,000 of Cannabis
Shop and employee festooned with resin

An unwitting scuba diver may have been finning around the Irish coast in the early 80s, totally unaware that inside his tank were twenty-three kilos of Moroccan cannabis resin, with a street value of more

The Creature from Neary's Lagoon

It began in 1982 with calls to the police about a mystery scuba diver who regularly disappeared into the mist-shrouded waters of Neary's Lagoon in Santa Cruz, California, just after daybreak. The diver would make his way through the chilly water 100 yards out to a small island that, for the last ten years, has been part of a city park and wildlife refuge. There, amid a thick growth of tall grass and cottonwood trees, police found a carefully cultivated marijuana plot. "It was pretty ingenious," said Santa Cruz police Sgt. Bill Aluffi, who needed a rowboat to reach the island. Aluffi found a 40-foot by 60-foot clearing, hacked out of dense tule grass and supporting forty thriving marijuana plants. Fully processed, Aluffi said, the harvest would bring about $80,000.

Who is the creature from Neary's Lagoon? Police don't know and say they have little hope of finding him. But, they've left him a note in the middle of the now barren minifarm. It reads "You are under arrest. (Signed) The Santa Cruz Police Department."

than $150,000. And the luckless diver was also unaware that his spare cylinder had another sixteen kilos secretly packaged inside.

The accidental discovery of the marijuana, which occurred when one of the cylinders exploded as an employee of a dive shop was refilling it, has sparked an international search by Dublin Drug Squad and Interpol.

Drug Squad authorities staked out the Dublin airport, following a tip that two scuba cylinders might contain contraband. They inspected the bottles, and found nothing suspicious, but continued their watch.

Although the two tanks later disappeared from the airport, officials believed that they had been stolen only for their intrinsic value as scuba tanks.

Des Mulreany, who works for the Great Outdoor Store, was visiting their Galway branch and brought a vanload of cylinders to their Dublin facility to be tested. One tank appeared to have a smaller inside diameter than normal, but the serial number indicated it was an American tank that should hold 80 cu. ft. of air. "I knew from my experience," Mulreany said, "that there was no way that 80 cubic feet would go into those bottles." He sent one to a colleague, Willie Siddel, who tests tanks at his facility in Dalkey, asking him to examine the bottle closely because "I felt there was something fishy about it."

An employee of Siddel's connected the cylinder to a compressor and a few minutes later the cylinder exploded, sending a shower of cannabis resin all over the room, sticking to the ceiling, the floor, the walls . . . and the employee. He suffered only a minor cut near his eye.

The authorities were called, of course, and upon examination of the second cylinder discovered a false bottom underneath a rubber protection cover. This part of the tank had been cut and threaded and the cannabis resin was then packed like a doughnut around an inner cylinder which held the air.

The Drug Squad interviewed the client who had left the tanks at the Galway shop; they believe that he was unaware that the cylinders carried the cannabis. Another man who sold the cylinders is now being questioned and authorities have expanded their search from Dublin and Galway to Paris, Morocco, and the United States.

As for the diver who was using the cannabis-laden tanks, with that kind of air contamination he must have seen some remarkable creatures below.

–Jack Foley, *San Jose News*

Divers planting marijuana are mild scofflaws compared to this dive shop owner in our next piece, which we carried in 2006.

The Yellow Fin in the Sand
The case of the dive store owner and his dead wife

In 1999, 43-year-old David Swain, the owner of Ocean State Scuba in Jamestown, RI, and his 46-year-old wife of nearly seven years, Shelley Tyre, chartered a sailboat in the British Virgin Islands with friends Christian and Bernice Thwaites and their son. The last day they were to dive they moored off Cooper's Island to dive two tugboat wrecks.

The couples had agreed that two adults would remain on the boat to watch the Thwaites' boy, so Tyre and Swain went into the water. Swain returned to the boat alone thirty-five minutes later, saying he was chilled. Christian Thwaites dropped into the water for his dive.

Moments later Thwaites spotted one of Shelley Tyre's yellow fins and looked for Tyre, figuring she would be grateful that he had found her fin. Instead, he found her lying on her back on the sandy bottom with her eyes and mouth open. Thwaites took Tyre to the surface, where he tried to perform CPR. Swain, who had been an emergency medical technician, helped lift his wife aboard, but did not try to resuscitate her. She was dead.

> *The pin holding one side of the mask strap in place was missing, indicating it had probably been ripped from the mask frame.*

Learning about the death, James Philip Brown, who runs Aquaventure in Tortola, thought it suspicious. Tyre and the Thwaites had visited his shop to rent gear and discuss where to dive. A day after Tyre died, Brown dived the wrecks looking for something that might explain the death. Brown found one of Tyre's fins embedded toe first in three inches of sand. He found her snorkel, sans mouthpiece, and her mask. On one side of the mask, the strap hung loose off its anchoring pin.

Brown locked Tyre's scuba gear in his office to await inspection by Tortola police. Two days later, Swain told him that he could get rid of the equipment, give it to a local diver or use it in the rental business. Brown refused.

Swain then fretted that the medical examiner was taking a long time to do an autopsy and asked if he knew anyone who might "expedite the process." Swain said that "the medical examiner might not know about diving accidents," and he wanted to talk to him before the autopsy. Swain's remarks seemed irregular to Brown, enough for him to approach Tortola police. But no charges were brought.

Shelley Tyre's parents asked Swain for an explanation of the death, but did not find him forthcoming. As more information came to light, and Swain continued to stonewall, they brought a wrongful death suit against him, which was heard over nine days in February 2006.

A Violent Struggle

During the trial, Bill Oliver, a mechanical engineer who designs diving equipment and is product manager for Sherwood, presented videos

Squid Fishermen's Bombs Rattle Night Divers

California scuba divers are upset with commercial squid fishermen, accusing them of jeopardizing night divers by detonating small explosives to protect their catch from sea lions. The bombs endanger the divers and ruin diving after dark, divers say.

"It sounded like elephants doing cannonballs over our heads," said San Diego diver Peter Ajtai, who was startled by the firecracker-like noisemakers while diving off La Jolla. "We could actually feel the percussion inside our bodies," he told Copley New Service in May 2004.

While the bombs aren't powerful enough to blow off a diver's finger, the percussive sound waves could damage eardrums or sinuses. Kristine Barksy, a U.S. Fish and Game Department biologist, said sound waves are amplified under water and can be disorienting to an unsuspecting diver. "You're down at night. It's all dark and then all of a sudden — BOOM!" she said. "It's very loud even if you're not close."

Federal law allows fishermen to use seal bombs to ward off sea lions and seals. Fisherman Donald Brockman said the bombs are made with a waterproof fuse and are filled with sand. Once, he accidentally detonated one in his hand. The only damage was a broken finger, he said. "It doesn't hurt the seals, it just spooks them."

Scuba divers would be wise to keep their distance when the squid fleet is working because the fishermen can't tell whether divers are in the water at night, Brockman said.

This reminds us of another incident reported by the AP in May 1998. A couple of Italian fishermen found a hand grenade, and decided to use it to enhance their catch by stunning fish in the Mediterranean. They spotted bubbles they thought disclosed a school of fish. So, one of the guys pulled the pin and lobbed in the grenade. Unfortunately, the bubbles were exhaust from a diver's regulator, and the blast killed him. The fishermen were charged with manslaughter. They complained there was no diver flag on the surface to indicate divers below.

of tests he conducted. He showed how Shelley Tyre's fin would have simply sunk, heel first, under normal conditions, and how the strap of her mask could have pulled free if it had been yanked from behind. When Brown found Tyre's fin, the heel strap was still fastened tight.

Oliver testified that only a strong "external force" could have pulled the fin off.

> Evidence suggested a "violent struggle with another individual."

Dr. Thomas Neuman, a diving medicine specialist, reviewed Tyre's medical records, and said the five-foot, one-inch woman weighed 120 pounds and was in good health. She had logged at least 352 dives, and had no reason to panic. Her tank was two-thirds full when it was found and the dive site was a "benign" sand location.

The chief medical examiner of Miami/Dade County, Bruce Hyma, testified that evidence suggested a "violent struggle with another individual." The pin holding one side of the mask strap in place was missing, indicating it had probably been ripped from the mask frame. Hyma, a diver for thirty-six years, said no medical condition would have interrupted Tyre's normal breathing. With her experience she could have effectuated a self-rescue if she had the opportunity. "Her air supply was shut off," he said, and he called it a "homicidal drowning."

Underwater forensic investigator Craig Jenni concluded that Swain had attacked his wife in 80 feet of water. Had Tyre encountered an emergency other than an attack, she would have dropped her weight belt and returned to the surface as fast as possible. But Tyre was found with her weight belt still on. Her primary and octopus regulators were working perfectly.

Based on air still in Tyre's tank when it was found, Jenni determined Tyre was underwater for about eight minutes before she stopped breathing. Divers normally swim about one foot per second while underwater, an important calculation considering what Swain said during his deposition: after a five-minute descent to the wrecks together, he set off alone and made one revolution around one of the sunken boats.

After considering the size of the wreck and Swain's own mapping of his swim, Jenni figured it would have taken Swain about three more minutes to get back to where he had left Tyre. "At that precise time,

Shelley was no longer breathing," said Jenni, and Swain was in her vicinity. Even if she were already unconscious, Swain would have had to see her, Jenni said. But he came up alone. "The only conclusion," said Jenni, "is David Swain attacked Shelley Tyre."

Keith Royle, a Tortola dive operator, had responded to the Mayday call. When he got to the sailboat, he jumped aboard and offered to perform CPR, but was told it wouldn't be necessary because Tyre was dead. He thought it unusual since he was taught "you do CPR until someone more qualified takes over."

Three hours after Tyre's death, Swain gave a written statement to the Tortola police, saying his wife had swum off and left him by the wrecks. When he could not see her, he went looking for her. However, in depositions taken in 2003 and 2004, Swain said they had dived together to the tugboats. Swain said it was common for them to split up — she counted fish and he took photographs. But, he then contradicted his statement to the police, saying he swam around one of the wrecks before moving toward a reef in shallower water. At some point, he said, he looked back and saw Tyre, the last time he saw her alive. When asked where was the dive computer he wore that day, which would have registered how long he was under the water and what depths he reached, Swain said. "I haven't a clue." He said he also could not remember where the photographs were that he took during the dive.

Had he drawn any conclusions about how his wife died?

"Nope," said Swain.

Swain's testimony was on videotape. Swain did not testify on his behalf and chose not to be represented by his own counsel during the trial.

Sex and Money

Why would a dive shop owner murder his wife and dive buddy? Before the death, Mary Grace Basler testified that she had rebuffed Swain's advances, telling him she wasn't interested because he was married, though he overnighted at her home once. Two weeks after Tyre died, Basler met Swain at a restaurant. In two months they were lovers, she said.

While a prenuptial agreement prevented Swain from receiving anything from Tyre if they divorced, after the death Swain collected

$570,000 from life insurance policies and Tyre's investments. By February 2003, he was in debt from taking extensive trips to the Caribbean and other cities. He currently faces debts of $189,000.

Swain chose to defend himself outside the courthouse. He said, "This is a tragic accident that is a personal matter between me and the Tyres" — his former in-laws. "I didn't do it . . . I feel for the Tyres . . . They have the pain to deal with. I have pain to deal with too. But the thought that we are going to work out this pain by going through this is absurd . . . This issue of money . . . is not something I want to be a part of."

Tyre's lawyer said it was not about money, "it's about justice . . . Tortola authorities won't do anything, and Rhode Island authorities can't, and so it's up to [the jury] to see that justice gets done."

The Verdict

During closing arguments, the jury heard Tyre's attorney tell how he believed Swain had killed his wife. Using a videotaped demonstration filmed underwater where one diver attacks another, he described how Swain had climbed onto Shelley Tyre's tank, ripped off her face mask, shut off her air supply, and held her down on the sandy bottom.

The eight member jury found Swain guilty and awarded Tyre's parents $3,534,943 for compensatory and punitive damages. The standard of proof for a civil jury is whether the "preponderance of evidence" leads them to believe that the alleged crime occurred. Jury foreman Robert Capello said the jurors were not convinced the attack happened as outlined, but "other than human intervention, how else could she have died? And who else was in the vicinity when it happened other than Swain?"

After the verdict, Swain said, "I would welcome a criminal trial." At least then "all evidence gets evaluated" and not just pieces. Swain is considering an appeal and has sued Shelley Tyre's parents for defamation.

– From our own interviews and reports by
Tom Mooney, *Providence Journal*

PS: In November, 2007, Swain was arrested by U.S. authorities. Attorneys said circumstantial evidence, including his behavior after her death, apparent financial motivation, and Tyre's gear showing signs of a violent struggle, was "overwhelming."

Swain was extradited to the British Virgin Islands and in November 2009, a jury found him guilty of murder. He was sentenced to twenty-five years in jail.

Indonesian Diving Intrigue, 1988 Style

Three Australians and a Brit, all scuba divers, were arrested in Indonesia on March 22, 1988, and accused of illegally seeking treasure in Indonesian waters in an area that contains at least six 18th century galleons. If found guilty, each could be fined up to $250,000 (but a sentence would not require jail time). Indonesian officials seemed interested in sending a clear signal to other divers who might seek treasures in Indonesian waters, so they seemed to be protracting the proceedings and detaining the divers.

But for Americans, the real story is that six Californians were arrested along with the others. They were not jailed, but detained on their boat and later moved to a hotel. In late May, four of the men escaped, stole a boat, and found their way to Singapore. The remaining two; twin brothers Bob and Bruce Lanham, escaped by similar means in late June.

Now we've been following stories about these divers in the international wire services and find the circumstances curious. Apparently the Americans and Australians chartered a boat — the *Budi Indah* — in Singapore and shipped out for a "diving holiday." About 25 miles out to sea, in a narrow strait between Singapore and the Indonesian island of Riau, armed Indonesian officials came aboard and arrested them.

The men not only pleaded innocent to all charges, but during their detention the twins engaged in a hunger strike to publicize their plight. One of the escaped divers, Cliff Craft, a building inspector from Whittier, California, was quoted as saying that he and the others were on a two-week diving holiday in international waters and they were not acting illegally when they used sophisticated gear — a side scan sonar — to locate a reef and drop a buoy. Peter Howes, an Australian electrical technician who arranged the charter, said "we never even got in the water and we weren't looking for old wrecks."

Indonesian officials bought none of that, believing that the men were indeed looking for sunken treasure that lies in waters Indonesia declares as an "Economic Zone." The Indonesians are bent on keeping hunters away from these wrecks after two years ago accusing a British treasure hunter of pillaging $15 million from a wreck sunk in 1752.

But, there's still a matter left to be cleared up. A Ventura County, California, district attorney reported to the Associated Press that before Cliff Craft departed for Singapore and his pleasure diving trip, he had been charged with pillaging an underwater wreck off California's Channel Island National Park. Craft, and most of the other Americans, were identified by the *Los Angeles Times* as members of the "California Wreck Divers Club."

One of our chapters in this book is about whether diving makes you crazy. Here are two 2004 cases where it's apparent that it makes you stupid:

Scuba Scofflaw I: In 2001, Mark W. Samples walked into a St. Paul credit union and stole $70,000 at gun point. He then donned scuba gear and hid in the Mississippi River for eight hours while police searched nearby streets, later drifting downstream to his car. Police solved the crime and Samples claimed insanity, due to post-traumatic stress disorder resulting from the Iraqi missile attack on the USS Stark. Prosecutors said he was sane enough to go diving for eight hours, and he was convicted in April 2004.

Scuba Scofflaw II: Then there was the guy in Olympia, WA, who in April 2004, held up a bank while wearing a wet suit under his clothes. The man, Charles Coma, led police on a two-mile car pursuit, then plowed through a chain-link fence and crashed into a tree. He fled wearing a weight belt and toting a tank and regulator over his shoulder. He managed to get close enough to Puget Sound to toss the backpack into the water before officers tackled him. "No truth to the rumor he was running in flippers," a police spokesperson said, although officers found a pair of fins inside the car after making the arrest.

Men with Big Abs

California's red abalone, a single-shelled mollusk that clings to rocks, can't be commercially taken since they and related species have nearly been wiped out. Free divers can take twenty-four a year or three a day, but only for personal consumption. Since abs are worth as much as $100 apiece on the black market on the streets of San Francisco, $200 if they can be exported to Japan, plenty of divers go for them, though the risk of fines is big.

In April 2002, a Vietnamese diver was fined $30,000 and given eleven months in jail for poaching abalone off the Sonoma Coast. His five cohorts, who either poached or sold the abalone to restaurants, split another $40,000 in fines and seven months in jail.

Police confiscated fifty-three red abalones, which he had shucked underwater.

In another case, scuba diver Larry St. Clair is out on $40,000 bail, awaiting trial for abalone poaching in Mendocino. Officials saw him go under and then come up fifty minutes later with a full goody bag, and they apprehended him as he fled in his wetsuit. Police confiscated fifty-three red abalones, which he had shucked underwater, his 2001 Dodge pickup, an inflatable boat, extra tanks, and ice chests. Alledgedly, he had poached thousands of abalone in ten months, selling them for up to $40 each in San Francisco's Chinatown.

State Fish and Game wardens received an anonymous tip about two divers, and then spotted John Quinliven of Ukiah. Wardens said that after receiving the tip, they saw Quinliven on the Mendocino coast, transferring numerous abalone into two coolers. They followed him to Santa Rosa, watched him pass the abalone to Dung Le, and then arrested the two. The two were found with twenty-nine red abalone. Wardens confiscated $1,100 in cash and the two cars the men used to transport the abalone.

Then there is Joel Robert of Santa Cruz, once a commercial diver who sat on the state's Commercial Abalone Advisory Committee, railed against abalone poachers on CNN, and told a reporter that if he or his diving partner came across any poachers, they "would have to deal with us."

Unbeknown to Roberts, reports the *San Jose Mercury News*, in 1999 Department of Fish and Game wardens watched John Funkey, a local surfer, rent a Rent-a-Wreck van and drive to Roberts' house near the Santa Cruz boardwalk. They followed the two men and watched them as they made their eighteenth dive for abalone on the Sonoma Coast two nights during the off-season. They arrested them when they unloaded their illegal cargo near the San Francisco storage unit belonging to Goldmine Seafood Company. In exchange for a reduced sentence, Funkey testified against Goldmine owner Jimm Fong. Roberts, 39, was sentenced in June to three years in state prison, fined $25,800, and his fishing privileges have been revoked for life.

In Australia, they're just as tough. A fellow was recently fined U.S. $60,000 for attempting to sell more than 600 abalone, 581 over the personal limit.

One of the tragedies of diving is the diver who disappears on a dive, never to be seen again. There is no closure for the relatives, who are always left wondering what could have happened. Occasionally, however, those disappearing divers have a strange way of resurfacing, as did these three fellows.

Dead Diver Surfaces

Former Marco Island, FL, businessman Raymond David Young, 56, was two days away from being sentenced to prison for tax fraud when he disappeared in April 1993. Young's relatives said he'd gone scuba diving near the mouth of the Mississippi River in New Orleans, failed to resurface, and apparently drowned. In 2001 he was found living happily in Costa Rica. He was extradited and sentenced to seven years in prison and ordered to pay $3.8 million in unpaid taxes. Now his wife has been indicted for concealing him in Costa Rica and faces a five-year prison sentence.

You Can Run but You Cannot Hide

In the summer of 1986, 48-year-old Richard Smith Harley, an avid diver, moved to the Maldive Islands to enjoy the world-class reefs. The Maldives comprise 1300 beautiful tropical islands near Sri Lanka in the Indian Ocean. In this Islamic nation, there's little to do but sit in the sun and dive, dive, dive.

Harley, who arrived with his companion, Colette Golightly (yup, her real name; Google her for the *New York Times* story), soon found work as an instructor at the beautiful Bandos Island resort. Within a few months he had several instructors under his supervision and contracts to provide instruction at a couple of nearby resorts as well. The friendly "Mr. Richard," as he became known, quickly became a very popular and well-liked man on the island.

Although the Maldives advertise themselves as "the last paradise on earth" and "the best kept secret in the world" not all secrets can be kept there. Especially Harley's.

On December 26 he was arrested by local police and released into the custody of U.S. Marshalls. Richard Smith Harley, it seems, is actually David Friedland, an ex-New Jersey legislator who had been convicted of taking $360,000 in kickbacks on loans from Teamster pension funds he administered. Authorities claim that in 1985 he arranged a bogus diving accident off Grand Bahama Island, fled to Europe with a phony passport, and eventually ended up in the Maldives, about as far away from New Jersey as one can get.

Friedland could run, but he could not hide. Not even as a scuba instructor in the nation proclaiming itself in travel advertising to be "the best kept secret in the world."

Expensive Trip

The Florida diver who feigned his death while diving for lobster off Key West on August 8, 1998, has been ordered to repay $55,000 to rescue crews that searched for him in vain. Kerry Stephen Scheele was in the midst of a divorce and had taken out a $1 million life insurance policy that named his girlfriend as beneficiary when he staged his death. He admitted that after entering the water on August 8, he swam to shore, ditched his dive gear in the mangroves, and hitchhiked to his girlfriend's house in Wisconsin. Authorities arrested him after he allegedly talked his girlfriend into filing a claim on the policy.

So while these divers had scammed the authorities, or at least thought they had, here's a true tale of a Californian operating a dive boat in Belize who back in 1988 scammed starry-eyed divers — including a major travel agent and a very popular dive guide and eventual resort manager. He gets our award as the Bernie Madoff of the wet set, but in his Ponzi scheme he used the money of others to pay himself back.

The Sad Saga of *La Strega* Investors
worthless paper, useless liveaboard

Opportunity: Large liveaboard dive boats are the future of the dive vacation industry. An established, profitable operation with excellent tax advantages is expanding. Investors wanted—working partners needed in several fields. Substantial investment required.

The above advertisement appeared in the February 1989 issue of several dive publications. For sale is the Belize-based boat *La Strega*, owned by the Tonilla Corporation. In December 1989, we contacted the head of the corporation, Baxter Livingston, who told us that *La Strega* was showing a 20 percent return for its investors. (We will refer to the Tonilla Corporation just as *La Strega*.) Then, we received a letter from one of his investors, who wondered if he was being swindled. We tracked down nine other investors and the words of one, Stewart Williams, a video storeowner from Nebraska, summed up what we found. "I am out $55,000 that I will probably never see again."

> *"I am out $55,000 that I will probably never see again."*

We had several telephone conversations with Livingston, and then met with him in his Spartan upstairs office in Ventura, California. Downstairs is his travel agency, American Travel Leisure.

Livingston, in his fifties, with nearly silver hair, told us that he and his wife Nancy bought *La Strega* in 1980 for $125,000. They worked on it for two years then, he said, sold it for a million dollars. He carried the note, but the new owner "drove the boat into the ground and defaulted on the note and we took it back."

The Initial Investors

In 1984, Livingston began to seek investors. According to the prospectus, Livingston owned 86.6 percent of the 8,250 shares of stock in *La Strega*, which was worth $500,000. The financial projections claimed that *La Strega* had a profit of $37,000 through October 1984 and would earn more than $177,000 by October 1987. Hugh Parkey, manager of Turneffe Island resort, owned 10 percent. Art Travers, the owner of Poseidon Ventures travel agency, owned 3.4 percent.

Other investors were brought in. Grover Morris, Jr. of Oklahoma City read a dive magazine advertisement and in October 1987 flew to Ventura. Livingston told him "there was a 24 percent return on investment." Morris took his word and invested $15,000.

> When asked why he invested in the first place, Parkey said, "I was looking to get to swaying palm trees."

Truth is, by September 1987, *La Strega* was in debt $257,000, according to figures provided by other investors. Much of that debt was owed to Livingston. Four months later, Livingston had reduced his holdings to 52 percent by selling his own stock to new investors, a fact he did not disclose. (As you will read later, he had no stock to sell). However, he was getting cash for his stock and transferring the debt to others.)

Now You See Him, Now You Don't

We talked with many investors and what a mess we found. Art Travers was listed initially as a $17,000 investor, but Livingston later removed his name. Travers told *Undercurrent*, "I met with Livingston and told him that I wanted my $17,000 back and he told me that he wouldn't do that." Livingston told us that Travers' $17,000 was not for stock, but a deposit on his guarantee to fill 20 trips per year; Travers did not provide the bookings, so he defaulted. Travis scoffed at this, saying he would never guarantee bookings, and besides, Livingston had opened his own travel agency and took over bookings.

Hugh Parkey never received his stock certificates. "I gave Baxter $17,000 with an agreement that he would pay me $1,300/month to manage the boat and I would pay him $600 to pay off the stock. He ran short of funds and couldn't pay me so I couldn't pay for the stock. Next thing I know, he claims I defaulted on my contract." When asked why he invested in the first place, Parkey said, "I was looking to get to swaying palm trees."

Keeping *La Strega* Running

Livingston recruited the investors as working partners and many joined the *La Strega* crew for a salary. Each one-week dive charter needed about $5,000 to operate properly, but they only got about $3,500 from Livingston. Pat Savage of Eureka, CA (he invested $25,000 before seeing the boat) said that it operated with only one generator, "then it broke down and two charters were cancelled." Rick Snidtker, 36, of Miami Beach, FL, invested $40,000 in March 1988 for "a 3 percent share in *La Strega* and 5 percent of the *Tropic Bird*," another liveaboard owned by Livingston. Snidtker, a commercial diver, said the boat ran for three to four weeks with a bent rudder that was not attached at the bottom. Had it broken loose, the boat would have lost all control.

We asked Livingston about the vessel being unsafe. He said, "I am not a director so I don't know." However, in a later conversation he told us that "at the stockholders meeting [two years ago] they told me that I was spending too much money on the upkeep of the boat. They asked me to stop and I did." No investor recalls such a conversation.

To keep the boat running, several working partners said they put up their own cash. One claims that Livingston owes him and his wife $5,000 for two months' wages and out-of-pocket expenses. Another says, "I am out of pocket about $4,000, which includes some salary and some expenses." When asked about these charges, Livingston claimed one person was a drunk and another a thief. Others left the boat under the shroud of being accused of theft.

Who's Selling Shares, Who Pays the Freight?

With Livingston selling his shares, the cash goes to him, not to the boat, so it had to operate entirely on booking income (minus the 1/3 sales commission Livingston takes for booking *La Strega*). He also charged a management fee: more than $50,000 for one 21-month period. While he told *Undercurrent* that he sold his shares "to use the money for marketing," *La Strega* paid him $110,000 for marketing during one 21-month period.

None of this information was shared with investors. Says Stuart Williams: "It took more than two years and constant harassment from the investors before we were ever given any kind of financial statement. Imagine our surprise when we were told that the operation had lost more than $200,000 between January '86 and September '87." Livingston told us "it is impossible to provide audited reports" because in Belize most business is in cash and "they don't give receipts."

Most of the $257,000 shortfall through October 1987 has been covered by loans from Livingston, cash he has raised by selling off his own shares to investors. As a lender, he has assured himself of being paid ahead of the stockholders. The stockholders have talked about taking control of the company, but no one can pin down the actual number of shares outstanding.

As we were ready to go to press, we made a new discovery. Livingston probably owned no stock at all.

According to British Virgin Islands records, *La Strega* became owned by Livingston's Cayman corporation on April 21, 1988. Prior to that, BVI officials told us, Anna Swift of Arlington, VA. owned it. What stock had Livingston been selling?

We called Anna Swift and she said she had signed papers to be the sole owner, with Livingston as the guarantor. She put up the initial money and he sent her monthly checks and she paid off the note. She didn't know why. She said she has never seen the boat. "Baxter wouldn't let me go on it."

About 1985, she said, they still owed $67,000. She borrowed the money to pay off the boat. It remained in her name, she owned all of it, but she never got the stock certificates. "Baxter didn't own any."

When we told her that other people had bought stock in the boat, she said, "I never understood how people could be putting money in without getting stock. He didn't have any certificates. I never authorized the sale of any stock."

For unclear reasons, Swift signed over the boat to Livingston in 1988. When we asked her why she got involved, she replied, "He is married to my daughter. I don't know how he tricked me. You have to know Baxter."

She has a note from Livingston for $100,000. "I don't think I'll ever get it. I have to sell my house now. I can't afford to live here. They send me a little money now and then but I don't know when it is going to stop."

The New Owner

About the same time we were talking to Anna Swift, Roger Hubbard of Sacramento bought the remaining stock and controlling interest in *La Strega* from Livingston for $216,000, with $35,000 in cash and the rest due later. He accepted $326,000 in corporate liabilities, more than half of it due to Livingston. He was unaware at least ten other people thought they were investors

Shortly after the deal closed, Hubbard told us he traveled to Belize, only to learn that the *La Strega* bank account was overdrawn and several debts had not been disclosed. In addition, 140 passengers had paid Livingston for future trips that Hubbard would now be obliged to run. Hubbard learned from Livingston that the money had already been spent. Hubbard will only say that there was a "misunderstanding."

Before he closed the deal, Hubbard told us "I've never felt like Baxter's holding anything back. I don't think he's pulling a scam, unless it's a clever one. Since we will be holding much of his money back and putting up only $35,000, if he is, he is only creating problems for himself."

La Strega operated for a short while, then closed down.

PS: Baxter Livingston is a pseudonym. We Googled the real Baxter in 2010 and learned that he is still in the travel business, but his focus is Europe, well away from diving.

Chapter 9
Loony Laws and Litigation

When diving was still in its infancy, the sport inherited some bizarre local regulations. Undercurrent reader Robert W. Pelton of Greenback, TN, made a hobby of collecting loony laws affecting scuba diving. He told us they collected most of the laws "from friends, associates, lawyers and people we met in passing while my physician-wife and I resided in various parts of the United States. Others were garnered as we camped and toured and dived all over the world." Many were most initially aimed at swimming, but then applied to divers or snorkelers. Here is what we published in 1989.

No Kissing, Flirting or Onion Eating

Prohibited from reading comic books while getting ready to scuba dive? Not allowed to kiss an unchaperoned woman while underwater? Scuba divers banned from winking at women on the beach? These are a few of the situations covered by ludicrous scuba diving laws throughout the world. Most of these decrees were written and then forgotten with the swift passage of time. Many reflect attitudes of male lawmakers toward women decades ago. But relevant or ridiculous, these laws were still on the books, at least in 1989.

South Laguna, CA, retains an old piece of loony legislation ob-

Might as Well Leave Home Without It

Despite all the times we've been cautioned not to leave home without it, American Express cards might not provide all the benefits divers expect. In 1997, Buck J. Wynne, III, left Dallas for Lighthouse Reef Resort in Belize, charging his meals, accommodations, and American Airlines tickets on his American Express Gold Card.

After arrival, he and his family went diving on one of the resort's boats. The dive was arranged separately and was not included in Wynne's package. During the course of the dive, Wynne lost his regulator and inhaled water, and, although the divemaster came to his assistance, he drowned.

Since the American Express Gold Card insures Amex card members against accidental death or dismemberment while riding on a common carrier paid for with an American Express card, Wynne's widow filed a claim with Amex. However, Amex refused payment. She sued.

Amex's coverage provides that benefits are payable to the cardholder if he sustains an injury while boarding, riding as a passenger in, alighting from, or being hit by a common carrier, if he suffers a loss due to exposure, or if he disappears because of an accident on a covered trip.

In Wynne's case, however, the court ruled that the dive boat was not a common carrier: "A company which maintains boats for the sole and exclusive use of its own patrons is engaged in the business of a private carrier and is not subject to rules applicable to common carriers." Therefore, the court held that the "accident" that resulted in Wynne's death occurred while Wynne was diving, not while he was riding as a passenger in, boarding, exiting from, or being hit by a common carrier.

The U.S. District Court agreed with Amex and denied the benefits to Wynne's widow.

viously designed to protect its female scuba diving buffs. No married woman is allowed to scuba dive at Aliso Beach on the Sabbath "unless she's properly looked after."

New Castle, in the state of new South Wales, Australia, has a unique law regarding the Sabbath. Women who happen to be single, widowed or divorced are banned from scuba diving on Sunday. Any unattached female who takes part in such outlandish activities can be arrested, fined and given a jail term.

> No *woman while scuba diving,* *surfing or swimming is allowed* to wear *"any device or thing* *attached to her head, hair,* *headgear or hat, which device or* *thing is capable of lacerating the* *flesh of any other person . . . "*

In Carmel, CA, no woman while scuba diving, surfing or swimming is allowed to wear "any device or thing attached to her head, hair, headgear or hat, which device or thing is capable of lacerating the flesh of any other person with whom it may come in contact and which is not sufficiently guarded against the possibility of so doing, shall be adjudged a disorderly person." Was there a time when spearguns were built into headgear?

People on Oahu, HI, are prohibited from eating onions when going scuba diving in Waimea Bay between the hours of 7 A.M. and 7 P.M. And in Brisbane, Australia, citizens aren't allowed to go scuba diving within four hours after having eaten garlic!

Not allowed to flirt? That's right! In Santa Monica, CA, it's unlawful for any male scuba diver, swimmer, etc., while on a beach "to wink at any female person with whom he is unacquainted. No male person shall make remarks to or concerning, or cough or whistle at, or do any other act to attract the attention of any woman within a radius of one hundred yards."

A true scuba diving lover might enjoy living in Malibu, CA. An old piece of loony legislation stops local citizens from "sticking out a tongue" in the direction of a scuba diver, surfer, or any other person in or near the water.

Moustache wearers stay out of Puerto Escondido in the state of Oaxaca, Mexico. The law bans males with hair growing over their upper lip from ever teaching a woman to scuba dive — whatever the circumstances!

Puerto Vallarta, Mexico, has an ordinance against kisses between scuba divers (or anyone else found to be in water) which last "longer than three minutes."

Santa Cruz, CA, has an unusual law that should be of great interest to all scuba divers. No one can kiss a woman while she's diving unless she's "properly chaperoned!"

> *It's against the law to read comic books while waiting to dive.*

A teenager can be arrested in Hanalei, on Kauai, HI, if "silly and/or insulting faces" are made at anyone who is learning to surf, swim or scuba dive!

In Arista, in the state of Chiapas, Mexico, one old law prohibits a woman from chewing tobacco while scuba diving without first having a signed permit from her husband. Normandy Beach, NJ, scuba divers can chew tobacco if they choose. But they aren't allowed to dip snuff while diving.

Boisterous adults can be penalized in San Blas in the state of Nayarit, Mexico, should they "laugh out loud" while watching anyone scuba dive!

Kilauea, on Kauai, HI, has an odd statute that makes it illegal to read comic books while waiting to dive.

Be on guard when scuba diving around Hermosa Beach, CA. An old piece of legalese says "No man may place his arm around a woman without a good and lawful reason," while teaching her to scuba dive, swim or surf, etc.

Lastly, in Virginia Beach, VA, no man can go scuba diving without his spouse along, unless he's been married for more than twelve months.

Clergyman Henry Ward Beecher said it all when he summed up his view on the art of lawmaking: "We bury men when they are dead, but we try to embalm the dead body of the laws, keeping the corpse in sight long after the vitality has gone. It usually takes a hundred years to make a law; and then, after the law has done its work, it usually takes another hundred years to get rid of it."

While some of these regulations may still be on the books, we can't imagine any are enforced. At least, we sure hope not. That doesn't mean that some other Draconian measures haven't cropped up over time.

It's rare to see scuba diving get brought up in a national political debate, but after 9/11 everyone was skittish, and rightfully so. The media was filled with stories about how surreptitious divers could bring America to its knees, blowing up harbors, destroying bridges and dams, and who knows what else. Here's a story we ran in January 2003 that caused a bit of debate among our readers.

Post 9/11 Certifications

The FBI developed an interest in scuba divers shortly before Memorial Day 2003 when officials received information from Afghan war detainees that suggested an interest in underwater attacks. So it set out to identify every person who had taken diving lessons in the previous three years. Hundreds of dive shops and organizations gladly turned over their records, giving agents contact information for several million people.

"It certainly made sense to help them out," said Alison Matherly, marketing manager for the National Association of Underwater Instructors worldwide. "We're all in this together."

But just as the effort was wrapping up in July, the FBI ran into a two-man revolt. The owners of the Reef Seekers Dive Company in Beverly Hills, CA., balked at turning over the records of their clients, who include Tom Cruise and Tommy Lee Jones, even when officials came back with a subpoena asking for "any and all documents and other records relating to all noncertified divers and referrals from July 1, 1999, through July 16, 2002."

Faced with defending the request before a judge, the prosecutor handling the matter notified Reef Seekers' lawyer that he was withdrawing the subpoena. The company's records stayed put. "We're just a small business trying to make a living, and I do not relish the idea of standing up against the FBI," said Ken Kurtis, one of the owners of Reef Seekers. "But I think somebody's got to do it."

In this case, the government took a tiny step back. But across the country, sometimes to the dismay of civil libertarians, law enforcement officials are maneuvering to seize the information-gathering weapons they say they desperately need to thwart terrorist attacks. From New

York City to Seattle, police officials are looking to do away with rules that block them from spying on people and groups without evidence that a crime has been committed.

Cindy Cohn, legal director of the Electronic Frontier Foundation, which represented Reef Seekers, said, "If we are going to decide as a country that because of our worry about terrorism, we are willing to give up our basic privacy, we need an open and full debate on whether we want to make such a fundamental change."

The owners of Reef Seekers say they had lots of reasons to turn down the FBI. The name-gathering made little sense to begin with, they say, because terrorists would need training far beyond recreational scuba lessons. They also worried that the new law would allow the FBI to pass its client records to other agencies.

When word of their revolt got around, said Bill Wright, one of the owners, one man called Reef Seekers to applaud it, saying, "My 15-year-old daughter has taken diving lessons, and I don't want her records going to the FBI." He was in a distinct minority, Mr. Wright said. Several other callers said they hoped the shop would be the next target of a terrorist bombing.

– Excerpted from the *New York Times*, December 10, 2002

PS: Ken Kurtis told us that this first ran in the *Los Angeles Times*. "When asked what I thought about [the FBI requests,] without thinking I immediately replied, "It sounds like totalitarianism to me." Of course, that was their lead quote. We received more than one hundred nasty phone calls and messages (needless to say, no one with the guts to leave their name) including a couple 'I hope the terrorists come and kill you.' Lovely. Sure am glad I'm standing up for these folks' constitutional rights.

"When the *NY Times* article ran, we received got close to three hundred (no exaggeration) e-mails, letters, and phone calls congratulating us on our stance. Very different experience."

Today, in 2010, when people mention it, it's mostly in a positive light. Even those who might disagree, usually say, "I don't know that I agree with what you did, but I understand why and at least you stand by the courage of your convictions."

Of course, in the first couple of years after 9/11, fear abounded. The 9/11 terrorists had attended legitimate flight schools to learn to fly commercial jets, and reporters speculated on the parallel with dive stores. But experienced divers knew that what a terrorist had to learn to blow up ships in harbors or blast holes in dams wasn't going to be found in a PADI course at a local dive shop. But, that's a different issue.

With DEMA and the training agencies strongly resisting legislation, the dive industry is essentially self-regulated. Many of the accepted rules or standards (such as depth limits, alternative air sources and

Milking Cousteau

On a highway sign in Sonoma Country, CA, Clover-Stornetta Farms Inc. portrayed its Clo the Cow logo in a wetsuit and snorkeling gear, calling it "Jacques Cowsteau." The sign pointed the way to nearby Marine World, where the company's Clover dairy products are sold. When the Cousteau Society complained in July, the billboard was taken down. Nonetheless, in November, the Cousteau Society sued the dairy, seeking at least $1.2 million in damages. The 83-year-old Cousteau, whose only commercial product endorsements are for U.S. Divers and films, was made to look like a pitchman for Clover products and Marine World, the lawsuit said. It claimed the billboard had endangered support for the non-profit Cousteau Society, violated Cousteau's trademark and right to control exploitation of his name, and had exposed him and the organization to "public ridicule and embarrassment."

Not so, said Barbara Gallagher, a lawyer for the dairy. She said Cowsteau was no more likely to be mistaken for a human than "Christopher Cowlumbus," one of Clo's previous incarnations.

"It was meant to be in good fun, and certainly was not intended to bother somebody or gain any advantage by using their name," Gallagher said.

– Ben Davison

PS: Not long after our article was published, the Cousteau Society dropped its suit.

buddy diving) come from lawyers attempting to limit the liability of dive operators. We raised hell about those rules way back in August 1991.

Being Treated Like Kids
The new rules of diving

It seems like these days dive operators are creating more and more rules, so that experienced divers are getting less and less satisfaction. We're being treated like kids.

For the moment, I'm going to pick on just one rule. But there are plenty of others deserving attack, as well.

While we all know that cocktail hour is reserved for those who have stopped diving for the day, more and more liveaboards are extending this to mean that a single beer or a glass of wine at lunch will keep you out of the water the rest of the day.

Recently, one of our readers was so upset with the attitude of the staff of the *Sea Dancer* — and the fact that he was kept out of the water after a lunch-

> *Would it not be wiser to establish a rule requiring a diver to drink a dozen glasses of water a day?*

time beer — he is demanding his money back. "If you don't tell me ahead of time about such an idiotic rule," he says, "then you can't enforce it."

Excessive alcohol can impair judgment, but that's not the reason for prohibiting a lunchtime beer. As Chris Wachholz, marketing manager for DAN, says: "alcohol dehydrates a person, and that dehydration can lead to the bends. But we don't know the exact amount of alcohol that increases the risk."

We also know that caffeine dehydrates, which puts coffee and Coke on the same list. Furthermore, sun and salt water also dehydrate, as does the dry air pumped into your tank. We also know that drinking plenty of water hydrates, putting necessary water back into the system.

Nevertheless, prohibiting a beer or a glass of wine at lunch has become de rigueur among the new moralists of diving. Would it not be wiser to establish a rule requiring a diver to drink a dozen glasses of water a day?

Vice-Presidential Debate

When we wrote that two of our vice-presidents got certified in the early 90s, some readers thought we were taking sides.

We wrote that to preserve their family values, Danny and Marilyn Quayle and their three children took scuba lessons in 1989. The Quayles received their initial lessons in a Washington-area swimming pool under the leadership of NOAA staff, then underwent open-water training in Florida and Hawaii. The Secret Service would not allow the family to take commercial lessons and purchased for them wetsuits, watches and monogrammed warmup suits to avoid possible tampering. However, while the Quayles had once reimbursed the government for ski-lift tickets and other vacation expenses, they did not pay for the diving gear because they had no choice in equipment or training. Part of the tab was a $566 bill to fix an instructor's Rolex watch that became ensnared with the vice-president's gear.

Not long after, we wrote that VP Al Gore and his family took a resort course and explored Florida's Looe Key, while based on Little Palm Island, a resort twenty-eight miles northeast of Key West. There was no word as to whether he borrowed the Quayles' gear or taxpayers bought them monogrammed warmup suits.

Some readers thought our comments were political. Said a Fort Lauderdale subscriber: "You might be surprised about how many of your readers think 'Danny' would have made a much greater leader than the 'ozone man.' Aren't you proud to have favored the 'un-inhaler' and the fanatic ozone environmentalist? I pray for people like you. Who cares about a $566 dive watch. How about sane policies?"

Well, vice-presidents aren't all that important. As legend goes, John Nance Garner, FDR's VP in his first term, said "the vice presidency ain't worth a pitcher of warm spit" anyhow. But, that's only legend. Truth is, he didn't say "spit."

– Ben Davison

Winston McDermott, owner of the *Little Cayman Diver*, told us that: "Since we've been told that alcohol can dehydrate a person we limit the intake until after the diving. Now, if someone is only doing two or three tanks and wants a beer during lunch and is planning on taking a nap after lunch, we wouldn't usually deny that. But since it is the responsibility of the captain and crew to ensure the safety of the passengers, it is also up to them to determine if the passenger can have a beer or not."

Owners of boats under U.S. laws are claiming that they're governed by the notion that if alcoholic beverages are made available and an accident occurs, then the owner is liable, much like a bartender serving someone who gets drunk and becomes involved in an automobile accident.

So, rules get promulgated. Glen Egstrom, a past member of the NAUI Board and a member of the UCLA Kinesiology Department, says that although "I don't like to see drinking and diving, I also don't like to see rules like this. We have rules that have little or no basis in scientific fact, then find ourselves trying to defend them in a court of law."

Wayne Hasson, operations manager for the Aggressor fleet, told us that the *Kona Aggressor* has had a "no drinking and diving" rule since its inception because it is owned by Americans and operates in U.S. waters. "We have begun a no drinking and diving rule with our other boats because of the increased risk of decompression sickness," he says.

Hasson himself got bent a couple of years ago. "I made a dive to 110 feet for 20 minutes and then came up for a two-hour surface interval. During this time I had two beers. I then went back to 110 feet for 15 minutes and on the way up stopped to outgas at 30, 20 and 10 feet. Within 30 minutes of surfacing I was beginning to be paralyzed. DAN had me fill out a complete case study on the dive and their analysis was that the beers had dehydrated me and increased my risk of decompression sickness."

However, DAN is not pinning this case of DCS — or any case — on a couple of beers. "Increased risk" and "contributing factors" are not the same as causes.

Some non-U.S. boat owners are instigating the rule even without pressure from insurance companies. One operator told us that "if I allow someone to dive and drink the other passengers begin to question how safe my operation is."

Bret Gilliam, once the director of operations for *Ocean Spirit*, says that "the training agencies ought to be more concerned about turning out capable divers than with setting limits. I've been on many trips where the divers had more experience than the divemaster. Most of the accidents I've seen are due more to lack of watermanship skills than to having beer or diving below 100 feet."

Beer is an easy target when the real problem often lies with the inability of captains and staff to deal skillfully with their divers. Many are short on good people skills, so it is easier to establish a prohibition than to negotiate reasonable guidelines and let individuals make their own choices.

On one hand, we are taught that we must take care of ourselves, that we must make our own judgments about diving, that we cannot depend upon others. We, alone, are responsible.

On the other hand, the new "rules" of diving tell us that we are not responsible individuals and we cannot make our own choices, so we're being treated like kids.

The agents and the operators can't have it both ways. "Question Authority" says the bumper sticker. I think I will.

- Ben Davison

Self-regulation hasn't stopped some outrageous legal actions. Here are a few we found that turned into lawsuits.

Diving is Not for Everyone, Thankfully

In 1999, Emily Gilbert and other members of her family began taking scuba lessons from Above & Under Water, owned by Donald Milliken in Hoffman Estates, Illinois. The students are required to complete the PADI medical statement, and if they marked any of the enumerated conditions they must obtain physician approval to participate in the class. Gilbert answered "no" to all questions regarding behavioral health problems.

She passed three of five written tests and a water skills test but was required to retake certain written tests. She never scheduled them. Then, while practicing diving skills, she became frightened and would not complete the session. A couple of weeks later, same thing, only this time she began to cry and failed to complete the lesson.

A family member called Milliken to reschedule pool sessions and told him that Gilbert had a learning disability. Milliken said she could not continue unless she obtained clearance from her physician. Milliken contacted both PADI and DAN, and they concurred. Milliken told Gilbert that if she obtained her physician's approval, his wife (a divemaster) would work personally with her.

Instead of physician's approval, Gilbert presented a letter of recommendation from her high school counselor and a letter signed by both her high school psychologist and principal, saying she was able to participate in the scuba class. That wasn't enough for Milliken, and he did not allow her to continue.

So what's a girl to do? She filed a complaint with the Illinois Human Rights Commission, claiming that Milliken had denied her training because of her learning disability and that he had unlawfully discriminated against her based on her mental handicap. The commission dismissed her complaint, but she appealed.

In 2004, the Court threw out the complaint. Thankfully. Had she prevailed, every dive operation in the industry might have to keep an eye out for the next frivolous action.

Emily Gilbert v The Department of Human Rights, and Above & Under Water, Inc., 2003 WL (Ill.App. 1 Dist.) Sept. 30, 2003.

Only in California

In the summer of 2000, Renee Dirkx signed up for scuba lessons at a Sport Chalet store in Southern California. She was scheduled for a pool session but said "her back was fatigued," so her instructor, William Manrow, volunteered to perform a few manipulations on her back, or, as Dirkx testified, he painfully "cracked" it several times.

In November, she felt a pop in her back that was diagnosed as a disk extrusion and she had surgery. The following year she filed suit against Manrow and Sports Chalet, claiming Manrow's manipulations had caused her back injury. The jury ruled in her favor, but the case was appealed.

Manrow argued that, as any good instructor, he was only performing his "duty of care" by manipulating her back. The court said scuba instructors should not be manipulating the backs of their students.

He argued that his back manipulation was well within the course and scope of his employment with Sport Chalet. That made no sense to the court. He then claimed protection under the PADI liability release she signed. (Yes, the same type of release we divers sign that absolves a dive operation of any liability, even if they are negligent.)

The court decided that the liability release did not relate to "chiropractic manipulations" or stretching exercises performed outside the scuba class . . . and Manrow's arguments regarding the applicability of the release were irrelevant.

Dirkx was awarded $80,000 in economic damages, but in reading the case, we have no doubt that legal fees were far greater.

California Court of Appeal, Fourth District, Division3, California. DIRKX v MANROW, No. G031639.SuperCt.No. 01CC08728.

Insurance Company Tries to Stiff Diver's Widow

Insurance companies often go to great lengths to avoid paying benefits, if they can get away with it. Here's a brief summary of a case that was decided in 2003, after appeals, in which Hartford Insurance Company did all it could to get out of paying the widow of a dead diver.

Larry Fuller, an Arkansas resident, was diving in Mexico with the Snorkel Center, aboard the dive boat *El Magnifico*, with eighteen other divers. He signaled the dive boat for assistance after experiencing trouble with his regulator, but drowned after grabbing the dive boat's ladder in an unsuccessful attempt to board the boat.

Fuller had common carrier travel insurance with Hartford, through his membership in the Exxon Travel Club. The policy provided coverage for injury that "occurs while [the insured] is . . . a passenger on, boarding, or alighting from a common carrier." Hartford refused Fuller's widow's claim for $500,000 in accidental death benefits under the policy, forcing her to sue.

Hartford argued, among other things, that Fuller's injury did not occur while he was boarding *El Magnifico*, as required by the policy. They claimed he was injured before attempting to board the dive boat, when he first experienced trouble with his regulator and his lungs began to fill with water.

The court slapped down that notion by saying, "We disagree with Hartford's attempt to parse the undisputed facts so finely. It appears Mr. Fuller's lungs were filling with water both before and after he grabbed the boat's ladder and attempted to board. Thus, his injury was an ongoing one and is not limited to the period preceding his fateful attempt to board the dive boat. The policy neither addresses nor excludes coverage for a continuing injury that starts before (and is still occurring while) an insured boards a common carrier."

Hartford also argued that there is no coverage unless both the "accident" (the event that caused the intake of water into Fuller's lungs) and the "injury" occur during the boarding process, because the policy required an injury to result "directly from accident." The court said, "the word 'directly' requires a causal relationship between accident and injury; not a simultaneous *temporal* relationship. Hartford could have written the policy in a manner that required the accident to occur during boarding, but did not."

Ms. Fuller was awarded $500,000 by the United States Court of Appeals, Eighth Circuit.

Of course, if you're going to sue a corporation, you'd better be sure you've got your story together, unlike a Southern Californian who took on Aqua Lung back in 2005:

Story Teller

In Santa Barbara, CA, Faramarz Bolour of Santa Maria, California, said he bought a buoyancy compensator with a Sea Quest Air Source, a power inflator manufactured by Aqua Lung. Bolour said the power inflator malfunctioned during a dive off Refugio Beach, causing him to surface rapidly and suffer an embolism.

He sued Aqua Lung and Santa Barbara Aquatics, where he said he bought the BCD, claiming to have suffered permanent physical and neurological injuries that impaired his earning capacity and damaged his relationship with his wife. He claimed negligence, product liability, and breach of warranty.

Aqua Lung said Bolour fabricated his claims. It contended that Bolour's story about purchasing the Aqua Lung product was a lie, that photographs he claimed to have taken before the accident had been tampered with, that the Aqua Lung product did not malfunction and that Bolour did not suffer a diving injury. To avoid trial, Aqua Lung offered $10,000, which Bolour rejected, instead demanding $ 3,000,000.

Eight expert witnesses testified for Bolour: six doctors addressed Bolour's alleged physical and neurological injuries, an engineer addressed the alleged defects in the Aqua Lung product, and a scuba diving expert testified on diving procedures and equipment. Nine experts testified for Aqua Lung: a physician certified in emergency and dive medicine, a mechanical engineer, an engineer designer of dive equipment, two neurologists, a physician certified in nuclear medicine, a neuropsychologist, a photography expert and an expert on scuba diving procedures. Six of them testified for Santa Barbara Aquatics.

According to the *National Law Journal*, after a fourteen-day trial, the jury found 10-2 for the defense on product defect and 11-1 for the defense on negligence. Bolour was ordered to pay court costs, including expert witness fees for both Aqua Lung and Santa Barbara Aquatics. Bolour appealed last year, but the original decision was upheld, with Bolour ordered to pay Aqua Lung's costs of $98,000 and $65,000 to Santa Barbara Aquatics — a stiff sum considering he could have walked with $10,000.

There was a day, most readers will not recall, when a diver's depth was recorded by a mechanical depth gauge. They were a mainstay of every diver's equipment until the early 90s, when computers became affordable and reliable. And while that mechanical depth gauge was affordable, it wasn't so reliable

Bent Diver Wins $2.3 Million Suit
Depth Gauge Inaccuracy an Issue

Before computers, divers carried mechanical depth gauges. U.S. Navy tests found that gauges can vary wildly at a variety of depths, although manufacturers attempt to set quality control standards for gauges from ±1 to ±3 feet. The manufacturers seldom indicate the tolerance in the literature provided the diver and, of course, the Navy found that many gauges vary far beyond these limits. What this might mean legally should a diver get hurt was an issue in a 1976 case in Los Angeles.

Mathew Hamilton, a Los Angeles County lifeguard, was permanently disabled after suffering the bends on a 120-foot dive near Santa

Catalina. He was on County business at the time, studying a possible site as an underwater preserve. Suffering still from "constant pain in his lower back, numbness, tingling in both hands and feet and a stumbling gait and headaches," he sued the County. In February 1983, he was awarded $2.3 million in damages.

The County considered taking action against U.S. Divers, which marketed the depth gauge Hamilton used. The gauge — a so-called "Navy gauge" which U S. Divers had stopped marketing in 1972 — had been manufactured to a ±5 percent tolerance. The gauge was tested and found to register within that tolerance. The County decided not to sue. The question we must ask, however, is what about the diver's assumptions about the gauge? If the manufacturer provides no information about the range of error to the consumer, would the diver not presume that 120 feet means 120 feet?

At the 5 percent tolerance levels assumed ten years ago, the U.S. Navy study of currently marketed gauges showed that nine out of 28 failed to meet that standard. Many more in the test failed to meet the ±3 feet manufacturer's standards.

Producing an accurate, shock resistant depth gauge for a price sport divers are willing to pay is apparently no small task. Nevertheless, the manufacturers and distributors of the gauges do little to tip us off to the potential — or real — error of their products. We wonder who will be the first to come out of the closet and treat the consumer as an adult by providing him with facts on the likelihood of error?

Chapter 10
What Happened to All the Fish?

These days, most divers must travel a very long way to see "big fish." Whether we're diving off Florida or California, Fiji or France, we've unfortunately had to grow accustomed to "so-called" aquarium diving. It's not always been that way, but the pioneer divers who had the first-hand opportunity to dive with enormous fish were not stewards of their environment, as an article we ran fifteen years ago describes.

Where the Big Fish Have Gone

If you were to see the first issue of *Skin Diver Magazine*, you might be horrified. We were. Bill Gleason, the editor, sent a copy of the December 1951 issue for our perusal.

Essentially, skin diving, as reported in those days, was a glorified spear fishing orgy, as virtually every article attests. One article describes a spear fishing competition in Los Angeles.

"The Sea Downers led the first hour with 68 3/4 pounds to the Dolphins' 44 1/2, but the Dolphins really picked up the cripples the next trip to come out winners with 120 pounds to the Sea Downer's 97 pounds." The fish ranged from rockfish to bass.

An article about La Paz, Mexico, says "large Grooper [sic] were fairly abundant, averaging between 100-150 pounds." Another article, about skin divers (who used "Aqualungs," as well) frolicking in Baja waters, tells why the fish disappeared.

"Jack came by on his way to shore with an eighty-seven-pound spotted eagle ray he had just speared . . . Jack had just left when we spotted a hawksbill turtle on the bottom between some rocks and tried to catch it by hand, but approached it too quickly and frightened it away. While Doc and I were interested in the turtle, Chuck, about 150 yards farther out, spotted a huge jewfish. He immediately dove and shot it with his gas gun, but the spear simply bounced off . . . He came back with his gas gun fitted with a detonating head. The gun worked all right, but the denoting head didn't go off [this fish gets chased 45 minutes and shot half a dozen times before it succumbs] . . . all this terrific action stops when the detonating head went off and at last the fish floated up to the surface — belly up . . . Its weight was just

A Cousteau Shark Slaughter

In his book, *The Living Sea*, Jacques Cousteau wrote that his ship, *Calypso*, accidentally ran over a newborn sperm whale. The creature was horribly sliced by *Calypso's* twin propellers. The water turned crimson. Cousteau's crew ended the suffering with a rifle shot to the brain. More than twenty sharks moved in to feed, which today we would consider perfectly understandable scavenging behavior.

But Cousteau, the most renowned naturalist of his time, felt his stomach turn: "On deck our men had watched them devouring the whale and were overcome with the hatred of sharks that lies so close under the skin of a sailor. When we finished filming, the crew ran around grabbing anything with which they could punish a shark — crowbars, fire axes, gaffs, and tuna hooks — and they got down onto the diving platform to thrust, knock, slash and hook sharks. They hauled flipping sharks onto the deck in a production line and finished them off . . . "

What changed our view? The popularity of scuba diving. Scientists and recreational divers eventually came to understand the shark in its own realm.

– John Balzar, Los Angeles Times

220 pounds . . . Paul caught a nice hawksbill turtle by hand. He also shot at a manta ray, but the spear glanced off its head and fell down between the two arms on each side of its mouth. When the manta ray took off, the spear caught and Paul was pulled so fast through the water that he was glad it came loose . . . Doc got his spear into a fish weighing between 200 and 300 pounds, but it got away . . . Ten minutes later he got one about 180 pounds, but the spear pulled out . . . Paul speared a man-eating-type shark about 12 feet in length and Mel got movies of it rolling until it broke the line . . . Chuck speared a 120-pound jewfish, which turned on him and attacked. It took his whole knee in its mouth and left a nasty circle of bleeding toothmarks . . . When it made another rush right at his face . . . he pushed frantically on the edge of its big thick lips with his left hand and drove his hunting knife upward into its throat . . . Ted brought in a whole raft load of all sorts of interesting and unusual marine species which he had found in the water around one of the small islands."

"Paul caught a nice hawksbill turtle by hand. He also shot at a manta ray . . ."

If you want to know what happened to the inshore marine life of Baja — or Florida or California or everywhere else, for that matter — now you know. This sort of stuff went on for nearly three decades. In fact, it's still going on.

When the larger fish of a species get killed off, the gene pool changes, the average size of the fish shrinks, and the species becomes threatened. And while you might think that our fellow spearfishermen have stopped pillaging, a few big egos remain.

The *St. Petersburg* (FL) *Times* reported in July 2004 that a local diver, macho man Dan MacMahon, had speared a 400-pound Warsaw grouper in 425 feet of water. The Warsaw grouper is listed as "Critically Endangered" by the World Conservation Union.

In a lurid account posted on www.spearboard.com, then circulated and criticized on other bulletin boards, MacMahon describes his kill as a "mission." He had spent the last year "plotting and planning" to "finally get the big Warsaw I've wanted all my life." When he reached a wreck on the bottom, MacMahon says, "There were a half-dozen Warsaws in the 40-100 lb. range close to us when I spotted the monster facing me about 100 feet away."

When the fish approached him, MacMahon boasts, "I pointed my 52-inch SS Hornet and slammed a free shaft into the sweet spot." When the fish "started shaking back and forth," says MacMahon, "I slammed shaft number two into his head." Then, as a coup de grace, he recalls, "I put a PH [power head] on my kill spike and slammed into his head." After wrestling the huge fish to the surface, it took four men and a block and tackle to get it on the boat.

"What an awesome dive," says MacMahon. "There's (sic) just too few moments like this in ones (sic) life." To which we can only add, "good thing."

Trophy hunting for endangered species or in marine reserves is unconscionable in an era with so much pressure on fish populations worldwide. Terry Maas, legendary spear fisherman, author and video maker, points out that a 430-pound, slow-growing California giant black sea bass would be seventy-five-years old. He compares that venerable specimen with a 400-pound bluefin tuna, only eleven years old, that he took while free diving. "Obviously," Maas concludes, "tuna, with their rapid growth, can replace large adults in their population in one-seventh the time it takes black sea bass populations to replace a similarly sized fish."

News reports of an 1,100-pound tiger shark being reeled in during a recent "monster shark derby" at Martha's Vineyard, MA, point out that taking trophy fish is hardly exclusive to spear fishermen. Yet, we divers have a special relationship to the fish in the sea, and with that comes a special responsibility to protect them. That means giving your time or money to organizations that work hard to protect the oceans. There's not a lot of time.

A frequently overlooked problem is the collection of fish from the reefs so they can swim around in a glass zoo to entertain armchair divers in the comfort of their living rooms. Larry Clinton researched this piece for us in 2004, and if anything, the problem has worsened.

Divers and Home Aquariums: If You Want to Conserve Reefs, Why do You Have that Aquarium?

"We who dive along the Kona Coast have seen a drastic and definite reduction in our tropical fish populations over the past few years, due in part, at least, to the tropical fish collectors' increasing numbers." So says Dick Dresie, aka "Dick the Diver," who conducts shore dives at Hawaii's most popular sites. His concerns are being echoed by divers and conservationists worldwide.

Rene Umberger, who leads tours with her company, Octopus Reef, says "the entire southern Maui coastline has been impacted by fish collecting, including Ulua Beach, Makena Landing and Five Graves."

In Indonesia, near Bali's Barat National Park, the Wildlife Conservation Society has seen a considerable decline in aquarium species. At Helen Reef in Palau and Komodo National Park in Indonesia, collectors squirt cyanide into crevices where fish hide. The poison stuns the fish, making them easier to catch, but large numbers of the weakened fish die in transit, so far more fish are collected than necessary to allow for a "fatality margin." The poisons destroy reef ecosystems by killing non-target animals, including coral and invertebrates. In the Philippines, 70 percent of ornamental reef fish are caught with cyanide. At Hat Island in Vanuatu in the South Pacific, dive operators say 38,000 fish were taken within one month last year.

While fish collecting is a source of income for collectors, a U.N. report confirms that the aquarium trade uses damaging techniques to collect the animals, over-harvest some species, and inadequately handles and transports fish, resulting in a high mortality rate.

The roster of nations exporting marine ornamentals reads like a diver's wish list. Besides those already mentioned, commercial divers in Florida, Australia, Tonga, the Solomon Islands, Fiji, the Maldives, Samoa, Micronesia, Mexico, Sulawesi, Kenya and throughout the Caribbean collect marine animals for export. Many work the same reefs that we divers travel thousands of miles to visit.

Americans Collect Half the Reef Fish Taken

Tropical fish sales have soared since the release of the Oscar-winning animated feature *Finding Nemo*. Blithely ignoring the movie's message, hobbyists have rushed to set up saltwater aquariums stocked with beautiful fish, corals and invertebrates.

More than 20 million tropical fish are sold for aquariums each year, 98 percent captured in the wild. The trade brings in $330 million a year, according to a new report from the U.N. Environment Program entitled *From Ocean to Aquarium*. As many as two million people worldwide keep marine aquariums, 600,000 in the United States alone. Americans buy 50 percent of the marine fish captured and 80 per cent of the stony corals.

Of the 4,000 species of fish that live on coral reefs, 1,471 species are traded worldwide. Damselfish make up almost half, with angelfish, surgeonfish, wrasses, gobies and butterfly fish accounting for another 25-30 percent The most traded species are blue-green damselfish and clown anemone fish.

Seahorses form faithful long-term pair bonds, mating exclusively with one partner. If a collector separates a pair, the reproductive cycle ends.

Once captured, many ornamental fish quickly belly up, and many species that survive the long journeys aren't suited to home tanks. The bluestreak cleaner wrasse and the spectacular mandarin fish are commonly traded, though they do not acclimate well to aquariums. Foureye butterflyfish, harlequin filefish and Hawaiian cleaner wrasse are also popular, despite their restrictive dietary requirements. Baby nurse sharks are popular with aquarists though they are highly predatory, often eating other organisms in the same tank. If they live long enough, they'll eventually outgrow home aquariums. (Try flushing one of those down the toilet!)

How Collectors Destroy Reefs

Those who collect marine organisms in the wild tend to work alone or in small groups, either self-employed or working for a wholesaler/ exporter. In Sri Lanka and the Maldives, collectors use hand nets. In Australia, the Pacific and Florida, they often use larger barrier, drop, or fence nets. Branching corals, which provide shelter to chromis and other small critters, are often snapped off to extract fish hiding among them.

Although poisons like cyanide are illegal in most countries, the UN report notes that "the high premium paid (often large bribes), the ease with which a great number of fish can be caught . . . the often-poor law enforcement and high levels of corruption have allowed the use of poison to spread rapidly throughout the Asia-Pacific region and have made the eradication of this highly destructive technique nearly impossible."

For most species, juveniles are targeted due to their distinctive coloration, ease of maintenance and small size. However, where juveniles are consistently heavily harvested, adult populations suffer as only a limited number of young will grow to reach adult size. Some species are endemic to certain waters (such as the scribbled angelfish of Australia and Papua New Guinea). Others are naturally rare, occurring only in restricted locations, or naturally occur in lower numbers in some habitats. Ironically, increased rarity creates higher prices.

Merely 2 percent of the marine aquarium fish traded are cultured — the rest come from the wild.

Banggai cardinalfish are captured for their beauty and easy adaptation to aquariums. They live in the reef and seagrass of the Banggai Islands off the east coast of central Sulawesi, Indonesia. They have the lowest fecundity rate of their species and a low dispersal rate of their eggs. They've been proposed for listing as "Critically Endangered." Seahorses form faithful long-term pair bonds, mating exclusively with one partner. If a collector separates a pair, the reproductive cycle ends. Males of many coral reef fish species, such as mandarin fish, are preferred due to their distinctive coloration. But, concludes the report, "Selectively harvesting males of particular populations on a regular basis may lead to reproductive failure and ultimately populations collapse due to heavily biased sex ratios in remaining schools."

Sometimes unwanted aquarium fish are released into local waters, taking hold as alien species. Examples include Moorish idols, sailfin tangs, bursa triggerfish and racoon butterflyfish. Six lionfish were accidentally released in Biscayne Bay, Florida, from an aquarium during Hurricane Andrew in 1992 and divers are now seeing lionfish as far north as the Carolinas. *Editor's Note: In 2010, they are prolific throughout the Caribbean and depleting endemic fish.*

The Trade in Live Coral, Sponges and Anemones

Besides fish, 140 species of stony coral and 60 different soft corals are traded worldwide, perhaps as many as 12 million chunks a year. Some, like carnation coral, lack the ability to create food through photosynthesis and must filter particles and nutrients in the water; in aquariums, they usually die within a few weeks.

More than 500 species of invertebrates — sponges, mollusks, shrimps and anemones — are also traded as marine ornamentals. The annual trade estimate is as high as 10 million animals. Collectors harvesting corals and other immobile invertebrates often use hookahs and carry hammers, iron crowbars, chisels or screwdrivers to remove colonies. The most popular invertebrates mainly feed on algae, parasites or dead tissue (e.g., cleaner shrimp) and dead animals (e.g., hermit crabs). Removing them from their natural habitats reduces diversity on harvested reefs, once their cleaning services are no longer available.

Fiji is the world's primary supplier of live rock (covered with decorative coralline algae and other tiny invertebrates). Each year, 800 tons are harvested from the edges of Fiji's reefs or within shallow lagoons — about 95 percent destined for the U.S. Much harvested live rock, subsequently considered unsuitable for export, is discarded and thrown back into the sea. Large-scale removal of live rock, the result of hundreds of years of accretion, can undermine the structure of coral reefs. Some harvesting areas in Fiji have been converted into rubble and may never recover.

Some political jurisdictions have established restrictions. Florida, for example, prohibits collection from certain sites (marine reserves or other restricted areas like those in Hawaii). Many prohibit certain capture methods (such as cyanide in Indonesia). Some set size limits for individual species, and require permits or licenses. However, rules and regulations vary from one country to the next, as does enforcement.

Should a Conservation-Minded Diver Have a Home Aquarium?

Here's the question for divers. Should we, who have seen firsthand just how important it is to conserve reefs, have saltwater aquariums?

We think not, unless they are stocked with farm-raised species. Eric Borneman, author of *Aquarium Corals: Selection, Husbandry, and Natural History* says: "be aware of what wild collected species are common, and which are not, and always purchase sustainably collected aquacultured (tank-raised) or maricultured (cultivated in their natural environment). Merely 2 percent of the marine aquarium fish traded are cultured — the rest come from the wild. Only a few cultured species are available, primarily clownfish, dottybacks, and gobies. As Borneman says, "they may cost you a bit more, but these specimens will be selected and bred to thrive in captivity, so you can expect them to enjoy longer and less stressful lives than wild transplants." It's our view that even stores certified by The Marine Aquarium Council (MAC), which develops standards for quality wild-caught products and sustainable practices, are not an appropriate destination for divers who know personally the beauty of a wild reef.

One simple and basic debate that has thrived since the 90s was whether divers should feed fish. This piece we published (it was originally an article in the South Pacific Underwater Medicine Journal *by Bill Douglas) explained the problem, which has only grown worse.*

Pavlov's Sharks

In June 1996 at a popular fish-feeding site on the Great Barrier Reef, a 21-year-old female had her left arm shredded and subsequently amputated because of an unprovoked attack by a six-foot moray eel. In the same area a large potato cod seized a snorkeler by the head. The snorkeler drowned.

Entertaining scuba divers by fish feeding is big business. In South Australia and South Africa groups of divers experience thrilling encounters with the great white shark, which can be observed from the relative safety of an underwater cage lowered from the boat. An appetizing cocktail of blood, fish oil and raw meat entices these huge carnivores to approach the divers. At some South Pacific dive destinations, feeding reef sharks follows similar lines.

With this experience, sharks lose their natural caution and could be conditioned to associate humans with food. Altered behavior and movement patterns such as "downstream circling" have been observed in great white sharks. Researchers using ultrasonic tracking devices found that following the cessation of chumming, the sharks crisscrossed for several miles downstream of the baiting station for up to twelve hours, apparently searching for food.

The increasing practice of feeding marine animals should be seriously examined on the basis of potential injury to both humans and animals. The lessons of Pavlov's dogs and Skinner's rats appear to have been completely forgotten.

About the same time Douglas was writing his article, an interesting battle in Florida pitted the American dive industry — those folks who make money by selling us gear and taking us diving — against virtually every Florida and national conservation organization — the single exception being PADI's Project Aware — and a large majority of sport divers and even spearfishers. Here's an important story we did in 2000 detailing the industry's fight against Florida's effort to ban fish feeding — and, therefore, organized shark dives.

American Political Forces Behind Fish Feeding: The Dive Industry

Despite thirty years of commercial marine animal feeds for divers and snorkellers in as many as forty countries by more than two hundred operations, there are plenty of people who want it stopped. At stake is a big industry. It's claimed that thirty feeding operators in the Bahamas generated $65 million last year, and that stingray feeds are responsible for half the diving dollars spent in Grand Cayman.

The controversy most recently flared in Florida, where the state Fish and Wildlife Conservation Commission (FWCC) voted unanimously in February 2000 to develop a rule to ban fish feeding. Immediately, moneyed interests in the dive industry — PADI, DEMA (Diving Equipment and Marketing Association), Rodale's *Scuba Diving Magazine* and others — organized to overturn the ruling. Their opponents were environmental groups and spearfishers — who worried that human-fed sharks would see them as bait.

On September 7, 2000, after the FWCC listened to these groups, they ignored their previous ruling and decided not to ban fish feeding, urging the sides to work together and come up with a plan for consideration in May 2001. Afterwards, an article in the *Ft. Lauderdale Sun Times* called the decision "a colossal cop-out or a cave-in to special interests," i.e. the dive industry.

The Arguments For and Against

Risk to humans and marine creatures: Pro-feeding groups point out that with more than a million shark feed dives there has yet to be a fatality. *(Editors note: that is no longer true in 2010.)* Anti-feeding factions say this ignores the divers who have been injured because of feeds. They argue that the pro-feeding side has been disingenuous. For example, Richard Finkus, a Florida dive shop owner who has taken

Fish Bite

A fish bite has infected a human with a marine bacterium previously unknown to cause human disease, reports *New Scientist Magazine.*

The victim, a 55-year-old woman, was diving in the Maldives when a fish, which she couldn't identify, bit her on the ankle. The infection caused serious swelling, requiring her to undertake a regimen of intravenous antibiotics until she recovered fully.

The bacterium couldn't be identified until DNA tests discovered *Halomonas venusta.* Says a microbiologist from the University of Tasmania, "it's an example of how exotic pathogens can do unexpected things. She was lucky because this organism is comparatively harmless." (See the *Journal of Clinical Microbiology,* vol 37, p3123)

hundreds on feeding dives, told the Commission that, "If done in an organized and responsible manner, these dives are 100 percent safe with no harm to animals, the environment, or to divers or snorkelers." Yet, more than ten years ago, Doug Perrine, a marine biologist and photojournalist, reported that many divers feeding fish, or even diving in organized feeding sites, have sustained lacerations of faces, hands, arms and torsos, and even loss of fingers.

Jeff Torode, co-owner of South Florida Diving Headquarters and a proponent of feeding, sustained a serious hand injury while feeding eels. A Boca Raton man diving near a feeding area, but not himself feeding, had a large moray bite him on the leg. After a supervised grouper feed at Walker's Cay, a regularly fed barracuda bit a diver's fingers as he made the sign for shark, requiring fifteen stitches.

The September *Skin Diver Magazine* contains an interview with Key Largo's Spencer Slate. When asked his craziest stunt, he replied: "The time Perry, the moray eel, bit me. I was so mad that I punched him in the nose. He responded by biting me again, only this time caused seventeen stitches worth of hurt and it was caught on tape." Slate admits to being bitten more than fifty times across the span of his feedings, but jokes that: "We always sell more video tapes of the dive on days I get bit."

More than a dozen injuries have occurred on Bahama's shark feeds, including a German woman who was bitten on the head at a shark feeding site on a nonfeeding day. In the Maldives an operator who feeds by hand and mouth has been bitten four times by sharks, once so severely he was evacuated to the U.S. for treatment.

George Burgess, a noted University of Florida shark researcher, has opined: "Sooner or later, some tourist will suffer a very serious injury or die during one of these operations. It's not a matter of conjecture. It will happen. It's just a matter of time." *(Editor's Note: In 2008, a diver died after being bit on the thigh during a shark feeding frenzy on a liveaboard trip to the Bahamas.)*

Alteration of long-term behavior: The pro-feeding camp contends that marine animals are opportunistic feeders, and the small amount of food offered does not foster dependency. However, they offer no

Shark Bite

A severe shark bite on a Florida fish feeding expedition came to light the day after the Florida FWCC hearing, though the victim, Andrea Nani, was attacked long before the hearing. She told *Undercurrent* that she was aboard a commercial snorkel boat at a nurse shark feeding area in Big Pine Key. She said the charter captain told her family that nurse sharks were "harmless and had no teeth." They threw food scraps in the water to attract the sharks and told their customers to go snorkel.

Within seconds of entering the water, Ms. Nani was attacked by a five-foot nurse shark that wouldn't let go of her leg. Her husband jumped in the water to free her. She said the captain told her she had a "superficial" wound and wanted to finish cooking dinner for the people on board before taking her to shore. She arrived on shore ninety minutes later and the boat operator had not called ahead for medical assistance; it took another hour to get to a hospital, where medical personnel told her that air evacuation would have helped them save some flesh.

Well-fed Sharks: An Easy Target

Stella Maris resort in the Bahamas has attracted a lot of business in the early 90s due to its shark feedings. Guides use bait to attract the critters, and tourist divers watch the frenzy. As many as eighteen sharks have appeared.

Then, a long line Bahamanian boat swept through the area where they fed the sharks. Jeorg Friese, a Stella Maris owner, told *Undercurrent* that when the fishermen left "Shark Reef had no sharks. We kept going back and leaving bait but for six weeks no sharks came. Now they are slowly coming back. First there were three, and now there are eight. Our concern is not only the sharks but the reef ecology."

evidence.

The other side has some science. In a paper to the FWCC, Dr. William Alevizon, scientific advisor to Florida-based Reef Relief, comments that land-dwelling opportunistic predators such as bears, and marine counterparts such as dolphins, conditioned by regular feeding, lose their natural wariness of humans and become aggressive toward them. Bear feeds have long been banned in National Parks, and dolphin feeds have been banned by the National Marine Fisheries Service. Fed dolphins eventually stop discriminating safe from unsafe feed sources. That's why they get trapped in shrimp trawling nets.

Of course, any diver knows that when sharks congregate at the sound of boats approaching, or grouper and barracuda closely approach when a BC pocket is opened or hand extended, or eels leave hiding places to greet you, they are not behaving as fish unaffected by humans. It's not natural.

Impact on the environment: Anti-feed factions say that the unnatural aggregation of sharks or large predators in a small area will eventually reduce stocks of nearby fish in the creatures' food chain. More aggressive species have been observed dominating and reducing populations of less aggressive fishes in feeding areas.

Proponents say these feeds allow divers to become educated about sharks, thereby increasing appreciation and promoting protection. Anti-feed proponents argue that divers already appreciate sea creatures and any boost they get from feeding them is inconsequential.

The Raw Politics

For this Florida fight, PADI retained an attorney-lobbyist to orchestrate the pro-feeding campaign. PADI's position is viewed by some as an abrogation of the responsibilities implied by Project AWARE, advertised as the dive industry's leading nonprofit organization operating on behalf of the aquatic environment and its international Protect the Sharks public awareness campaign.

In July, *Scuba Diving's* editor, David Taylor, promoted feeding in the magazine, offering an on-line petition for divers to oppose the FWCC effort to ban feeding. The Florida-based ScubaRadio sponsored a luxury bus, replete with free food, beverages and prizes, that took divers to the September FWCC hearing because " . . . what the commission needs to hear is your personal experience with this type of diving and your objections to the proposed ban."

One of the more interesting events involved Dr. Russell Nelson, head of the Florida Division of Fisheries. On July 7, Nelson presented comments that concluded: "Staff does not recommend regulatory action at this time." Instead, they recommended forming a working group of interested constituencies to develop voluntary controls. A few days later, the *Sun-Sentinel* reported that, by his own admission, Dr. Nelson had visited pornographic websites on his state computer and on state time. Dr. Nelson resigned, but did not remain unemployed for long. In September, he released a report for DEMA concluding that total prohibition of feeds by the FWCC was not warranted and at best the FWCC should look to " . . . the voluntary adoption of industry standards and specifically the use of special management areas and public information and education efforts."

The Outcome

The FWCC met in a grueling day-long session on September 7 to hear massive testimony of widely varying quality. It voted to suspend consideration until May 2001, recommending that all factions work together to arrive at methods of feeding that minimally impact the environment. In short, the pro-feeding side prevailed.

The day following the vote, John Stewart, in charge of marketing for DEMA, told *Undercurrent* that the pro-feeding coalition has full

$5,000 Reward Offered for Rogue Spearfisher

The owner of Body Glove, a major wetsuit manufacturer, has posted a $5,000 reward to catch a California poacher who speared a 350-pound giant sea bass that may be a century old. Bob Meistrell put up the money when he got word that the protected, friendly giant was spotted off Santa Catalina Island, in mid June 2001, on the shoreward side of the island with a spear lodged in its body. Later, another diver pulled out the spear, and eventually other divers reported that the wound was healing.

Overfishing led the number of the giant sea bass to plummet until it became protected in 1982. The population is bouncing back, much to the delight of divers who can often get a close-up look. "They've become like puppy dogs," said Meistrell. "They swim right up to you. People pet 'em."

Harming the fish is a misdemeanor that carries a maximum sentence of six months in jail, a $2,000 fine and the seizure of the marine equipment used in the crime.

Meistrell said he and his twin brother each speared a giant sea bass in Mexico in the 1950s, when doing so was legal. "We were young and stupid," he said. His attitude has changed markedly since then. Recently he saw a man diving with his son who illegally speared a lobster. Not only was the catch out of season, but it was laden with tens of thousands of eggs. After Meistrell told him the error of his ways the spearfisherman apologized and said "well, I'm glad you stayed calm." Meistrell said he answered: "You were lucky I didn't have a spear gun."

– Leon Drouin Keith, Associated Press

intention of launching a work group that will be "inclusionary, not exclusionary." He indicated that the deliberations will be entirely public, and hoped to have recommendations to the FWCC by next April. He indicated they will focus on making feeds maximally safe for divers, marine creatures and the environment.

A spokesperson for the losing side was less enthusiastic, telling

Undercurrent: "It's a real disappointment to see the body responsible for protecting Florida's marine life respond in the way they did to the kind of dog-and-pony show orchestrated by the dive industry."

In May 2001, the dive industry put forward guidelines produced by the Global Interactive Marine Experiences Council (GIMEC), an entity formed by Florida marine feeding interests and others. GIMEC reportedly developed its guidelines in consultation with dive operators, operator associations, environmentalists, marine biologists and shark behavior experts. Absent were any members of the faction that supports a ban, the Humane Society of the U.S., Reef Relief, Defenders of Wildlife, and the World Wildlife Fund. Groups like the Coral Reef Alliance (CORAL) and REEF, which have industry members on their boards and depend on industry goodwill, dodged the fracas. The only environmental group in favor of feeding sharks is the PADI-sponsored Project Aware.

And so, while we weren't impressed by DEMA's and PADI's arguments, we weren't alone. Concerned that their recommendations did not adequately protect marine resources or the diving public, the FWCC directed state biologists and other staff to review and refine the proposed guidelines. In September, the FWCC voted to ban all fish feeding effective January 1, 2002.

Bob Dimond, President of the Marine Safety Group (MSG), a Florida nonprofit that has fought for two years in support of the decision, stated "Divers all over the state will once again be able to enjoy the natural beauty of the undersea world without being continually 'mugged' by aggressive fish seeking handouts."

PS: The dive industry vowed to continue the fight in Florida's courts, but lost its appeals. In 2010 the ban still stands. Shark feeding continues in the Bahamas and many other locales around the world.

It took a long time for divers to worry much about how our feeding can harm the fish, not just how they may harm us. Dive instructor and attorney, John Fine, the author of many books and articles about diving and the sea, was one of the first to point out why divers should not feed fish in this 1994 article.

Feeding Fish Underwater: A Shortcut to Their Death

"Let me tell you a funny story that happened in Australia . . . "

It wasn't really a funny story the diver recounted with a smirk, it was another tale of fish feeding with the eventual punch line leading to the agonizing death of a tamed potato cod. The story the diver told began with the common practice of duffers squirting cheese spread into the water to attract fish. That done, they went on to feeding eggs to large, domesticated potato cod. So accustomed to receiving food from the divers, the fish banished their instincts and gulped down anything that was presented.

One diver went down with a dive light, not attached to his hand with a lanyard. As the large fish approached for its feeding, somehow the diver's small plastic dive light was pulled into the fish's open mouth. Ha ha ha!

That fish was dead. The only thing that remained for it was the slow agony of the process. Putting aside the fact that most divers mean well, most have no appreciation at all of the consequences of their actions.

Feeding fish underwater is cute. It is a wonderful way photographers can obtain those beautiful and appealing pictures of fish that normally remain aloof. It also gives divers a chance to interact with marine animals, but the food taken below is often harmful to the digestive systems of the marine animals and the "tamed" fish are endangered by foreign articles that they ingest accidentally. The "tamed" fish are set up for killing by ruthless spearfishermen.

Norine Rouse, world-renowned dive instructor and conservationist in south Florida, guides divers off Palm Beach's reefs. She once befriended a moray eel. The animal could be caressed in her arms. One day Norine dove on the spot only to find the tame moray impaled on a spear, left to die on the reef, some diver's sport. Norine thereafter refused to "tame" these creatures.

It's been said that if one wants to do an animal a favor, throw a stone at it. Well, perhaps there is some relevance to that sour view of human conduct. In another case, in the same Bay Islands of Honduras where groupers spawn each year, dive instructors routinely fed the large animals that were regular territorial residents on their favorite reefs. One day the groupers were gone, speared by local fishermen who heard the fish were there and were easy targets.

Like the diver's flashlight, carelessness has accounted for an increasing number of deaths among tamed marine animals. In Saba

I'd Rather Fast

The most unappealing product at the 1993 DEMA trade show was Aqua Worms (yes, that's the real name), some sort of plastic looking stuff that was actually formulated by people who specialize in making cattle feed. To attract and feed fish, a diver releases a worm-like substance from an aerosol can, much like shaving cream. A single can, at $5.95, supposedly provides enough formulated worms for a single dive.

Multi Systems International, which is trying to market this stuff to dive shops, writes in its sales brochure: "Our experience from worldwide dive testing has shown that once a diver has tried Aqua Worms he will usually become a devoted user of the product."

Thanks for the offer, but I don't eat anything my grandmother wouldn't recognize as food. Fish shouldn't either.

it was reported that divers routinely fed Vienna sausages and other "unreal" food to groupers off the reefs. One tamed yellowfin grouper was even called "sweetlips," the Saba Marine Park Newsletter reports. One day divers discovered the blade of a knife sticking out of the fish. Somehow a diver's knife was ingested by the fish, which shortly thereafter disappeared.

Unreal food taken below, like the assortment of cheese spray cans and table scraps, eggs and other non-natural marine animal food sources have damaged the digestive systems of animals that have been made dependent on the routine dole. Waves of divers, boatload after boatload, invade the same sites to see the cute fish swim up and take food out of their hands.

No divers would squirt cheese into their own fish tanks at home, yet these same divers go wild on a diving holiday. Instructors in the Caribbean, who have long encouraged these fish feeding practices, have recently changed their opinions on the wisdom of the practice. "Cheese kills," one dive guide said, insisting that sardines taken from a freezer where they had been fresh-frozen, thawed to water temperature, and fed to the animals with prudence to prevent overfeeding, was the only way to satisfy his diving guests yet protect the species he tamed.

"We are responsible for what we have tamed," is the paraphrased lesson learned from Antoine de Saint Exupery's *The Little Prince*. As divers, we have a special responsibility to the underwater world and to not do things that imperil our charges in the deep.

The important rule taught all beginners in diving has always been "look but don't touch." As we've come to know the gentle sea, there has been more touching. Coming to appreciate marine animals in the wild is an important aspect of undersea exploration, and with care and good judgment, divers can enjoy wonderful interaction with marine species, get great pictures and still act responsibly. In 1992, we sought opinions from several experts on the best ways to interact with sea life.

Dances with Wolf Eels: Opinions on the Stressing of Underwater Animals

Divers have gone from being afraid to touch anything underwater to being comfortable — too comfortable, in fact — touching almost all marine animals. We've lost our fear of morays and whales and, to a great extent, even sharks. We feel perfectly comfortable with wolf eels and frogfish and scorpionfish and sea snakes.

Some photographers root out critters from the reef for their lenses; some divers pursue any animal for the sake of touching or holding it; some divers feed fish Cheez Whiz and dog food, and some divers never touch a thing.

Just how one should treat animals underwater is a matter for debate. We all agree they shouldn't be harmed, but what constitutes harming an animal?

Dee Scarr, part-time Bonaire resident, has become known for her gentle approach to sea critters. Through her Touch the Sea course and several books, she advocates a view of animals that has become increasingly popular for caring divers.

* * * * *

For many people the only question about touching a marine animal is, "Will the animal hurt me?" But there is another question: "Can I hurt the animal?"

When a diver picks up a frogfish or a batfish or a seahorse, the animal usually struggles, but stops struggling as soon as it is released. I don't think it's too imaginative to conclude that the animal was stressed until being released — or that it would have been most comfortable if never handled in the first place.

If something comes toward us that we're interested in, or feel neutral about, we stay put. If we're afraid, we run away. That's what filefish and porcupinefish and triggerfish are doing when divers chase them — they're trying to escape a potential predator.

Animals that have to be chased to be caught are being stressed. Although gentle stroking with wet hands won't hurt the mucus coating that helps protect them from disease (especially since they can always swim away), holding them firmly as they struggle requires pressure, which is likely to damage their mucus coating and leave them vulnerable to diseases.

I'm concerned about all animals under the sea, not just fish. Consider a ghost shrimp, removed from its anemone by a diver who, trying to be gentle, cups it in his hand. The shrimp scoots downward off the hand, only to drift slowly downward, completely unprotected. Should it manage to reach the bottom without being gobbled down by a Spanish hogfish, it's in the middle of nowhere. It needs protection, but other shrimp in the local anemones may not allow it in. It may never finish its life normally . . . all because the diver wasn't satisfied with just taking a closer look.

And what about the flamingo tongue, whose camouflage is provided not by the shell itself, but by the mantle that covers the shell and secretes a substance to keep the shell shiny, clean and growing. Some divers touch it to make the mantle retract to display the bare creamsicle-colored shell. That can damage it. Others drop it to the bottom, preventing it from returning to its source of food or its mate.

Stress

Stressed animals are more vulnerable to predation and are also less likely to breed.

Animals whose defense mechanisms have been used up — such as an octopus or a squid's ink — or broken off — such as a lobster's antennae or a crab's claws — have no defense mechanisms left to use against threatening predators, and are thus more likely to succumb.

These effects of stress are serious, but not particularly noticeable to divers who aren't taking reef population counts. What can be obvious to divers is behavioral changes. For example: when people dive uncommonly dived areas, porcupinefish just watch them, unconcerned. But, on popular reefs, porcupinefish flee at the sight of a diver. They have learned to avoid divers because they don't want to be grabbed and inflated.

How can we adjust our behaviors to avoid stressing the very critters we love?

- We must stop chasing and catching and poking and holding — in short, we must stop trying to dominate our marine friends.

- We must turn ourselves into marine animals. Let's make our buoyancy control good enough to stimulate the curiosity of a trunkfish. Let's imagine what it's like to be a trumpetfish well enough to be accepted by the gang at the gorgonian. Let's approach a porcupinefish so unthreateningly that it allows us to stroke it. Let's imagine what it would be like to be a cleaner station client — and act our imagination well enough to be cleaned by shrimps or gobies.

When we meet these challenges, we'll become accepted members of the undersea neighborhood.

* * * * *

What is the right way to treat animals? In 1992, we asked the most knowledgeable divers we knew for their points-of-view.

Dr. John McCosker, Director, Steinhart Aquarium, California Academy of Sciences:

"We don't know how to measure or define how, or if, a fish is stressed. Human curiosity is a strong urge and to tell divers not to touch or feel an animal is to ignore reality.

"Naturally this does not include harming the animal, which would happen if a triggerfish were pulled out of a hole after the trigger has been activated.

"Who is to say that a turtle or a manta does not enjoy being ridden? The only way to judge that is to find out if the animal stays around after you do it. That is the way we learn about animals. The majority of people will never dive and see underwater animal life.

But photographers who return home and show their slides to their friends and neighbors expose these nondivers to animals that they would never have known about.

"Ten years ago we had more people diving and shooting fish. Today there are more photographers. That is a step ahead in the preservation of the sea life. Even if stressed, at least they are still alive."

Al Giddings, cinematographer, *The Deep*:

"When we shoot for natural science, we leave the animal in its natural habitat. We don't move it because that would change the animal's environment. When we shoot for feature films, we do not use real animals. The moray eel in 'The Deep' was a mechanical eel."

> "I have done everything that I now preach against . . . feeding fish . . . moving animals to get a better shot . . . sloppy buoyancy control . . . holding onto coral . . . lying on coral. . ."

"I have mixed feelings about dolphins and whales, such as the orca, being in aquaria. I hate to see them in captivity, but if they were not where many average people could see them, I doubt that legislation designed for their protection would receive the wide public support that it does now."

Chris Newbert, author, *Within the Rainbowed Sea:*

"I do not see any difference between a professional photographer and an amateur. I make my living taking pictures, and nothing I do is worth killing an animal for.

"I have fed fish in the past, but I don't now. It changes the animals' lifestyle and can lead to dependence upon divers feeding them. Nature has established what the animal does, and I don't think we should try to change things.

"I have done everything that I now preach against . . . feeding fish . . . moving animals to get a better shot . . . sloppy buoyancy control . . . holding onto coral . . . lying on coral . . . not looking where my gauges are in relation to the reef, things like that. Now if I do not or cannot get a shot that I want, I know that there will be another day in the water when I will get it. My stalking skills improve all the time."

David Doubilet, author of *Light in the Sea* and *National Geographic* feature photographer:

"I don't think that there is a photographer that hasn't stressed a fish, particularly the puffer. I call it the 'tortured fish picture.' Now that I have had more experience, if I see such a picture in someone's portfolio I stop looking.

"Suppose your assignment is to get a shot of sharks and you do not have the time to wait for them to appear. You have to compress time and behavior into the period when you have air in your tank. I would prefer to stalk sharks, and do if time permits.

"I think that most of the better photographers have at one time been spearfishermen. They stalked their prey and learned their habits. Now they apply what they learned to taking photographs. I don't mean to suggest that budding photographers take up spearfishing; only that they should learn about the habits and habitats of the animals they take pictures of.

"In order to move an animal, you have to know something about that animal. To move a starfish to fire coral is not one of the things you do unless you don't understand the animal. Moving an animal isn't just picking it up from one place and putting it in another. You have to know how to pick up the animal so that it is not damaged or killed in the process. Sometimes that is the only way to get a shot.

"But you don't just put the animal out there take your picture and leave it unprotected. If you have moved it to a natural location, with protection and the ability to feed, that is usually okay. But I try to put everything back as I found it.

"One photographer does more damage to the coral than a boat load of sightseeing divers. I try to control my buoyancy, and if given the opportunity, I prefer to be in sand. But to get some shots you must be at least on the level with that animal. And that is where coral damage occurs, particularly if there is surge or currents.

"Do I do it intentionally? No."

We divers and photographers didn't always behave so sensitively to the ocean's critters, at least not until Jacques Cousteau began to preach to us about caring for the oceans, but, even the good Captain took a long time to learn that with his career came a responsibility, as our review of a 1989 biography pointed out:

The Greening of Jacques Cousteau: A Revealing, Unauthorized Biography Published in 1989

For several hours each day, Jean-Michel Cousteau stands in front of a US Divers logo at the Diving Equipment and Marketing Association trade show, patiently greeting hundreds of eager people. After a few pleasantries, he throws his arms around a shoulder so that a hired photographer may snap a picture for the passerby. Cousteau, dressed impeccably in a French-tailored suit, looks more a businessman than an adventurer, though his thick mane and beard proffer some suggestion of the sea.

In reality, the people gather not for surrogate Jean-Michel, but rather for "Cousteau," the name. It's no secret that the 52-year-old son of Jacques is but a stand-in for his famous father. Like the son of any good politician, Jean-Michel is preparing himself to head the empire by criss-crossing the nation to build a constituency, speaking wherever he is invited, shaking hands wherever one reaches out. Someday, the 80-year-old senior Cousteau will not be there to thrill the multitudes.

For the better part of his life, Jean-Michel operated in the shadow of number one son, Philippe, a charismatic and talented film maker to whom the Captain expected one day to hand the keys to the *Calypso*. But the dashing Philippe died in an airplane crash in 1979, leaving the more managerial, less adventurous Jean-Michel as heir apparent. It will not be easy for him to follow in the footsteps of his father, a film maker and a poet, a policy molder and a beloved public figure, no matter how many hands he shakes.

It will not be easy because the Captain has touched all of us so deeply.

Jacques Cousteau began as an inventor and adventurer, creating the first commercial regulator and subsequently developing dry suits and other diving accessories. After he became interested in photography, he joined forces with MIT professor Ernest Edgerton, the father of underwater photography, to create cameras and lights capable of bringing authentic underwater photography to television. In 1956 his film, *Silent World*, left audiences in awe, bringing him international fame. He became the first truly "international citizen" and the deification process had begun.

His subsequent films and books taught us about our ocean and our planet. To many, he is seen as the moving force behind today's worldwide environmental movement. He has spoken out to save the Amazon, to stop polluting oceans, and most recently to preserve Antarctica. He has moved people and moved governments. Jacques Cousteau is saving our planet.

Perhaps not as much as we have come to believe, writes Richard Munson in the newly published biography, *Cousteau: the Captain and his World; a Personal Portrait* (William Morrow and Co, 1989). The author fleshes out Cousteau in such a way to confirm our beliefs about the good captain: the teamwork on the *Calypso*, the dreams and development of the wind ship *Alcyone*, the details behind hours of filming.

Munson demystifies Cousteau by taking us behind the scenes to learn that the Captain is, in some respects, a Jacques-come-lately to the environmental movement, following far behind the leadership of groups like Greenpeace and others. He is first and foremost a filmmaker, not at all reticent to do whatever it takes to produce the right footage.

Although Cousteau himself refused to be interviewed for the book, the author has pulled together a fascinating portrait by relying on a plethora of publications written by Cousteau himself, articles in the *Calypso Log* (the journal of the Cousteau Society), articles in other publications, as well as fresh information from people around the Captain. The result is a reasonably balanced but revealing account of Cousteau's life, his idiosyncrasies and inconsistencies, his entrepreneurialism and environmentalism, his public image and private intentions.

In the 1930s and 40s in France, Cousteau devoted much of his time to inventing devices to enable him to dive. He purchased *Calypso* in 1950 and became an instant celebrity in 1956, with the release of *The Silent World*. For the next ten years — in fact during much of his life — Cousteau used the *Calypso* and his crew for commercial tasks, ranging from oil exploration to undersea mapping. In the mid 1960s he began filming the *Undersea World of Jacques Cousteau*, which would eventually take him and his crew for a four-year 250,000 mile voyage, resulting in twenty hours of shows and several publications.

Although the public was enraptured by these films, some critics were not. They charged that Cousteau portrayed himself as a scientist, a teller of truths, when in fact he was producing entertainment. Cousteau himself seemed to agree, by saying that "We are not documentary, we are adventure . . . The entire environmental content of my film is wrapped into adventure, with the same heroes."

Indeed, as a filmmaker. Cousteau took many liberties inconsistent with his public image. For example, Munson writes that "while viewers were led to believe that Calypso's divers waited patiently to witness a dramatic battle between large octopuses, in reality Cousteau provoked the fight by pushing two males together."

Another time, while the Captain argued against the "idea of removing animals from their natural environment, especially marine mammals like these, who are so obviously attached to their freedom and so active in the water," his divers netted two sea lions to train to

Ahhhh . . .

It wasn't that long ago that divers would frequently see Caribbean fishermen with trussed turtles heading to market. In the mid-80s, Al Catalfumo of the Bonaire Scuba Center at Hotel Bonaire was escorting a group of dive store owners around the island when they came upon a small cove where a local fisherman had caught a 70-pound sea turtle. "When I looked over, one of these women was pouring sea water on the turtle which was lying on its back all tied up. Our hearts went out to that creature," said Catalfumo. "It's not illegal for local fishermen to catch turtles on the island, but I thought of all the times one of our divers latched on to the shell of a sea turtle and went for a ride."

With this in mind, everyone chipped in and bought the turtle from the fisherman for $70. They took it back to the hotel, untied the ropes and placed it at the water's edge. "We waited but the turtle didn't move," said Catalfumo, "so we nudged it a little; then all of a sudden, it began to move, and within seconds it was forty yards off shore."

dive with them. He drove them in automobiles back and forth on the streets of Puerto Rico, where they constantly tried to escape. One, the author reports "fell into a rage, not unlike a child's tantrum, and proceeded to cover the crew and the automobile with excrement." Eventually the two sea lions were filmed faithfully following Cousteau divers and returning to the ship, allowing the Captain to conclude that "two marine mammals were our willing companions in the sea." He never acknowledged, according to Munson, that "in his quest for dramatic footage he had imprisoned a marine mammal, taught it tricks, and watched helplessly as it died in captivity."

> *In his quest for dramatic footage he had imprisoned a marine mammal, taught it tricks, and watched helplessly as it died in captivity.*

Munson gives us plenty of opportunities to view the dirty laundry of the Cousteau team, but eventually the laundry comes clean. In effect, we see Cousteau go through a metamorphosis that perhaps most of us went through in the last two decades.

In Cousteau's early days, he had no compunction about harpooning whales to mark them so he could ensure that a surfacing whale was the same one who dived ("a very superficial kind of wound," he said, "one that does not harm the animal in the slightest") or for spearing manta rays for food and pleasure. In the 1960s, he promoted undersea industrial projects, periodically exploded undersea bombs to help scientists locate mineral resources, and helped an aluminum company locate an "acceptable" deepwater dumping site for its toxic wastes.

But just as you and I have learned to love our planet, the Captain has learned as well, and Munson chronicles, if you will, the greening of Jacques Cousteau. Pictures of the earth from outer space helped Cousteau conceptualize his "Water Planet" image and call it to the attention of the public. He started speaking out against harming marine mammals and the undersea environment. He began to deplore the dumping of toxins in the ocean and by the mid 1970s his television productions began dealing more with social and environmental problems than undersea life. By the 1980s he was viewed as a worldwide leader in the environmental movement. The elimination of nuclear war became his number one priority.

Chapter 10: What Happened to All The Fish?

Though Cousteau now speaks out, he has generally avoided controversy and has had few legitimate political battles. Neither he nor the Society lobbies or joins political coalitions. "Rather than attack the political system, as he proposed to do when the society was founded, he ignores it," Munson writes. "Rather than mobilize his members to solve social or environmental problems, he has decided simply to identify the challenges in his films and books. And rather than advocate policy alternatives, the Cousteau Society has become primarily a film production company." Most recently, however, Cousteau has lashed out strongly at those nations that would exploit Antarctica, and his outspoken antics — he walked off the set of one live television show to protest a pro-development point of view — have played a crucial role in getting the French government to oppose Antarctic development.

Upon finishing Munson's book, one will no doubt be left with a different and more complete picture of a man who is arguably viewed as our personal guardian of the seas, if not the entire planet.

There is no need to deify Jacques Cousteau. Instead, there is great value to seeing how human, how inconsistent, how compassionate, how entrepreneurial he can be. It's valuable to see the man change; where he once was paid to seek a toxic dump site, he now issues memos to tell the *Calypso* crew to stop throwing beer cans into the pristine waters of Papua New Guinea.

In this biography of Jacques Cousteau there is a biography of all of us who have come to learn in the last two decades that the planet must be saved. Cousteau learned, and what he has learned he has shared with all of us. Now, it's time for the rest of us to take action.

And for the future of Cousteau and his Society? Munson writes:

"Ever curious and optimistic, Cousteau still dreams. He wants, for example, to build and launch *Calypso II*, a more sophisticated research vessel. He would love to compose the music for one of his films. He talks of flying in the space shuttle. The Captain pauses at the end of such suggestions, laughs, and says, 'You know, I think I'll do it all.'

"Cousteau's only enemy is time."

– Ben Davison

Chapter 11
Brave New Gear

In 1970, a diver used a watch and a depth gauge and carried a waterproof set of U.S. Navy Decompression tables with him in case he didn't follow his prearranged time and depth dive plan. To gain buoyancy underwater, he inflated his BC orally. Between dives, he used his dive tables to compute the time and depth for the next dive, depending upon the length of the surface interval. There were no dive computers. There was, however, the Scubapro SOS Decompression Meter, a mechanical device that some divers swore by. It had no science behind it and relied on increasing pressure to collapse a small bag to push air through a tube to move a needle, allegedly showing no-decompression time limits. We once wrote a story describing how it produced false tables. We disclosed that Scubapro covered up the facts and divers were getting bent. A few years later Scubapro stopped selling the SOS.

In 1985 we asked an equipment manufacturing visionary to predict technological advances in the year 2000. While a few stabs had been made to produce a decompression computer, none had made it to the market. The only significant new equipment was a bottom timer that recorded minutes once you submerged (but only of a single dive) and a BC inflator that connected to the tank. Here is what our visionary hoped to see by the year 2000. You might be surprised by what panned out . . . and wonder why some of these ideas still haven't made it to market.

The Diver of the Future
Equipment for the Year 2000

Ralph Osterhaut, the president of Tekna, and one of the truly innovative minds in the diving business, has speculated about the diver of the future. Upon first examination, Osterhaut's remarkable vision might seem to extend far beyond the year 2000. In the next 15 years, we may very well find that Osterhaut's future is indeed our reality.

Masks

Masks will become smaller and lighter: 6–10 oz. They will be made of translucent silicone flanged with structural resin frames and instant strap locking mechanisms, allowing adjustment during a dive. They will undergo a transition to ultra-compact 16-18 oz. full-face masks with instantly removable second-stage regulators weighing only 4-6 oz. This will eliminate jaw fatigue resulting from prolonged dives and greater distances traveled underwater when using self-propelled vehicles.

Next will come wireless diver-to-diver communications as an integral part of full face masks in the form of an FM single side band transceiver with a microphone in the mask and an earphone in a disc-like unit attached to the head strap. Small lightweight headlights with krypton or xenon bulbs will be integrated into the mask, allowing 2-4 hours of white light wherever you look.

Fins

The next generation will be composite fins of translucent thermoplastic elastomer, stiffened with boron/graphite epoxy ribs. At less than 1.25 lbs/blade, they will be incredibly light weight, yet have the highest stiffness and strain-stored energy recovery of any material known. With the added convenience of heel straps and foot pockets that instantly adjust for length and width, the fin customizes to the user. Kicking effort is reduced by 40-50 percent.

Snorkels

The next trend will be toward low-drag configurations including airfoil cross-sections and collapsible designs to help the snorkel "disappear" when not needed.

Suits

Wetsuits are unlikely to see any significant change in the next five years. The greater progress will come in dry suits, with dramatically better thermal insulation and more mobility. Today, their principal drawback is the added weight required to neutralize the buoyancy of the air layer between suit and body, and their annoying tendency to allow the air to shift back and forth from the upper to lower extremities when one changes attitude underwater. The solution will come by compartmentalizing the air throughout the suit. Flexible weave fabric with ultra-low durometer urethane waterproof coatings will allow this. Body hugging designs will allow a high degree of freedom while remaining absolutely water tight.

Tanks

There is recurring talk of 4500 psi tanks to get more air, but that is unlikely. Aluminum dominates the tank market due to its immunity to rust, but it cannot hold the pressure unless it is "filament wound," a process that drives up the price enormously. Moreover, the majority of dive shop compressors are designed for 3500 psi, not 5000 psi (but this could be overcome by using a high-pressure booster).

The solution to getting more time underwater is not more air, but more efficient use of what we have. That will come by a combination of dive computers that monitor air consumption, more efficient fins, lower drag equipment and the use of self-propelled diver vehicles that eliminate kicking.

Regulators

The bulk, weight and greater effort of conventional regulators will give way to servo-assisted designs. Their breathing effort is typically 50 percent less, and they do not get harder to breathe with depth. The next major change might be in the form of fully self-adjusting tiny servo-regulators that have synthetic ruby and sapphire combined with titanium-nitrided valve mechanisms that never wear, corrode, or change in performance and seldom if ever need service or replacement. Their inhalation and exhaust diaphragms will be of near inert fluorelastomeric compounds that are immune to deterioration.

Buoyancy Compensators

Ultimately, dual bags will give way to nearly indestructible single bag, glue-free, highly flexible thermoplastic elastomers. The buoyancy chambers will be modular and "snap-fit" in design, allowing dive stores to custom fit the chamber lengths and plumbing to the individual diver. The "Modular BC" will be cheaper and lighter, have lower drag and be more rugged.

> *There is no way to reduce respiratory work in regulators or kicking efforts in fins to match or even approach the reduction in air consumption by the work reduction an underwater vehicle affords.*

The big breakthrough will be automatic depth control. Fully controlled by an 8-bit microcomputer, this automatic inflator/deflator device will allow the diver to hover at any depth by simply pressing a button on this chest-mounted module. It will sense the water pressure and convert it to a signal that maintains the depth setting by slightly inflating or deflating the buoyancy modules if the diver begins to rise or sink. This "smart" controller will never cause an ascent faster than 60 feet/minute or descent faster than 75 feet/minute. It could be manually overridden in an instant by pushing the depth controller lever up or down to a newly selected depth.

Vehicles

With the advent of low cost, high reliability diver vehicles, the sport will make its biggest leap in more than a decade. The added capacity to effortlessly go three to five times as fast, travel ten times as far, and cut air consumption in half will change the role of the sport diver from one of being a temporary hydrospace intruder whose forays are measured in minutes, to one of an explorer who pilots his way through hydrospace for hours, charting the unexplored reefs, wrecks and caves.

There is no way to reduce respiratory work in regulators or kicking efforts in fins to match or even approach the reduction in air consumption by the work reduction an underwater vehicle affords. One might liken the difference in effort between running ten miles and riding on a motor scooter for ten miles.

This new wave of vehicles will be so quiet that they will be virtually undetectable. These undersea shuttles will spawn a new generation of instruments, such as a pictographic representation of a battery showing the level of charge remaining and bit-mapped graphics that show the relative position and actual heading from the starting point. An artificial flight map will be a guide to a safe return; simply pushing a button will generate the proper heading for the fastest way home.

Gauges

The microelectronic revolution is about to descend on the sport diving industry. Tiny digital dive timers powered by 4-bit mono-chip microcomputers are paving the way for sophisticated highly integrated 8-bit microcomputer driven instruments. They will reliably manage the inputs from multiple sensors such as high and low pressure transducers and thermistors. The result will be digitally displayed information that is instantly recognizable by its pictograph shapes. For example, tank pressure will be read out in actual psi. It will also be displayed in the form of a scuba tank with the level dropping as one consumes air. Remaining air time will be computed for breathing rate and pressure drop and digitally displayed in a window next to an hourglass.

Decompression status will be read out in the form of remaining no-decom time, not only in minutes but also in the manner of a human form that "fills up" with nitrogen as we approach our no decompression time limits.

Ultimately, well-designed displays should allow the diver to glance at the tank and see that it is not empty, and glance at the body and see that it is not full. The balance of the information is more technical support data for decision making beyond "Am I OK?" As an example: The no decompression time and remaining air time numbers tell the diver he should perhaps ascend to shallower depths to increase his bottom time and lower his air consumption.

Useful decompression computers will have to be based on the multi-level dive concept where decompression status is based on actual time at actual depth. This will safely allow the diver more no-decompression time in multi-level dives, but provide no advantage in staged dives, based on, say, the U.S. Navy tables. However, if a diver gets into decompression, he will be penalized as though he were stage diving.

Clearly, the efficiency comes in staying within the computer's no-decompression limits, which will use tissue saturation ratios more conservative than the old U.S. Navy's.

These new generation computers will store the "last one hundred dives" allowing them to be recalled and reconstructed on an IBM PC interface unit. At any worldwide decompression site one would simply plug a tiny connector into an access port of the instrument for a readout.

The Future Diver

Now, with these small paint drops of coming technology on your brush, let's race our minds forward to that world of dream and possibility we might call "what could happen," and paint a landscape that might be like this:

Before beginning your dive flight, you check your equipment and your partner's. Placing your magnetic encoding module against your instrument console, you enter your three-digit code, so as to be able to "communicate" with each other undersea. Just before you jump from the boat, you each set your Automatic Depth Control Monitor (ADCM) to 45 feet. As you slip beneath the waves, you sink automatically at 75 ft. per minute, until smoothly stopping with flawless buoyancy trim in virtual suspension at 45 feet. Beneath the boat a silent transponder sends an encoded signal for your navigational fix on return. You press a button on the side of your mask and the snorkel disappears into itself.

As you turn to your partner and call out his name, your vox-activated transceiver delivers your voice clearly and crisply through the water through a pulse-coded modulation scheme, immune to background noise. As you look toward your desired direction of travel, you softly say "display." The display of your Digital Total Dive Computer appears in "infinity" out through your mask as the digitized information from the computer has been fed through an optical character generator and down a fiber optic link that projects the "image" through a self-focus lens at the transflective mirror and onto the surface of your cornea. Wherever you look, the image follows for up to fifteen seconds.

Pressing the button on your tiny diver vehicle, your retractable cruise seat deploys to comfortably position you for your five-mile flight over the reefs. As you bank over reefs and sandy bottoms, you are periodically "updated" from tiny transponders buried undersea as to your locale and the immediate things of interest by a soft, synthesized voice that disappears as you fly on.

Stopping at hemispherical way stations anchored at 35 feet, you lift your head up into the "pocket" of fresh air driven constantly into it by its floating surface action pump. You unsnap your contoured flat food canister and press its pressure compensating valve to allow access to its rewards before continuing your journey. With your distilled water injection regulator, you never feel thirsty as it automatically replenishes your body with the fluid lost through osmotic pressure.

As you look toward your desired direction of travel, you softly say "display" and the display of your Digital Total Dive Computer appears in "infinity" out through your mask as the digitized information from the computer has been fed through an optical character generator and down a fiber optic link that projects the "image" through a self-focus lens at the transflective mirror and onto the surface of your cornea.

Noticing a deep reef, you head down to ink-blue water. As ambient light drops, your "Auto-sensing" Xenon mask light turns on, "correcting" the flora and fauna colors. Sensing it's time to return, you say "display partner" and your Heads Up Display (HUD) reveals he too, needs to return according to your No-Decompression Time Status. Slowly you spin in a circle, until your HUD indicates the exact heading home and your Estimated Time of Arrival (ETA).

As you surface at the boat, twenty-eight minutes later, you are comforted by the thought that the highlights of your journey were captured by your two-cubic-inch mask-mounted, low light, charge-injected camera, which stored the images in its magnetic bubble memory for playback later. On board, you press a tiny printer module against the Total Dive Computer, for a graphic reconstruction of your "Dive Profile" in ninety seconds.

Impossible, you say? Or worse — unneeded! Remember, we are but adventuresome pilots when undersea who must use wisdom, caution and harnessed technology to allow us our safe sojourns in this breathtaking innerspace. If we let suspicion, and the comfort of the known — the "old ways" of diving — govern our possibilities, we won't be able to reach for the "sky" and venture into that world of reefs, caves, valleys and cliffs that lies just beyond our present grasp . . . but in our reach with the equipment of tomorrow.

Ralph Osterhout left the recreational dive industry in 1990, moving on to entrepreneurial stints in consumer electronics, defense contracting and technology. Today he runs Osterhout Design Group in San Francisco.

Nice Tries
A human gill

In the mid-80s, we reported that researchers at Duke University announced that they had been able to extract oxygen directly from water. A major hoopla followed, centering on the possibility of creating lightweight tanks that divers would never have to refill. Actually, it was more like a human gill. Aquanautics, a San Francisco company that was created to buy the technology, claimed that not only would divers benefit, but the technology could be used to provide air to submarines so they would never have to surface. With all the hope, it went from a penny stock to as high as $3.50 a share, which in a moment of foolishness we pointed out to our readers.

We followed its development, but it never went far. Eventually, Aquanautics president Ross Buckinham told *Undercurrent* that their technology could be applied to scuba, but "the scuba market potential is much too small for us to consider."

They eventually introduced a beer cap which absorbs oxygen from the air inside the bottle, keeping the beer fresh several months longer. Then they filed for bankruptcy and went out of business. And we lost our $5000 investment.

This goal is still being pursued by other dreamers, as we reported in 2006 from an article by Lakshmi Sandhana, in the BBC News.

An Artificial Gill for Divers?

Israeli inventor Alon Bodner has developed an underwater breathing system that literally squeezes oxygen directly from seawater, doing away with the need for tanks.

Called "LikeAFish," the battery-powered artificial gill extracts small amounts of dissolved air that exist in water to deliver it to the diver. It uses a high-speed centrifuge to lower the pressure of seawater in a small sealed chamber. The dissolved air escapes back into a gaseous state — much as carbon dioxide is liberated from a soft drink when you pop the bottle cap. The air is then transferred into a small, impermeable lightweight bag, for the diver to breathe.

Bodner's system must circulate 200 quarts of water per minute to accommodate the breathing needs of an average diver, he says. A one-kilo battery should be able to supply a diver with one hour of dive time.

Today, his system exists as a laboratory model with approved European patents and U.S. patents pending. He eventually plans to reduce the size of the apparatus to a small, lightweight vest for divers.

Some people, like Mike Rowley, a British Sub Aqua Club Instructor, aren't so sure it will serve divers. Bodner makes the assumption that a closed-circuit rebreather diver will use a quart of oxygen per minute. However, heavy swimming against a strong current can require at least

Tiny Bubbles

The big loser at the DEMA show in the early 90s was the Dive Bubble. Its display was a focal point in the trade show hall that year, with a giant columnar glass tank filled with water, a scuba diver, and hundreds of colorful plastic balls (smaller than a ping-pong ball) whirling around. The small Dive Bubble balls are to be carried in a clip-on case attached to one of your regulator hoses. Before surfacing, the diver is to release one of these balls and then follow it to the surface in order to maintain the correct ascent speed, the same rate your plastic bubble would rise.

To no one's surprise, this idea never floated.

Don't Fill it with Vodka

Is not SCUDA, the Self Contained Underwater Drinking Apparatus, the silliest piece of diving gear to hit the market in 1992? SCUDA is a 12-ounce beverage pouch with its own mouthpiece — you use in place of your current regulator mouthpiece. Whenever you want a little bit of liquid, just squeeze the bag. Drymouth not withstanding, why a diver needs to wet his whistle during an hour dive escapes us.

3.5 quarts/minute. Says Bodner, the device will need "some form of reserve capacity to enable it to cope with lengthy periods of high oxygen metabolism." That would mean a much larger device, perhaps too large to make it practical for divers.

Craig Billingham, a technical diving instructor, says to get the time one gets from a rebreather or twin tanks, you will need a lot of batteries. "Also, batteries and seawater don't mix. It isn't a case of if it leaks but when."

Bodner says that it would be undesirable to use the system if the water lacks oxygen or is polluted. A small compressed air tank built into the system could act as a reserve in case of battery failure. He says a fully functional prototype is about two years away.

Chapter 12
If the Bends Don't Get You
Then the Mask Squeeze Might

Decompression Sickness ("the bends") is relatively rare. According to Diver's Alert Network, DCS "occurs in approximately one-thousand U.S. scuba divers each year." Yet, because of the emphasis on this threat in open water certification classes, it remains the most talked-about malady in the diving community.

However, one aspect of bends seldom discussed is enough to make all but the most uncautious divers a bit more careful underwater.

Unspeakable Issues in Diving?
Time for a little candor

Can bends affect sexual activity? Many people who push the tables believe they can overcome minor bends problems, but can decompression sickness inhibit sex?

In August 1986 we asked Hugh M. Greer, M.D., who is with the Neurology Department at Santa Barbara Medical Foundation Clinic. Dr. Greer started diving in 1954, when he served with the U.S. Navy Underwater Demolition Team.

Sex And Diving:

Ordinarily, I wouldn't touch this with a ten-foot pole-spear, but the editor twisted my arm. To this date, there is no scientific basis to believe that diving improves one's sex-life. Of course, I have heard some sea stories around the bar, but if you believe those . . .

Diving doesn't hurt your sex-life either, unless you get bent. Although it doesn't happen very often, it can be a grim story.

> *Diving doesn't hurt your sex-life either, unless you get bent.*

The spinal cord is the principal target of serious decompression sickness, and it usually happens in the lumbar region, about at the belt-line or below. Injury to the spinal cord causes paralysis (paraplegia) below the level of injury.

A lesser degree of injury, partial weakness, is called paraparesis. This means varying degrees of weakness and loss of sensation in both legs and in the trunk up to the area of injury. The spinal cord serves bowel and bladder control, as well as sexual function. Serious injury to the spinal cord produces spastic paralysis of both legs, complete loss of bowel and bladder control, and loss of sexual function. Lesser injuries produce lesser, and not necessarily uniform, deficits. In general, if bladder function is impaired, sexual function is lost as well.

Treatment will not necessarily fix this, even if the chamber is nearby and treatment is prolonged and intensive. Nerve tissue has no tolerance for injury, and once the nerve cells are really gone, hyperbaric treatment will not bring them back.

Some recovery takes place after most spinal cord injuries from decompression sickness. However, persistent disability is common. Rehabilitation often enables the patient to walk, with or without a cane or braces. All of us know bends victims in wheelchairs. There are techniques for improving bowel and bladder control, and most patients who regain the use of their legs learn to handle these sphincter functions.

Unhappily, sexual function is less likely to return. Males are often unable to achieve an erection, or to sustain one, or finally, to have an orgasm. Female victims of spinal DCS are similarly affected.

The good news is that you don't have to get bent. Nearly all serious DCS involves definite violation of the computer tables. Observing a redundant decompression stop, even in the most benign dive schedule, makes good sense.

Of course, we've all been warned about flying after diving. DAN suggests a minimum preflight surface interval of twelve hours after a single no-decompression dive, and at least eighteen hours after dives requiring decompression stops . . . even though they caution that these surface intervals "do not guarantee avoidance of DCS." But what about climbing to altitude on a mountainous island after a dive, we asked in a 1991 article about the Caribbean island of Saba.

Getting Bent on Saba

Does diving while staying at Saba hotels, which sit as high as 1500 feet, increase the risk of decompression sickness? Moreover, what about climbing the mountain after diving? The summit is 2900 feet, and most divers would avoid flying that high in an airplane after a dive.

Joel Dovenbarger at DAN told us, "with only seven or eight cases, we don't have enough data to suggest a profile that will minimize the potential risk. It may be that the dive operations have factored in the altitude in their suggested profiles."

Dr. Jack Buchanan, who operates the decompression chamber on Saba, said that two cases involved divers who made two daily dives and then climbed the mountain, despite signs he posted urging divers to avoid the climb. Buchanan does believe that the altitude and exertion caused them to bubble. He added, however, that DAN had conducted Doppler tests on divers staying at Captain's Quarters and did not detect any unusual bubbling.

Divers can do many things to decrease the odds of getting bent. Improving our physical condition is at the top of the list. As we reported in 2003, this becomes increasingly important as we age.

Gray Around the Gills
Are you ever too old to dive?

With the Baby Boomers getting up in years and developing bad backs, creaky knees, and reduced endurance, the question arises: when is one too old to dive? Duke University Medical Center researchers have concluded that as long as older divers remain healthy, the gradual decline in pulmonary function that comes with age is not significant

Cozumel Warning

During the early and middle part of the Caribbean hurricane season — say into September — it's not unusual for divers to face strong and unpredictable currents, including vertical ones. Since May, there have been a number of reports of heavy downwellings and roller coaster-like horizontal currents.

One day in July 2000, groups of divers at southern sites such as Palancar Caves and Santa Rosa Wall, ran into downcurrents as shallow as 15 feet and some divers were uncontrollably sucked from 60 feet to more than 100 feet deep.

Five divers from a group on the Santa Rosa Wall sustained DCS, including both Types I and II, and required multiple chamber treatments. At least one diver from another group joined them for recompression, and others may have sustained Type I DCS and did not seek treatment.

Be properly trained, be aware, be tuned in to local knowledge. Be careful out there.

enough to bench them.

Using Duke's hyperbaric chambers, the researchers studied the effect of age on the body's ability to balance oxygen and carbon dioxide levels under pressures experienced during normal dives. Carbon dioxide retention is a major safety issue for divers, particularly during heavy exertion and with high breathing resistance either from the regulator or due to lung disease. It can cause mental confusion, seizures, and even loss of consciousness while diving, the researchers said

"We found that even at a depth of 60 feet with moderate exercise, healthy older people experience increased levels of retained carbon dioxide that was statistically significant from at the surface, but clinically insignificant compared with younger subjects," said lead author Heather Frederick, M.D.

Richard Moon, M.D. clinical director of the Duke Center for Hyperbaric Medicine and Environmental Physiology, added, "Even while exercising, the older group performed similarly in all measures as the young people. It was a real shock to me that they did just as well as the younger participants."

But there are some caveats. The Duke study focused only on carbon dioxide retention and not on decompression sickness. Susceptibility to DCS increases with age, so older divers would be wise to follow conservative practices such as avoiding repetitive deep dives and rough conditions. Take up less taxing interests (such as photography). And breathe nitrox while keeping the dive computer in the air mode.

Ernest Campbell, M.D., (www.scuba-doc.com) says, 'To my knowledge there is no specified age limit to sport diving. Chronological age and physiological age can differ markedly, and each individual ticks to his own genetic clock. However, most elderly divers are not capable of sustaining the workload required by all but the least physically demanding dives. The majority of elderly divers do not exercise regularly or adequately. Physical training can definitely minimize the decline in physical capacity in older divers."

Older divers have a higher incidence of chronic ailments such as cardiovascular disease and chronic lung disease. Arteriosclerosis affects the blood flow to the brain, heart, kidneys, and limb muscles and their functions. Campbell suggests "Appropriate evaluations of the heart and coronary arteries with exercise testing are useful in older divers." Besides strength and endurance, flexibility is important when maneuvering in and out of the water.

Ronald T. Garry, M.D., of Harvard Medical School, surveyed 99 active divers aged 70 or over. Despite multiple medical problems, 99% of respondents rated their health as "excellent" or "good." They took an average of 4.3 medications per day, but only 4 percent felt their meds had a negative effect on their diving ability. A history of diving-related injuries was reported by 16 percent, with 75 percent of the injuries being middle ear barotraumas. The mean age at certification was 49.5 years, and 29 percent were certified at age 60 or older. They had an average of 24 years of diving experience, performed 52 dives in the previous year, 248 dives in the last five years, and 1314 lifetime dives per person. The vast majority (73 percent) felt that they were better divers now than when they were younger.

A 74-year-old male diver from Boynton Beach, FL, said, "I still dive five dives a day on liveaboards. I find going up ladders in rough waters difficult, but that, too, has never been easy." A 72-year-old female diver from Alta Loma, CA, noted, "My husband and I have always

Unfit Diver

Are you among those who do not think staying aerobically fit means much to a diver? Think again. Researchers have found a positive correlation between aerobic capacity and the amount of nitrogen expired. In testing three subjects, the subject with the highest aerobic capacity eliminated up to 15 percent more nitrogen than the one with the lowest capacity. While the data is insufficient to allow firm conclusions, it does indeed suggest that the higher the diver's level of physical fitness, the less nitrogen-bubble formation he will have—and the lower his likelihood of a bends hit will be.

(P. Ronning and G. Bolstad, XXIV Annual Scientific Meeting of the European Underwater and Baromedical Society, M. Gennser, ed., Stockholm, Sweden). 1/2000

been extremely cautious, sensible, conservative, aware divers. We still enjoy diving; however, there are two qualifications: no extreme or frequent deep diving and no strenuous diving, such as in excessive heavy current"

A 74-year-old male from Albia, IA, said, "I get in shape for a dive trip by working up to swimming one-hour laps with fins on." And a 75-year-old male from Kennett Square, PA, said that although "age has not reduced my comfort or confidence in diving, diminished agility and range of motion have necessitated some adjustments in the strenuousness or difficulty of dive activities undertaken."

Dr. Campbell points out that some savvy older divers arrange for a personal dive guide to help them suit up, don gear, manage their entrances and exits from the water, and accompany them during the dive. "The problem," says Campbell, "comes in getting us old GCFD's (geezer-codger-fogy-duffers) to recognize when the time comes to ask for help!"

The traditional treatment for DCS, of course, is done in a recompression chamber, which is great if there is one nearby and you have the insurance to cover it. Few people are aware that there is an alternate procedure if a chamber isn't available. We discussed it in 2001.

In-Water Recompression
The ignored emergency treatment

You've sustained a serious DCS hit hours by air from the nearest hyperbaric chamber. The air ambulance cannot fly due to weather, and even if it could, it's uncertain if the chamber is operational. What to do? Don't be surprised if your captain suggests sending you back down. While in-water recompression might sound like folk medicine, it is a valid emergency technique when performed under the direction of someone properly trained.

In-water recompression (IWR), not to be confused with re-entering the water to complete a missed deco obligation, is a legitimate emergency substitute for chamber recompression. It emulates hyperbaric treatment by taking the bent diver back to depth, while he breathes high concentrations of oxygen. Depending upon the method used, he may stay down as long as ninety minutes at thirty feet (though some methods go deeper and total time is longer).

Of course, the advent of IWR preceded the hyperbaric chamber. When a hardscrabble diver realized he could reduce surface pain by going back to depth, IWR got a foothold. Bent sponge divers off Key West possibly first used it in the late 1800s. Hawaiian black coral divers and Australian pearl divers returned to depth breathing compressed air. As oxygen became available, treatment improved considerably, though compressed air is still used — but not advisedly — when oxygen is unavailable.

Four IWR protocols have been developed to be applied after a diver experiences the first DCS symptoms. Commonly called the Australian, U.S. Navy, Hawaiian, and Pyle methods, each differs in submersion depth, time and ascent requirements.

The most popular method, the Australian procedure, mandates continuous breathing of 100 percent oxygen at a depth of 30 feet for 30 minutes for mild symptoms, up to 90 minutes for severe ones. Ascent rate is not to exceed one foot per 4 minutes, and inspiration of pure 0_2 is to continue for 12 hours.

All four have plenty of success stories.

Not surprisingly, major recreational dive training agencies are circumspect about IWR. IANTD founder Tom Mount told *Undercurrent* that the International Agency for Nitrox and Technical Divers does not yet teach IWR because of its lack of broad acceptance. He includes a caveat that IWR is only to be conducted by qualified and properly equipped individuals in remote areas, such as Bikini atoll, where a chamber is not available. Mount said that he had directed IWR on about 15 divers over the years, including his wife, during a trip to Roatan before a chamber was available there. He reported a startling 100 percent success rate.

> "If you've got a three-hour gap between the patient having symptoms and getting a MedEvac going, then you might as well use underwater (recompression) immediately."

Fatigue, cold, panic, seasickness or an exhausted gas supply can result in incomplete treatment, worsening of the DCS and possible O_2-induced convulsions and hypothermia. Joel Dovenbarger, VP of Medical Services at DAN, told *Undercurrent* that IWR should only be considered in remote areas where conventional and proven methods are unavailable, and where there are trained personnel and logistical support

Despite warnings, the sobering reality is that when Type II hits with serious vascular obstruction, irreversible brain damage can occur after 7 minutes; irreversible spinal cord damage after 15 minutes; and lung damage after 10-20 minutes. Research has consistently shown that the sooner DCS is treated, the more salubrious the outcome.

IWR has its champions. Dr. Ann Kristovich, Women Divers Hall of Fame, says that if travel time to a recompression chamber would take longer than 30 minutes, then she would use IWR. Australian Dr. Carl Edmonds told participants at an in-water recompression workshop that "if you've got a three-hour gap between the patient having symptoms and getting a MedEvac going, then you might as well use underwater (recompression) immediately."

The U.S. Navy method requires substantial amounts of pure O_2, and recommends using a 100 percent O_2 rebreather. The Navy recommends IWR when a hyperbaric facility is more than 12 hours away.

Data supporting IWR lacks scientific rigor, but is nevertheless impressive. An overwhelming majority of bent divers has come out of IWR either asymptomatic or improved, with only a fraction worsened or having an ambiguous result. Much of the reported IWR was done using compressed air rather than the recommended 100 percent O_2. Researcher Richard Pyle has compiled many case studies.

In the Central Pacific, a diver had partially completed his decompression following 15 minutes at 200 feet, when he saw an inquisitive tiger shark. He decided to abort decompression. After a rapid ascent from 40 feet, he hauled himself over the bow of the 17-foot Boston Whaler (without removing his gear) and instructed his startled companion to haul up the anchor and drive the boat rapidly to shallower water. By the time they re-anchored, the diver had increased pain in his left shoulder. He reentered the water and completed his decompression, emerging asymptomatic.

After ascending from his second 10-minute dive to 190 feet, a Hawaiian diver followed the decompression ceilings suggested by his dive computer. As he neared the end of the schedule, he suddenly noticed weakness and incoordination in both arms, and numbness in his right leg. He immediately descended to 80 feet where, after 3 minutes, the symptoms disappeared. After 8 minutes at 80 feet, he slowly ascended (his companion supplied him with fresh air tanks) over 50 minutes to 15 feet. He remained at this depth until his computer had "cleared." He felt tired after surfacing, but was otherwise asymptomatic.

Due to adverse weather, they could not transport him to the recompression chamber, 2,000 miles away, for an additional 12 hours. By this time, he was unable to walk and had cerebral symptoms. They returned him to the water to 27 feet, where he breathed 100 percent oxygen for 2 hours, then decompressed at 3 feet every 12 minutes (the Australian Method). Except for small areas of sensitivity on both legs, other symptoms had disappeared.

Although most of the reported attempts at IWR have used only air — and they have been successful — the practice is discouraged due to the risks of additional nitrogen loading.

Therefore, while IWR obviously requires much further study and adjustment, it may have a promising future under the unique set of circumstances for which it is designed. After all, breathing oxygen at depth is just what a hyperbaric chamber is all about.

The day may come when it's an accepted procedure to treat divers. But don't expect that anytime soon. As Richard Overlock, MD, told the recompression workshop, "there is such a horrendous bias against the concept of in-water recompression that nobody wants to admit they did it." Getting hard data will be a long time coming.

In addition to interviews, much of the material in this article comes from two sources: 1) *In-Water Recompression as an Emergency Field Treatment of Decompression Illness*, by Richard L. Pyle and David A. Youngblood, from the *Journal of the South Pacific Underwater Medical Society*, 1997. 2) *In Water Recompression, The Forty-Eight Workshops of the Undersea and Hyperbaric Medical Society*, published September 1999.

Deep Injury: Will Your Insurance Company Be There?

In August 2005, a British scuba diver got seriously bent in the Red Sea, and his insurance carrier refused to cover the nearly $70,000 in treatment costs. Lloyds TSB said 68-year-old Anthony Allen went deeper than the 30-meter limit stipulated in its small print. Allen's sons said doctors had told them their father's illness was caused by dehydration, and not the depth to which he dived. However, the tour company Allen was diving with confirmed that he reached a depth of 160 ft. before seeking medical assistance. According to the *London Evening Mail*, Allen was stuck in an Egyptian hospital for a month, and even faced prison if he couldn't pay his bill. Eventually the retired factory manager wiped out his life savings, and his sons arranged a loan so he could return home for further treatment.

Could this happen to a U.S. diver? Divers Alert Network also imposes a depth limit (130 ft/40m) on its least expensive Standard Diving Accident policy. Dick Clark, president of National Baromedical Services, which manages claims for DAN's insurer, says this policy is meant to provide affordable coverage for the occasional diver, who is not expected to make deep dives. DAN's higher-premium Preferred and Master Plans were created to cover more advanced divers, and have no depth limits. However, Clark points out that most decompression cases submitted to DAN involve dives deeper than 130 feet.

Clive Martin, who operates a hyperbaric chamber on Cyprus, emailed *Undercurrent* to point out a certain loophole in the Lloyd's coverage. One case of DCS at his facility involved a dive planned for 28 meters, but the diver became disoriented due to nitrogen narcosis, and actually went to 34 meters before getting bent. Says Martin, "Lloyds TSB had no option but to allow the claim, as they are playing with an unknown entity when it comes to narcosis as individuals' susceptibility levels differ greatly."

Says Clark, "To my knowledge, no DAN coverage has been denied due to depth limits" over the past decade. Clark adds, "The spirit of coverage will be applied in emergencies" if, for instance, a diver has to go deeper than 130 feet to rescue a buddy. Clark couldn't recall any DAN claims involving narcosis, but he says, "We would take each case under consideration, and would depend on eyewitness accounts to determine whether the event should be covered."

Next to the bends, divers most fear being entrapped and running out of breathing gas. We reported a number of these incidents in 2005.

No Way Up

Perhaps the most terrifying fate a scuba diver can experience is being trapped underwater with a dwindling air supply.

Northern California kelp proved a fatal attraction for Marie Murray (Salinas, CA). She and her brother made a shore-entry dive off Lover's Point, a popular site in Pacific Grove. When they became entangled in kelp, her brother broke free, but the 51-year-old Murray was not so fortunate. *The Los Angeles Times* reported that Ryan Masters, an avid diver who lives in Pacific Grove, was walking past when he heard Murray's brother frantically calling for help. Masters dove in, found Murray in the kelp and pulled her ashore. Besides wearing a weight belt, Murray was also wearing ankle weights, which might have contributed to her inability to free herself.

In overhead environments, divers are taught to follow the rule of thirds: use one-third of your air on the way in, one-third on the way out and keep one-third in reserve. An experienced technical diver with cave diving certification made a cave dive to 94 feet using a scooter for transit. A silt-out occurred during the dive, and he and his buddy became separated. The 42-year-old tech diver's body was recovered one hour later, and his breathing gas had been exhausted.

One certified cave diver with a history of narcolepsy (episodes of suddenly falling asleep in any situation), made a shore-entry solo dive into a freshwater spring system. He used a 34 percent nitrox mixture and planned the dive to 108 feet for 20 minutes. The 35-year-old diver's body was recovered in a restrictive area within the cave where the current was brisk. It appeared that he had been attempting to exit the cave system. He had plenty of gas available and no obstacle to leave. He may have just fallen asleep.

Throughout these reports, we see that virtually every fatality could have been avoided if the diver had made wiser decisions. Inexperience, panic, peer pressure and arrogance are thieves that can rob us of our better judgment. It's our responsibility to ourselves, our dive buddies

DCS and the Recovery of TWA Flight 800

After the crash of TWA Flight 800 off Long Island on July 17, 1996, Navy and civilian divers recovered the aircraft and the remains of 100 of the 230 victims.

Scuba divers made 3,992 no-decompression dives, to an average depth of 117 feet. Most were planned within no-decompression limits of either 120 feet for 15 minutes or 130 feet for 10 minutes, though a few employed decompression using computers. One third of the dives involved a 3-5 minute safety stop at 20-25 feet.

These dives were particularly stressful because of the long hours, the hazards, including 67-degree water and 15-foot visibility, and the presence of human remains. Several divers noted that their hearts were "pounding" in anticipation of finding the bodies. The remains of more than 100 victims were recovered by divers.

Even so, there were only three cases of DCS, one embolism and two cases of vascular headache, which can mimic DCS.

In recompression dives of up to 50 minutes, divers used suits heated with hot water. Interestingly, 14 of these resulted in five recompression treatments, so bottom times were reduced and more decompression time was given. In other incidents, researchers learned that "the use of hot-water suits is a contributory factor both to the overall incidence of DCS and to the proportion of Type 2 cases."

One thought for us ordinary divers: long hot showers after a dive are not a good idea.

and our loved ones to maintain our skills and fitness at levels that allow us to remain sharp and focused whenever we're in or on the water.

And then there are diving maladies so unique, you've probably never read about them anywhere else.

Swallowed Air

Have you ever considered that swallowed air can be hazardous to a diver? That a good belch before a dive may be a smart safety move?

Undercurrent subscriber Daniel Spitzer, MD, and fellow diver and surgeon Lee Fleisher, MD, encountered a unique and serious diving malady in a patient at Good Samaritan Hospital in Suffern, NY, back in 1998. As a warning to our fellow divers, they were kind enough to share it with us.

* * * * *

L.L., a previously healthy 34-year-old man, recently underwent emergency laparotomy — an incision through the abdominal wall — for repair of a gastric perforation.

Certified for fourteen years, L.L. had undertaken approximately seventy-five dives, all without incident. He arrived at the Turquoise Reef Resort in Providenciales, Turks and Caicos, in early February. Bad weather prevented diving for three days, during which he had no gastrointestinal symptoms such as diarrhea, constipation, nausea or stomach pain.

The morning before his first dive he had only a cup of coffee, though he normally eats a moderate breakfast. The dive was to 45 feet; during the descent he did not feel well, and tried to relax and control his breathing, since he felt he was sucking a great deal of air. He spent 5-10 minutes at depth, and then developed shortness of breath. He took a minute or two to ascend, and once on the surface, he had increased shortness of breath. He swam to the boat, where he needed to be dragged on board.

He noted that his abdomen was extremely distended and rock hard. An X-ray at the local health care facility revealed free air in his abdomen. On Provo, he underwent an emergency mini-laparotomy via a two-inch incision that released the air pressure and eased his breathing. He was then flown by MedEvac to Jackson Memorial Hospital in

Miami, where he was observed and released. He took a commercial flight back to New York.

Two days later, he collapsed and was taken to Good Samaritan Hospital. Free air was discovered in his abdomen, and he had a very low blood count from a gastrointestinal hemorrhage. He had a two-cm perforation in his stomach, with active bleeding, but no other abnormality. The perforation was repaired, and he has recovered.

The presumptive diagnosis is gastrointestinal barotrauma presumably due to swallowed air — something that we all do, but routinely belch it up easily. The gastric air ruptured into the abdominal cavity then expanded as L.L. ascended, causing abdominal distention, pressure on the diaphragm, and labored breathing. The mini-laparotomy released enough pressure to relieve most of his symptoms.

The textbook *Diving and Subaquatic Medicine* by Edmonds et. al. (1992) states that one case of a burst stomach, following a rapid and uncontrolled diving ascent, has been recorded — requiring surgical exploration and repair. Imbibing of carbonated beverages — although seemingly flat when drunk — may be a risk factor, according to Edmonds et. al.

And Dr. Spitzer wonders whether a second stage with too low a cracking pressure — one that almost pushes air into your mouth — might also be a risk factor.

Near-Fatal Mask Squeeze

Outfitted with communication devices, full-faced masks permit voice transmission between instructors and students and buddies: photographers, treasure hunters, exploring divers, marine biologists, and people who just can't resist talking about what they're seeing.

In 1994, a group of Midwest divers traveled to Gulf of Mexico off the Florida panhandle. While experienced in low visibility river and quarry diving, as well as ice and Great Lakes diving, some had not dived deeper than 40 feet.

One 63-year-old diver wore an AGA full face mask. He had gone to 85 feet on his first dive, and then 90 minutes later repeated it. On this second dive, he ascended to 35 feet, where he passed out (either from too much carbon dioxide, not enough oxygen, or both) and then sank back to the bottom, out of air. His companions rushed to him, found he was not breathing and ripped his face mask off to give him a spare regulator. But his mouth was so swollen, they couldn't insert the regulator.

They dropped his weight belt, ascended with him, and signaled to the boat. When he was hauled on board, his eyes and nose were swollen shut, and his lips were filled with blood blisters. His mouth was swollen tightly about his swollen, extruding tongue. He was not breathing and appeared nearly dead.

This was a near-terminal case of mask squeeze. With little or no airway, neither rescue breathing nor a normal oxygen system were of use. Fortunately, the boat was equipped with an oxygen respirator. By sealing the mask on his swollen face and activating the purge valve, pure oxygen could be forced into his lungs. Soon, he shuddered and began to breathe on his own, then began fighting the mask and complaining that he was all right. The only residual insult was temporarily blurred vision in one eye, due to ruptured blood vessels.

Watch that Giant Stride

Two of our readers returned from Bonaire in 2005 and wrote: "We dived 2-3 times a day for six days. At the resort, the pier was five feet above the water, and we used a giant stride to get in. The last day, my husband and I both experienced 'groin pulls' from the giant stride into the water. Two days later, I came down with the worst case of sciatica I have ever had! I ended up at the doctor's office, and was put on meds to ease the pain and stop the spasms. My right leg went numb to the touch and hurt like you know what! Have you ever done an article about problems with the giant stride?"

We haven't, but we asked Dr. Ern Campbell, aka Scuba Doc, what he thought of this injury. After all, sciatica is one painful problem. He told us:

The impact of jumping off a dock in full gear will apply a significant force to the intervertebral spaces. For a person with poor muscular development or an incipient disc herniation, the impact may cause a protrusion of the disc onto the nerve root(s), thereby causing sciatica, pain down the leg caused by irritation of the main sciatic nerve into the leg. Other things can cause irritation of or pressure on a nerve in the spine. Sometimes this may be a rough and enlarged part of a vertebra, brought about by aging, and sometimes rarer conditions, infections and tumors, are to blame.

Other injuries can occur. I've personally stepped onto a coral head from a moving boat swinging at anchor and scared the hell out of an unseen shark (and me) with another diver.

> *When he was hauled on board, his eyes and nose were swollen shut, and his lips were filled with blood blisters.*

But I've found these in the literature.

As a snorkel diver hit the water, the glass in his face mask shattered.

A diver under training made a stride entry, but his cylinder was not securely fastened and it struck the back of his head, causing a wound requiring stitches.

During a training drill at a Red Sea school, a diver suffered concussion when her first stage hit the back of her head during a stride entry As she hit the water, her BCD waist straps came undone, allowing her cylinder and valve to ride up her back.

A diver took a stride entry from a boat. He was carrying a surface marker buoy, and the buoyancy of the SMB pulled his right arm back and upwards, causing him to fully dislocate his shoulder, causing great pain.

A diver made a stride entry into the water at night. She had a torch on a lanyard attached to her right arm, and it struck her arm and fractured it.

It's conceivable that a giant stride entry could cause testicular injury in men; it would be helpful if we had a third hand to hold on to the cojones. Whether the backroll roll is any safer from a high transom or dock would be problematic.

Dead Air Spaces

In the early 90s, two highly experienced divers lost their lives in a seemingly easy dive in Florida. They were found under a dead air space. They had used only 500 psi from their cylinders.

Apparently, they stopped to talk things over in the dead air space. The carbon dioxide levels were within breathing limits, but the oxygen content was insufficient to support life.

Experienced divers have lost their lives diving in wrecks, caves and springs from what may seem like unexplained causes. But, in many cases, they removed their regulators from their mouths and breathed in the air pockets.

Some air pockets are ancient, some are trapped air in sinking ships, others have been formed from the exhaust bubbles of previous divers. If the gas mix in the dead air space has inadequate oxygen or excessive carbon dioxide, divers can get in trouble.

Excess carbon dioxide can cause severe confusion and drowsiness, eventual muscle spasms and rigidity. As the level of carbon dioxide in the body increases, the breathing rate will increase noticeably; shortness of breath can occur. The cure for excess carbon dioxide is fresh air. The aftereffects are headache, nausea, dizziness, and sore chest muscles.

The normal percentage of oxygen is 21 percent. At 16 percent, minor signs of hypoxia (inadequate oxygen in the blood) begin and, at 12 percent, serious signs develop. Below 10 percent, unconsciousness results and death can occur.

The diver inflicted with hypoxia may be totally unaware of the imminent crisis. A unique risk of hypoxia is that as it develops, it causes a false sense of euphoria that may preclude the diver from taking suitable action soon enough. Many divers know a similar phenomenon of sudden unconsciousness from shallow water blackout.

After one diver's death, several air samples were taken from the death site and analyzed for their oxygen content. One sample had 10.7 percent oxygen and another had 12.4 percent oxygen, enough to create nearly sudden unconsciousness. When unconscious, the diver drops out of the dead air space into the water and, without his regulator in his mouth, he drowns.

An experienced diving instructor who regularly free dived to 100 fsw would dive down to 47 ft. and enter a large dead air space just inside a cave. He would take a few breaths and return to the surface. One day, he made this particular dive several times and, as we watched, he fell unconscious as he reached the surface. Laying face down in the water, he did not respond to our calls, so we swam out and towed him to the beach. He was still unconscious; we administered 100 percent oxygen to him and he regained consciousness. Apparently, he received a bad gas mix in the dead air space.

The best way to avoid these problems is to inhale only from your regulator while you're in dead air space. You exhale while you talk in a dead air space, but inhaling must be from your regulator. In this way, you know your air supply has the correct gas mixture. You cannot vouch for any dead air spaces, because you can die using a gas mixture from a dead air space.

Author Gary Howland is an honor graduate of the U.S. Navy Underwater Swimmers school. He is a past president of both NAUI and the Institute of Diving with the Man in the Sea Museum.

Not-So-Dead Air Spaces

Dear *Undercurrent*:

Regarding Gary Howland's story about divers dying from breathing in closed air spaces (April issue), a few points deserve clarification.

It is unlikely that significant problems will result from excess CO_2, especially if it is from exhaled gases from other divers' exhaust. While breathing this amount of CO_2 may cause some shortness of breath, it would not likely cause the terrible effects often attributed to CO_2 .

The significant problem is hypoxia, or inadequate amount of oxygen in the blood. However, it is the partial pressure of oxygen, not the percentage of oxygen, that is important. Remember, there is still 21 percent oxygen on the summit of Everest. It was mentioned in the article that a sample from a cave contained 10.7 percent oxygen, but the depth was not mentioned. At 33 fsw, this would be equivalent to the 21 percent oxygen we are all accustomed to breathing. This may seem like a small point; however, it is the essence of the problem.

-John B. Feiner, M.D., Department of Anesthesia,
University of California, San Francisco

Dr. Feiner is right on target. We sit in our closed cars for hours with our exhaled CO_2. But, who knows what else generates CO_2 underwater? In dead air spaces, it is not really dead air, it is that you just die there. I define an air space that will not support human life as a dead air space.

Most of my experience with the low partial pressure of oxygen is from 800 hours in a B-17 flying above 18,000 feet, where I witnessed hypoxia in real time and in real terms. Low partial pressure of oxygen is the essence of the problem that Dr. Feiner said might seem a small problem to point out, but it scares the tar out of me, so I presented a paper to tell divers to keep their regulators in their mouths underwater. We know the partial pressure in our air supply.

The gas percentages uncovered by the Navy Experimental Diving Unit in samples taken from the dive site after the accident are not assumed to be those at the time of the accident. This discovery suggests being cautious in underwater gas pockets. – Gary Howland

Rebreathers Require Special Handling

Diving Medical Specialist David Sawatzky, MD, published a study in 2004 of 25 fatalities involving rebreathers, and has concluded that some fatalities are due to stupidity, some are from lack of experience, and some are similar to open-circuit accidents, such as myocardial infarction, arterial gas embolism, rare decompression illness, running out of breathing mix, and getting trapped. None of these deaths was the fault of the rebreather, Sawatzky concluded.

Unfortunately, as rebreathers become more popular, more divers are dying while using them. Rebreather rigs require meticulous maintenance, and errors in assembly may have tragic consequences, as with a very experienced 40-year-old technical diver who made a quarry dive at night using a rebreather with nitrox as his breathing gas. A group of twelve participated, and when the rest of the divers surfaced, one was missing. He was found, unresponsive, at 15 feet. An examination of the rebreather revealed that there was carbon dioxide absorbent throughout the rig, an oxygen sensor had been inserted incorrectly and was not functioning, and the oxygen addition valve was partially blocked, resulting in a 75 percent decrease in flow. There were also several loose connections.

Another techie, who liked to dive alone, pushed his luck too far on a wreck dive in a four-person buddy team. During the dive, the 58-year-old went off on his own. That did not alarm his buddies, since this was his habit. However, when he was found unconscious on the bottom in 104 ft., the rebreather was out of breathing gas, yet his "bailout" pony bottle was full. Solo diving adherents stress the need for self-reliance, but something prevented this diver from getting himself out of trouble.

That may also have been the case with an experienced advanced diver using a rebreather on a liveaboard. He did not appear to have a designated buddy, and had been prolonging his dives long after the other divers had exited the water. (Some of his previous dives lasted up to two hours.) But on his last dive, the 41-year-old diver never came back, and his body was never recovered.

David Rampersad, a certified instructor for the Scuba Network dive shop in Carle Place, NY, was found unconscious in four feet of water while testing a rebreather in a high school swimming pool. According to the *New York Daily News*, Rampersand had said he was having problems with his Azimuth semi-closed circuit rebreather and wanted to check it out. Three other dive instructors from the shop were teaching a class at the pool that day, and one spotted Rampersad unconscious, his mouthpiece out of his mouth. They pulled him out and attempted CPR, but he was pronounced dead at a nearby hospital.

It's clear that anyone using a rebreather needs specialized training and continued practice. Although we use them for fun, rebreathers and other scuba units are our most basic life support systems . . . not toys.

We divers love crystal clear water, so just the thought of diving near a sewer outfall is off putting, to say the least. So, we have to hand it to a certain breed of divers, who risk their lives not only by diving in dark and treacherous waters, but also by submerging themselves in the deadly bacteria swarming in city sewers.

The Worst Job in the Diving World

The next time you fume about your job, your boss or your desk in cubicle land, remember it could be worse—you could be a diver for a waste treatment plant. Even worse, you could be a treatment-plant diver in a Third World Country.

Reuters and the Agence France Presse profiled divers at a sewer treatment plant in Mexico City in 2007. They are paid just $400 a month to take the fetid plunge into the "pond," down to 30 meters. Mexico City's nine million people produce a staggering 9,250 gallons of wastewater every second. The divers' mission is to keep the flow on the go, pulling out whatever gets stuck in the grates, which has included human corpses, dead animals, entire cars, and abandoned furniture. In 1991, one diver, struggling to unclog a grate, managed to pull out a car tire, only to be sucked into the sewer system by water pressure and die.

It is so dark that the divers have to feel their way along the tunnel walls. "You cannot see a thing, you really only have your hands to see with," 43-year-old diver Luis Covarrubias told Agence France Press.

The equipment is low-tech—the crew works in plastic suits and wears gloves they hitch onto the suit with tape. Top that with more than twenty pounds of headgear, and a set of rustic tubes for breathing and talking to the surface. At the end of every shift, divers scrub their suits with detergent to remove the stink of urine and rotten waste. The disinfection process: A few buckets of tap water tossed over their heads.

Constant breathing of the fumes and contact with the sludge can be toxic, but some divers believe they have earned some immunity. "This is just a job like any other," said Covarrubias. "It just has some risks that we know how to handle.

Many divers are former dive instructors. Julio Cesar Cu, one of ten brothers from a poor family, was an instructor who didn't have enough money to study oceanography, so he took the sewer-diving job and has been immersed in the brown stuff ever since. But, as he told Reuters, he doesn't mind it. "I like diving as a sport. As a job, I like it even more. I do a job that benefits a lot of people."

– Vanessa Richardson

So, let's say you have survived all the hazards mentioned here (and then some). When you have finally hung up your fins and you are ready to take that great final plunge, here's an option we uncovered in 2008:

Think You've Made Your Last Dive?

Let your eternal reef give you one more for eternity

If you're in the Miami area and feel like diving, here's a site to explore. Take a boat from Key Biscayne and set your GPS coordinates to 25.41.412 N, 80.05.445 W. Head 3.25 miles east until you see mooring buoys. Jump out and descend to 45 feet. There you'll find the first phase of the most unusual artificial reef ever sunk in Miami-Dade County waters. It's a half-acre network of concrete pathways and benches, bronze columns and statues that serves as a haven for fish — and a graveyard for people.

The Neptune Memorial Reef is an artistic portrayal of the lost city of Atlantis. Thinly coated with marine growth and guarded by lions, it already has attracted amberjack, mutton and gray snapper, angelfish, grunt, even a scorpionfish pretending to be a statue of itself. The ornate arches and balustrades also serve as final resting places for the cremated remains of several people.

> "He came over for dinner in 1998 and asked if I could put his ashes in a reef ball and place them on a reef."

It's one of a number of artificial reefs that also serve as final resting places for divers, fishermen and general water-lovers – and their pets, too. Eternal Reefs, the creator of "reef balls," pioneered the idea 10 years ago in Florida and is now building memorial reefs along the Eastern Seaboard.

Before you scoff, consider that the family of Caribbean dive pioneer Bert Kilbride thought it a good idea. After the "Last Pirate of the Caribbean" died on January 8, 2008, at age 93, his ash remains were mixed with cement designed for underwater use and fitted into a mold. A copper and bronze plaque was installed with his name, dates of birth and death, and a memorial message. A diver then placed his mold atop a column of the Neptune Reef's main gate, a place of high honor because of his contributions to the sea. "I think he would feel very honored," his son Gary Kilbride told the Associated Press. "This is somebody who has been connected to the sea his whole life."

The Neptune Society, a cremation services company based in Fort Lauderdale, has invested $2 million in the reef, designed by sculptor Kim Brandell. To pay for the project, the society is selling "placements," the columns, statues and molds containing cremated remains, priced at an average of $2,000. Project manager Jim Hutslar says that when completed in eight years, the reef will cover 16 acres and have room for 125,000 remains. Molds for remains can be shaped into starfish, seashell and brain coral. Those interested in making this Atlantis their eternal home can get details at www.nmreef.com.

Because it's in open waters, living divers can visit too. The Neptune Society has contracted with some local dive shops like Key Divers in

Key Biscayne and Tarpon Dive Center in Miami to include it on their dive trips. It may become a big tourist attraction for divers.

The first person to be officially buried within a reef was Carleton Glen Palmer, father-in-law of Eternal Reefs founder Don Brawley. Brawley had pioneered the concept of "reef balls," eco-friendly concrete designed for sea life to attach and grow on, and it has become a standard for coral regrowth projects worldwide, but it was Palmer who thought of an alternative use for them. "He came over for dinner in 1998 and asked if I could put his ashes in a reef ball and place them on a reef," said Brawley. "He said, 'I can think of nothing better than spending eternity with all that action going on around me — just make sure the location has lots of red snapper and grouper.'" Palmer died a few months later, so Brawley mixed his remains into reef ball concrete and got permission from local officials to place it on an artificial reef he was working on in Sarasota, Florida. Palmer got his wish — the Sarasota reef, now with more than 100 memorial reef balls, is teeming with life. "When I told the story to friends and business associates, they asked, 'How can I do that, and how much does it cost?'"

"As soon as we place the reefs, fish move in immediately and start laying eggs."

So far, Eternal Reefs has buried 800 people. "If we could get just two percent of people who decide to be cremated to put their remains in the reef balls," Brawley told *Undercurrent*, "we could build 15,000 to 20,000 reefs a year at no cost to the government."

There are no official fish counts but Eternal Reefs president Chuck Kizina says that a decade of setting reefs is making an impact. "As soon as we place the reefs, fish move in immediately and start laying eggs. Then come groups of smaller bait fish, crabs start living underneath and corals start bridging the reef placements."

Placements range from $4,995 for an Atlantis memorial reef ball to $995 for a community reef memorial. Unfortunately, you can't pick your location in advance, because reef-building permits are controlled by the Army Corps of Engineers. Eternal Reefs also doesn't make individual reef placements because it's too inefficient and doesn't build up the reefs. "As soon as five people sign up for burials, we put the dates and schedule out there, and with a little luck, we fill it up," saws

Brawley.

For people who want to be buried together, Eternal Reefs recommends saving some ashes from the first to go so that a communal memorial can be built with ashes from both parties in the same place. It also offers "Pearl for Pets," a reef ball memorial for house pets up to 150 pounds for $895, but Brawley says most pets are mixed in with their masters. And don't have second thoughts – once the reef ball goes in the water, it stays there, and is guaranteed to last for 500 years.

Eternal Reefs now has memorial sites in Miami and Sarasota, FL, Charleston, SC, Ocean City and Chesapeake Bay, MD, and Ocean City, NJ. The reason for the East Coast prevalence is because each state there has marine fisheries commissions with an artificial reef coordinator that helps Eternal Reefs get the work done. There are no reef coordinators in the Pacific states, which can be red-tape heavy when it comes to anything coast related, but Brawley hopes to announce West Coast memorial reefs soon. For details, go to www.eternalreefs.com.

– Vanessa Richardson

Chapter 13
Undercurrent Travel Reviews

I started *Undercurrent* because my first dive trip to the tropics in 1975 was a big disappointment. I subscribed to *Skin Diver Magazine* and read a glowing report of a Jamaica dive resort, so my girlfriend and I pooled what little money we had and headed there. I expected picture book reefs with fish as long as I was, but what I found was beat up coral, few fish, and none much more than a foot long. As I sat on their postage-stamp beach that was covered with sea urchins (*Skin Diver* had a picture of a beach in the article, but it was 30 miles away and they made no mention of the distance), re-reading the *Skin Diver* article I saw several ads for the resort. Spend good money on advertising and a glowing report would be the result.

I decided right there to start *Undercurrent*, reviewing resorts without announcing my presence, spending my own money, and describing my experience exactly as it happened. A few writers joined me and followed the rules. If the concept were valid, I would get enough subscribers to support it. But I would take no advertising.

In my 35 years of reporting, I can say that I have never even taken a free dive and always paid for everything. I can also say that I don't believe anyone ever knew I was Ben Davison (that's a *nom de plume*, by the way), and or realized I was writing a story. Now, that's fodder for another book, but let me get on with this one.

All *Undercurrent* reviews follow a certain style, and if I didn't write the review, I surely edited it. In the early days, I'd write the story on my Olivetti typewriter in my resort room at night, hence the use of a typewriter font in the printed issue. We provided more than a thousand reviews over the years. I'm aware of half-a-dozen resorts that went out of business after we wrote about them, and I'm aware of many more struggling resorts and even liveaboards that survive even today after we put them on divers' maps.

While at least a third of each issue is devoted to travel reviews, I'm including only one in this book. It's a story within a story, which we featured in April 1989. When you finish reading it, I'll tell you more.

Precious Island, Cayman Islands
Can You Top This ?

Dear Reader,

April May Precious is the most unique and exotic name I've run across, but then so is the woman who sports it. She pulled a yellowed copy of the 1978 <u>World Almanac</u> off the bookshelf in the main house of her extraordinary new and intimate diving retreat on Petit Cayman, 42 miles south, south-west of Grand Cayman. "See, I wouldn't pull your leg, nice leg that it is," she said and pointed at page 779: "Miss America Contest, 1976. . . April May Precious, 19, Mississippi, third runner up."

Precious, of course, is just that. In the midst of a modeling career that had her commuting between New York, Paris and Stockholm, she was invited to Townsville, Australia, to shoot the 1985 <u>Sports Illustrated</u> swimsuit issue. While several overcast days were interfering with her shoot, she took a resort course and was so impressed that she tracked down Mike Ball Watersports to get certified. It changed her life forever. "At 28, I was beginning to get too old to be an international cover girl" she said, brushing her soft brown sun-streaked hair away from her blue eyes. "My BA from Cornell was in business and I'd taken several graduate courses in financial management, so I had already been flirting with various business ideas. The minute I got certified, I knew this was it." She threw her head back and laughed. "So I called my daddy."

Regal M. Precious is just the right daddy to have. About ten lines short of Fortune's list of the 100 most wealthy men in America, Papa Precious has spent his spare time picking up quaint pieces of real estate throughout the Carribbean. In 1965, he bought unsettled Tortuga Cayes on Tortuga Banks. It includes four cayes of an acre or less -- where Ridley Turtles spawn (now a preserve) -- and the 102-acre Petit Brac, which he has kept private and untouched. (The Aggressor Fleet has sought permission to dive here, which he refused.) Then, twenty years later, in 1986, he deeded the Cayes to daddy's favorite daughter. Precious Island was born.

In April, Precious Island will be open for business. Right after the January DEMA show, eight lucky journalists were given a week sneak preview (I paid my own way, as is Undercurrent policy, but others didn't). April May, who is now 33, has been living here with a small construction crew for 18 months, guiding the careful construction of her personal paradise ("I built that fireplace with my bare hands," she is quick to point out, "and laid every piece of wood in this floor.") Although her daddy gave her the island, she's building it out with the money she earned from her $2500-a-day modeling assignments and subsequent investments. Nearly finished are ten thatched-roof, two-bedroom cottages (which she calls "bures" after her Fiji experience) finished with the finest woods ("not one piece from the rainforests," she proudly claims) and decorated with colorful Haitian paintings and Cuna Indian molas. White wicker furniture and king sized beds fill out the warm and won- derful rooms. And, oh, how I liked those rooms ... and the service. In the morning, a gentle- man -- Henry Bodden -- in a starched white coat tapped lightly on my porch door, then left a pot of steaming coffee, fresh mango juice, and a copy of "The Precious Paper," her daily MacIntosh mis- sive. It contained weather information ("A cold weather front is coming down from the states, so it may drop to 70° tonight; if it does I'll light up the fireplace in the lodge, and bring out the pillows and brandy, so we can cozily spin stories of our day's dives"), dive choices ("my recommen- dation for today is Precious Mounds, where at 120 feet you'll think you're in the South Pacific; if you want to stay below 100 feet, have your boatman take you to Grouper Gardens; you won't be able to count them all and there's bound to be a Goliath Grouper or two"); and the dinner menu ("Kingsley will fish for cobia today, and tonight we'll dust it in flour and nutmeg and add my secret spices, sauté it lightly, and serve it with garlic mashed potatoes, fresh corn on the cob, and my special Jamaican breadfruit/dasheen puree. And for new arrival Billy Joe -- Say hello to him in Bure #7 -- I'll even have a little okra cooked up....")

Let's talk diving, though. That's why I came. When I disembarked from the silky-smooth sixty- minute hovercraft trip from Georgetown harbor, I was introduced to Henry, who was to serve as my personal valet for the duration of the stay (he could provide snacks and drinks, straighten the room, hang my clothes, even be my dive buddy if I needed one -- anything, I was to learn). He smiled graciously and took my belongings to my bure and my dive bag to the dock. When I arrived the first morning at the dock, my BC was strapped to the tank, my gear laid out on a locker on the deck so I could check it all out, and once I did Henry took it aboard. <u>No more than six divers are taken on any of their five Radons.</u> On mine I was joined Sydd Finch, a writer from <u>Diver</u>, a British magazine, and his consort, and Maryalice Martin, a freelance journalist. April May, who leads about half the dives, piloted our boat. She gave us a briefing and we were soon underway.

Four hundred yards off shore, Henry grabbed the anchor and jumped overboard, dropping to 50 feet to place it gently in the sand. I fell over backward, dropped to 40 feet, gave the OK sign, and headed directly toward two large mounds covered with softly swaying gorgonians. <u>As I slid between them I saw a boulder move; it was a grouper, easily as long as a man and three times as thick; I approached slowly, and when I reached five feet, he opened his enormous mouth; even at that distance, I could feel the water pull me toward him.</u> No thanks, buster, and I headed over the wall. And there, at 120 feet, was a parade of pelagics. In twenty minutes, more than thirty sharks cruised by; they were mostly reef sharks, but a couple of bulls joined in and two hammerheads cruised by in tandem, no more than 20 feet away. Several amberjacks streamed in from the distance as three eagle rays drifted by, and then three manta. April May Precious slipped out into the blue and slowly turned somersaults with the mantas. They swooped around and over her for a few minutes, then disappeared. An enormous ocean sunfish, at least six feet in diameter, fluttered by and I grabbed the bottom fin for a short ride. Believe me, I was absolutely stoked.

Only in the South Pacific have I seen diving
like this. We made a couple dozen wall dives and
the experience of the first repeated itself time
and time again. Once, <u>in fact, a twelve foot mar-
lin streamed past, no more than 30 feet away. On
another time, a school of tuna, two hundred or
more, came by the wall, with a score of dolphins
above</u>. Above the reefs there were plenty of queen
angels and queen triggers. When we looked for
smaller critters, April May pointed out seahorses
and, on one dive alone, three frogfish! What was
missing? Nothing. Nothing. Nothing.

On shore, I passed enjoyable hours walking the
isolated beach, snorkeling in Blue Lagoon (April
said she "loved the movie") or walking through
the cool forest. (There are parrots and mon-
keys in this ecological miracle! Quite a treat.)
Yes, it's all here, every dream imaginable. One
night, after an exceptional dinner beginning with
a sea cucumber soup (don't gag, it's a Far East
staple, and splendid), a salad made with greens
from their hydroponic garden, poached durgon in a
sauce of white wine and butter and sprinkled with
fresh urchin roe, and freshly baked coconut bread,
I ambled out on the deck, which extends twenty
feet over the lagoon. I could see the guests in
the house watching videos from the day, chatting
and enjoying themselves, but I wanted a moment to
be alone, to soak in what is the most remarkable
place run by, arguably, the most incredible woman
ever to don a dive skin and become a NAUI instructor. "What man wouldn't give his left ...."
I began to think, when I felt a hand on my shoulder. "Mind if I join you?" April May asked. She
had brought two 1963 Sandeman Ports and two cof-
fees, so we sat and sipped for well over an hour.

Lesser men would melt in front of the brainy

and beautiful April May Precious, but I kept my cool, being the objective writer that I am. "Man, am I lucky," she said. "My own island, my own diving lodge, my own bar and restaurant. And diving, diving, diving. I am sooo happy." Her perfectly natural face needed no makeup other than the moonlight to make her the most striking woman I've seen. She kicked her very long legs up on the deck railing and threw her head back. <u>"And, most of all, I'm with people I love. Divers. I mean, what better lot could there be? We love the sea, we talk about it all the time.</u> Oh, I'm still going to Paris once a year. Go diving in the South Pacific now and then. But this will always be home. Where in the Caribbean can you sit at 120 feet at the Point and see such a parade every day? You know," she said, "the only thing missing for me here is the right man. But if I'm going to find that special guy, what better place? My dream man must be a diver. And sooner or later, every diver in the world will pass through here for the diving we have. So I'll find him."

She looked my way and smiled. I stuttered a bit, but finally said, "Well, maybe he's here tonight ... in the lodge, uh, right here maybe." She smiled again. "Gee, that would be wonderful, wouldn't it," she said softly. She stood, silhouetted in the full moon, brushed her hair back, and said, "See you tomorrow at 120 feet."

Diver's Compass: Precious Island opens April 1; bures are $1500 for 8 days, seven nights; add $500 for each additional guest up to three; all meals, plus three tanks a day, plus night dives every other night are included; . . .shore dives can be taken any time, but the depths don't exceed 50-60 feet. . . . There are new DACOR BCs for free use; Delphi computers are $10/day. . . .

PS: As I was getting ready to leave, I stopped to chat with Don and Deborah Marshall of Seattle, who had arrived the day before, with Deborah's sister, Janey, in tow. All three happened to be travel agents, hard core divers and world travelers. "This place is the best, isn't it?" Deborah asked. "The diving is sensational and the luxury here is a real surprise." She leaned a little closer to speak in hushed tones. "And, I'll tell you, my sister is ready to move in. All these great divers come down here to ogle April May and there are plenty left over for Janey. She said she'll take April May's rejects just any old day," Deborah said with a laugh. "I guess this is the first legitimate diving resort for, well, mature, single, serious divers. Should have been here before I married this guy," she said, poking Don in the ribs. He only shrugged.

Yeah, I suppose that's all true. But this is no Club Med, this is serious diving. Maybe April May will meet her man, maybe guests will meet their mates. Me, I'll go back in a New York minute, you can be assured, but not to dream. I'll go back to watch the parade, both underwater and on land. I got the message. April May's special guy didn't happen to be there the night I was.

— Ben Davison

Well, dear readers, are you ready to pack up and go?

So were nearly a thousand readers. At the conclusion of the original article, I wrote that until April May reaches agreement with a stateside representative," reservations could be made by calling a number that I listed. When readers called, the voice mail message said to go back to the article and read the first letter of every paragraph. I suggest that you do that now.

Boy, did I get letters. Most everyone had a great laugh but a few were steaming. You see, they had cancelled pre-booked trips as soon as they read the article, and then called to make reservations. Oh, oh.

A year later, I was sitting in Ambua Lodge in the New Guinea highlands with some friends, talking to a couple at the bar. They had just gotten off a liveaboard and started talking about *Undercurrent*. They related to my friend and me the story of April May Precious; how they were sucked in, but had a great laugh. My friend, after a couple of beers, couldn't resist telling them that I was the guy who wrote the article, Ben Davison.

The fellow looked at me, pulled his glasses down over his nose, looked again, then said, "well, now I understand why April May's special guy wasn't there the night you were."

May I wish you good diving.

The Authors

Ben Davison wore jeans and a sweatshirt when he began diving in the 55°F water under Seattle's Fauntleroy ferry dock. He started *Undercurrent* after a 1975 *Skin Diver Magazine* article proclaimed the wonders of Jamaican reefs, which he found quite the opposite. To avoid conflicts of interest, *Undercurrent* accepts no advertising. While writing *Undercurrent*, he was a partner and creative director in two fund raising consulting firms; his clients included Greenpeace International, Defenders of Wildlife, the Simon Wiesenthal Center, The Cousteau Society, the Sierra Club, and many public television and radio stations. As West Coast director of Common Cause, he directed the initiative campaign that created California's Fair Campaign Practices Commission. He holds a doctorate in public administration from the University of Southern California. He is now working with colleagues in the UK to establish the International Court for the Environment to adjudicate international environmental and climate issues. His articles have appeared in *Men's Journal, Outside* and many diving publications.

Larry Clinton, the son of swing era songwriter and bandleader Larry Clinton Sr., began his diving in Long Island Sound in the late 50s as a member of the Five Fathoms Club of Roslyn H.S., America's first high school dive club. During spring break, he and his friends would drive to Marathon, FL, to camp on the beach and dive in borrowed boats. After graduating from Tufts University in Massachusetts, he settled in the San Francisco Bay Area, and learned to love the kelp forests. Besides freelance journalism and magazine editing, he has worked in financial services marketing. In the 70s, he wrote the definitive *Complete Outfitting & Source Book for Sport Diving*, and has written for *Skin Diver Magazine, Scuba Times, Coastal Living, Lonely Planet Books,* and *San Francisco Magazine.* He is senior editor for *Undercurrent,* a long-time member of the Historical Diving Society, a regular volunteer at the Marine Mammal Center where he rescues seals and sea lions. He has made more than 1300 dives in two dozen countries, and regularly plucks abalone in Northern California to feed his friends.

Ken Smith has allowed Ben Davison to take the heat as well as the credit for every last word that has appeared in *Undercurrent.*